so *that*
happened

Jon Cryer

so *that* happened

 NEW AMERICAN LIBRARY

New American Library
Published by the Penguin Group
Penguin Group (USA) LLC, 375 Hudson Street,
New York, New York 10014

USA | Canada | UK | Ireland | Australia | New Zealand | India | South Africa | China
penguin.com
A Penguin Random House Company

First published by New American Library,
a division of Penguin Group (USA) LLC

First Printing, April 2015

REGISTERED TRADEMARK—MARCA REGISTRADA

LIBRARY OF CONGRESS CATALOGING-IN-PUBLICATION DATA:
Cryer, Jon, 1965–
So that happened/Jon Cryer.
p.   cm.
ISBN 978-0-451-47235-9
1. Cryer, Jon, 1965–   2. Actors—United States—Biography.   I. Title.
PN2287.C6855A3   2015
791.4502'8092—dc23   2014046319
[B]

Printed in the United States of America
1   3   5   7   9   10   8   6   4   2

Set in Bulmer MT
Designed by Spring Hoteling

To my beautiful children,
Charlie and Daisy

(Please don't read the part
about the prostitute.)

"Sweetheart, you'll find
mediocre people do exceptional things all the time."

—OK Go, "What to Do"

Contents

Contents

Contents

A Note on the Use of Profanity

When I started this book I truly believed that I did not curse very much. That I added a dash of salty language to a slab of comedic irony only when it was urgently necessary. For flavor. But the process of writing it has brought me to the realization that what I tend to offer up is actually a sodium-packed canned ham of expletives of dubious necessity. For that I'm desperately sorry. I've endeavored to reduce their use wherever possible, but I'm afraid many remain. If you purchased this book hoping it'd be appropriate to read for your "Family Showbiz Bio Reading Night," I suggest you take this moment to reconsider.

Prologue

"Goddammit."

"Cut, cut, *cut*!"

The director yanks off his headphones and wearily barks, "I'm pretty sure doves don't shit sideways! Am I right? Anybody?!"

The special-effects guy (Allen, I think) is at a loss for words. Really, how does one respond to that question? The cast, dressed in tasteless formal wear for a mideighties suburban American wedding, break character and start to mill about restlessly.

There is a moment of tense silence while some of us consider a reply to the director's odd dove query. But fortunately, our fearless leader breaks the tension by answering himself. "That's what I thought."

We are shooting outside a wedding chapel in Phoenix, Arizona, during the summer of 1983, and it's incredibly, unbearably, fucktastically hot. My white polyester tux is sodden with sweat and adhering to every contour of my body. The reason Bob, our director, is asking about the physics of bird ejecta is because in this particular shot, the animal

1

wranglers were supposed to release some doves, and when those doves flew over the wedding party, they were supposed to shit on us as we exited the chapel. Sadly, the actual doves, ignorant of their cue, indifferent to the wishes of the director, as well as unconcerned about their chance at screen stardom, did not cooperate and empty their bowels upon us.

So the special effects guy (ninety-five percent sure it's Allen), ever resourceful, had jury-rigged an elaborate backup system of pressurized containers to squirt fake dove poo on the wedding party from either side of the camera. But no matter how he tried, said poo would rain onto the partiers with a noticeably wide arc. This made Bob unhappy. Apparently he felt any discerning moviegoer would immediately notice the crap's flight path, and their sense of cinematic verisimilitude would be forever compromised. Bob was turning out to be the Stanley Kubrick of turd-trajectory perfectionists.

Not that Bob is being an asshole about it. He seems irritated, yet kind of amused. The Bob in question is actually a Robert: Robert Altman, the acclaimed director of *MASH*, *Nashville*, and *McCabe & Mrs. Miller*. So if any director has earned the right to be an asshole about doves shitting on people, it'd be him.

The movie is *O.C. and Stiggs*, and it is intended to be Bob's subversive take on American suburban torpor dressed up as an accessible youth comedy. The story is about how the two titular teenagers abuse, accost, and generally annoy an atrociously clueless nouveau riche family, the Schwabs. I play Randall Schwab Jr., idiot scion of the brood, while Jane Curtin of *Saturday Night Live* fame and Paul Dooley from *Breaking Away* play my parents. Also in the film are Dennis Hopper, Cynthia Nixon, and Ray Walston.

This is my first day of shooting on my very first movie role.

In a fucking Robert Altman movie.

I am quite literally vibrating with excitement, anticipation, and abject terror.

The scene we are shooting is Randall's sister Lenore's wedding.

Pretty much the entire cast is in it. So on my first day I get to work with both a director I revere, as well as performers I've admired for ages. I'm in the big leagues. I'm getting my chance to find out how the actors who've made it ply their trade. To discover exactly how one of the all-time great directors makes his genius manifest. It's going to be amazing. If only they can figure out how to get this bird-shit thing to work.

The crux of the scene, as Bob imagines it, is that the Schwab family emerges from the chapel, followed by the auspicious release of a flock of doves, signifying to all that our clan is the gauchest of the gauche in terms of egregious displays of suburban American wealth, at which point—big joke!—the doves would poop on us. Take that, richies!

But as I said, this guano business is easier said than done. So after Bob's minor outburst, he emerges from his trailer, where he's been watching us on video monitors, with a certain if-you-want-something-done-right-you-have-to-do-it-yourself determination. He confers with his special-effects guy (it's possible it's Steve), who runs off and hurriedly gathers a large yellow mixing bowl and several ingredients easily found in a refrigerator or pantry. He throws the assortment into the bowl and mixes fiercely. Meanwhile Bob motions to one of the grips, who grabs a ladder and rushes in. The special-effects guy (thanks, IMDb, definitely Allen) hands Bob the bowl and Bob sighs.

With filmic reality on the line, it is now evident that someone will have to go vertical and rain this new faux poo from a proper angle over the assembled wedding guests. And that that someone will be none other than five-time Academy Award–nominated director Robert Altman himself.

Imagine, if you will, this master American filmmaker—the man behind *The Player*, *Short Cuts*, and *Gosford Park*—climbing a rickety aluminum ladder, perching his shall we say portly frame on the top while a crew member nervously holds the ladder in place, and, as his actors step out from flung-open chapel doors, hurling down on us healthy dollops of *very* realistic-looking ersatz bird feces (see the Appendix for the recipe) with steady, consistent authority.

As cameras roll, Bob lobs bogus excreta with the artistry of Jackson Pollock. Or perhaps Georges Seurat is a more appropriate comparison: Like Seurat's pointillist masterpieces, not a blob is out of place. But I start to notice a curious phenomenon. I haven't been hit and, for lack of a better description, I'm feeling left out. My gut tells me the audience will really enjoy seeing my character get nailed. So I begin jockeying into position to put myself in the line of poop fire, much the same way an outfielder adjusts to get under a fly ball. I look around and realize that all of the actors I was looking forward to working with, the ones I truly respected, are doing it too! There's Jane Curtin gliding sideways to snag a faceful of avian dookie, Paul Dooley expertly catching some on the shoulder, and future *Sex and the City* star Cynthia Nixon animatedly yakking with a background performer as she stealthily positions herself to receive an admirably viscous splotch in her hair.

Looking around at this surreal scene, I could not help but marvel at the caliber of performer hoping to get shat on by Bob Altman. I thought, *Welcome to showbiz, Jon.*

And as it turned out, this wouldn't even be the weirdest day of my career.

Not even close.

Chapter 1
A Child Slave for Zestabs

I don't remember the first time I was on television.

If that sounds a little strange, it should. I grew up during a time when an appearance on TV was a fairly exotic, noteworthy occurrence. I also don't remember even wanting to be an actor then, which should have made it all the more bizarre.

For your perusal, I submit this:

This is me circa 1969. Clearly I was looking down the barrel of a future already limited by my glaring failure to master the arcane arts of the common hairbrush. As you can see, I had no earthly reason to expect a career in the entertainment industry.

Yet I was blessed. Blessed with moxie, stick-to-itiveness, spunk, an off-kilter grin, lousy posture, an anxious nature, discolored teeth, zero muscle tone, asthma, an assortment of vocal tics, low self-esteem, a muffin top (before they even called it that), and dandruff. As well as the two things that made up for almost all of it: an appreciation for the surreal, and a near-delusional ignorance of my own limitations.

All I needed was fate to throw some happy accidents, odd occurrences, and utter fiascoes my way, and I'd be off and running.

The first of them is the one I can't even really remember.

You can decide if it means anything in the larger scheme of things. I've had to rely on my mother for a lot of the details, since she was there for it.

Actually, I like starting with a story involving my mother, because she's an amazing woman. This was the late 1960s in my hometown of New York City, when my parents—Gretchen and David Cryer—were still together. The estimable Gretchen Cryer was, in fact, a double threat—actress and playwright. A triple threat soon after, if you count having to raise two kids, a daughter and a son, after my parents divorced.

At any rate, playing moms in television spots certainly helped pay the bills, and one day she landed a commercial for a multivitamin called Zestabs, an over-the-counter brand aimed at families that would now be called "vintage." Although not the way wine is so judiciously labeled. In other words, if you find a dusty bottle of Zestabs in your grandmother's medicine cabinet, do not decant it and serve with lamb chops. Sell it on eBay to some hipster who wants it for his apothecary table.

Anyway, Zestabs not only wanted Mom for their commercial; they wanted her for the whole campaign, too, so this was a real score back then. TV! Print ads! Store displays! The bottle label, too! Mom would be the new face of vitamins. And maybe also . . .

She was asked, "Do you have any kids?"

"I sure do," she said. "Two. A girl and a boy."

"Great," said Zestabs. (I don't have a person for this part of the conversation, just a faceless brand, but hey, corporations are people, too, apparently.) "We need two kids. They don't have to say or do anything. You'll just stand there and say the copy, with your arms around each of them."

Mom came home to our apartment on the Upper West Side, brimming with enthusiasm about the offer. First she probably had to get my sister, Robin, then six years old, to stop beating the crap out of her younger brother (I was four at the time). I picture my mother excitedly throwing open the front door to reveal my sister in a prepunch tableau, eyes wide, holding me up by my collar, fist clenched and arm cocked. But once she pried me out of my sister's freakishly-strong-for-a-first-grader grip and the proper admonitions were taken care of, she laid the news on us.

"Kids, we have this wonderful chance to be in a commercial together! Want to do it?"

At the same time I said, "*Yes!*" Robin began screaming and crying and bolted for corners of the apartment unknown, which necessitated a peacekeeping mission on Mom's part to reassure her that children aren't taken from home against their will and forced to hawk products, as though Madison Avenue had its own version of the child catcher from *Chitty Chitty Bang Bang.*

But me? Make me a child-labor slave for Zestabs! Give me a new sister, too, while you're at it! (I got one, in fact, a nice blond girl they hired for the commercial, named Jennifer.)

My first salaried job, people. And really, what did I even know of the business then? I knew my parents had something to do with performing. I'd hang out backstage sometimes during the original run of the Broadway musical *1776*, which both Mom and Dad were in, and marvel at the fact that adults were deeply involved in the act of playing and pretend. Women wore big hoop skirts, bizarre undergarments, and tall wigs; men wore tons of makeup and fancy old-timey suits; they sang and spoke loudly, then walked offstage and briefly turned into normal people again, drinking

Cokes and swearing and bumping into one another before scurrying back onstage to pretend again. It was like being on another planet, one that seemed way more fun than this one.

I don't know if at the age of four I could have put all that together as part of what being in a commercial was, but my saying yes so insistently meant the desire to perform was in me somewhere.

I was so excited about the commercial, in fact, that the morning of the shoot, as a special gift for everyone, I showed up with giant red blotches all over my face and skin. Yes, my four-year-old body—overwhelmed by the mixture of nervousness, anticipation, and enthusiasm coursing through it—turned me into a Dr. Seuss creature. Had we been shooting a commercial for a skin-rejuvenating soap, I'd have made an incredible "before" picture.

But this was a vitamin commercial in the 1960s, and all I was supposed to do was look happy and say nothing next to my mother— plenty of training in the bag there—and yet somehow already this neat little opportunity had taken an unforeseen left turn.

Luckily everyone was, according to Mom, very accommodating and understanding, and after a sufficient period of calmness the blotches subsided. We shot the commercial, everything went smoothly, the ad aired, and children everywhere got their recommended daily doses of vitaminy goodness because I looked clean, cheerful, healthy, and not in any way like this vitamin gave you shingles. With my paycheck, Mom started a bank account for me instead of blowing it all on hats, which was smart, I thought. Plus, when we'd go to the drugstore, I could go to the vitamin aisle and see a display-stand version of myself and Mother and some random blond girl staring back at me, which even then I thought was a little peculiar. I'm sure Robin kicked the cardboard me every chance she got.

And yet I wouldn't call my Zestabs experience the Bug. You know, the "acting bug" you always read about in interviews, which equates the desire to play characters with, of all things, a presumably incurable disease. That particular infection happened years later, when I was persuaded to go to a summer camp for the performing arts. But the Zestabs commercial certainly let me know that even when something sounds smooth and fun and exciting, you'd better be ready for splotches.

Zestabs, meanwhile, with their sights now directly on the young, went on to make chocolate-flavored vitamins and to use Mighty Mouse in its ads and labeling, eventually inspiring the Flintstones brand of chewable vitamins, before fading as a relic of cartoon-inspired marketing of over-the-counter drugs to children. Zestabs retired to Arizona, married a discontinued breakfast cereal, and lived out its days on a ranch.

But me, I was just beginning. . . .

Chapter 2
Things Were Wonderful Before You Came

In the 1960s, nobody wanted to live above Ninety-sixth Street. But one of the Bob Fosse dancers in the musical *Little Me* told my mother, who had a five-line part in the show as Miss Hepplewhite, that an apartment was opening up for rent in a building on One Hundred Third Street. Mom was pregnant at the time with my older sister, Robin. She and my dad needed more space, so they moved in. I was born two years later. I couldn't tell you if any of the friendly winos who frequently peed in the mailroom area of the building sent my mother flowers in the hospital or anything. I assume not.

It was pretty action-packed on our block, crime-wise. One time a prostitute jumped off the roof. We knew a kid who got shot in a building down the street. There were bullet holes in the Plexiglas front doors. Elevator muggings were known to happen.

Most grimly colorful of all was what occurred next door with friendly Mr. Green, a septuagenarian who enjoyed bringing over pots of oxtail soup for Mom, on whom he undoubtedly had a crush. Mr. Green liked to season his specialty with rosemary, and he also liked to pay for sex, hosting the occasional hooker from time to time. (Not sure if oxtail soup was offered to those ladies—I'd like to think he saved that delicacy for Gretchen Cryer.)

One night Mom heard the unmistakable pop of a gunshot next door. She ran out the door in time to see a woman fleeing down the stairs. Mom called the police, who arrived to find Mr. Green tied to his bed, quite literally holding a smoking gun, and a dead man on the floor. It seems one of Mr. Green's regulars had brought along her bruiser of a boyfriend, under the impression that this little old client had money hidden somewhere. Boyfriend tied Mr. Green up and started taking the place apart. While this was happening, even with his arms tightly bound, Mr. Green managed to reach under his mattress and find his gun. Then, from arm's length, using only his wrist to aim, without even being able to see down the barrel, he squeezed off a single shot. Boyfriend caught it right between the eyes. From then on, even though Mr. Green was as warm and jovial as he had always been during his oxtail-soup deliveries, all of our interactions acquired an (I'm sure unintentional) air of menace.

"Tell your mother she shouldn't use too much salt."

"Y-y-y-yes, sir, I'll tell her," I'd stammer.

Getting to P.S. 75 each day without getting threatened for lunch money involved some planning, especially if Mom needed me to pick up groceries on the way home. My scheme was: The twenty for the groceries went into my shoe, while a small amount of money was split between the upper pockets. Sure enough, my mother recalls coming home once and finding her already chipper son in a further state of unnatural exhilaration, so described because I was blurting out, "Mom! Mom! I got mugged! I got mugged!" What made me happy? The older kids who robbed me got only the fifty cents in my pocket. Suckas! The shoe twenty was untouched! Chicken for everyone tonight, thanks to my crime-fighting ingenuity.

The neighborhood was rough, but in our building there was a sense of community, especially because it was full of artists. It was a real bohemian enclave. Opera singers, jazz musicians, writers, and actors enlivened the faded grandeur of the prewar apartments. The place was also full of young male dancers, a good two-thirds of whom perished during the AIDS crisis. This was a devastating time for everyone in the building. Even then I was dimly aware that this was what it must have been like to live through the plague.

Two stories above us was a Jewish family, the Dennises: Robert Dennis, a composer who wrote for dance companies, collaborated on the music for the notorious nudie revue *Oh! Calcutta!* His wife, Marsha, was an opinionated, smart, lefty intellectual. Their three sons were Gary, David, and Eric, and I was close with the whole family. Though I'm not Jewish (or a Republican, Wikipedia!), so much of their New York Jewish sensibility informed my sense of humor—the fatalism, coupled with irony, wrapped in a sturdy shield of toughness—that I like to say I was raised by a pack of wild Jews.

As building babies, David Dennis and I knew each other from birth. We even shared that clichéd moment in which we sized each other up as toddlers from behind our mothers' legs. As we grew up, we were always either at his family's place or mine, and if not there, the park. I felt so comfortable with the Dennises, whose door was always open, that at dinner I was known to get up and help myself to more food without ever asking for seconds. (I learned many years later that this breach of etiquette was a source of amusement for Bob and Marsha.) Outside the building, David and I would hang at Riverside Park, maybe run wild in the art deco apartment building facing the park, or make our way to the roof, where fireworks lit inside launched paper airplanes made for cheap thrills. Closer to the ground, we'd hurl water balloons from my family's first-floor window, a choice vantage point not only for accuracy, but for gauging reactions.

As a child I was forever working against a lack of confidence, a sense that I was never truly comfortable in social situations. I really was a dyed-in-the-wool nerd: easily paralyzed by nervousness, lost in my own thoughts, unsure what to say, embarrassed when I did say something because of the vocal tics I had, and likely to be punched in the face by Puerto Rican girls for saying something I didn't realize was an insult.

When fourth-grade Vanessa from P.S. 75 started peppering me with slaps and small punches seemingly out of nowhere, her face coiled in anger, I barely knew what to do, and certainly my brain wasn't functioning well enough to tell my limbs to get in front of my face, or my lungs to breathe. I could only retreat to a corner of my mind in which I endlessly repeated, *How did this happen? How did this come to pass?* I can now shout into the past at my ten-year-old self: *You said something to piss her off, dummy.* Add another characteristic to the list of nerd qualities: situational unawareness.

It made David a strangely inspiring friend to have around. He was more athletic than I was, a terrific ice-skater, with a wall adorned with champion emblems: patches, medals and the like. He accomplished this, though, in spite of the fact that he was born with a birth defect: One leg was shorter than the other, and one of his feet was thinner and had only three toes. Even after David had an operation at twelve to prevent the onset of scoliosis by surgically extending his leg—an excruciatingly painful process that involved stretching his leg half a millimeter a day with a racklike apparatus—he could still beat me at footraces. I'd make Bionic Man jokes. My well-used comic excuse at the time was, "My leg hurts too!" David always appreciated that I never treated him differently because of his leg, which eventually required use of a cane. Then again, that kind of humor came directly from him and his family.

David and I were inseparable. My older sister, Robin, and I, on the other hand, nearly always needed to be separated. She and I had a pretty contentious relationship from very early on. She has been known to flat-out state, "Things were wonderful before you came." We were at each other's throats on a regular basis, and it drove Mom crazy; you could tell that at times she feared for our lives. Dinner was a barrage of insults, starting with my sister's pet name for me, King Uh-huh, a dig at an involuntary little laugh I occasionally add to the end of sentences. At any rate, I grew up with a sibling who could be counted on to crush any sign of confidence I ever showed, or just remove Mom's huge antique wrench from the wall and hurl it at me. Mom openly took my side, too, which I'm sure didn't make things any better for me in Robin's eyes.

Two things positively altered my and Robin's relationship, though. One was the time Sis had me pinned, ready to whale on me, when I somehow managed to bite her hard on the arm. It was a nasty mark, too, a real tooth tattoo. The mouse had roared, it seemed. I'd finally drawn a boundary. The second was just the natural course of adolescence. She began socializing outside the home, which took higher priority in her to-do list than tormenting me.

Key to that was her close friendship with a girl named Shelly, who eventually moved in with us. Robin and Shelly had that us-against-the-world kinship that made them love Aerosmith, Cheap Trick, and Yes more than anybody else, spurred them to dye their hair similarly, and probably (because I have no confirmation on this) get high together. When Shelly's free-spirit single mom wanted to marry a Trinidadian and move to his homeland, Shelly balked because she really wanted to attend the High School of Music & Art, which had accepted her. She asked my mother if she could live with us, and Mom loved the idea. There was plenty of room—we had four bedrooms—and maybe more important, when Shelly was around, Robin was less inclined to treat me like a detainee in a black-ops site.

I still remember Shelly's simple and gently spoken, cruelty-defusing words, and how they transformed the air, turning our home into a land of peacemaking and harmony: "Robin, don't do that."

Shelly was also pretty, and often traversed the apartment scantily clad, which made her a welcome guest in my eyes. Our building was so old that it still had keyholes on doors, and I may have, a time or two in front of Shelly's room, incurred a crippling injury that required me to stoop and turn my head in the direction of her door's keyhole, whereupon I might have seen some things I wasn't supposed to. The problem with getting caught and claiming injury, of course, is that you have to fake that pain for at least forty-five minutes afterward.

Ultimately Shelly was the UN to our Serbia and Croatia, which really brought unity to the household. But Robin also changed. She became less confrontational, and began to look at me as a fixer-upper instead of a punching bag. Perhaps realizing her little brother was entering pubescence with a target on his back—I was the definition of nerd-in-training: nonathletic, smallish, generally timid, and quick to spout know-it-all information as a defense mechanism—she actively worked at helping me socially. She even took me to my first concert, the Thompson Twins at the Ritz, and dressed me to boot in teen-hipster duds from the clothing store where she'd started working. Although she still enjoyed making fun of me, my early teens were marked by a lasting détente at Chez Cryer. War crimes would not be prosecuted. Trade talks were negotiated. The occasional diplomatic slight was forgiven.

Of course, much of the reason Robin and I had a trial by fire as fractious siblings was because as latchkey kids, we often had the run of the house. We became particularly independent during my preteen years, when Mom began to taste success with the musical *I'm Getting My Act Together and Taking It on the Road*, which Mom wrote the book and lyrics for and starred in, with music by Nancy Ford, her longtime collaborator.

It's worth taking a moment to note that it's no small feat to make a living in New York as a playwright, much less a female one, and Mom's been at it for more than fifty years now. The 1970 rock musical she wrote with Nancy, *The Last Sweet Days of Isaac*, won multiple theater awards, and in 1972 they opened a show on Broadway called *Shelter*.

Getting My Act Together was autobiographical for Mom. It told the story of an actress approaching middle age who finds new life singing songs about female liberation, and in 1978 the legendary theater producer Joe Papp put it up at the Public Theater.

When *The New York Times* panned it in a truly rotten, dismissive review, I vividly recall finding my mom crying by herself in her darkened bedroom. She'd worked so hard on it, it was such a personal story, and we had been enduring some lean financial years for a while. I remember Mom sitting us all down at the table and giving us the grim news that there would be no allowance for a while. My dad, who by that point had moved to Los Angeles and was a struggling actor with a new family, didn't have the money to pay child support, so it was all on our single mom. In that light, knowing that the *Times'* influence was enough to kill a show outright, the news did not look good for our getting out of financial straits. But Joe Papp, unbowed and perhaps reminded of how much preview audiences loved it, let the show run for six weeks. By the end of that run, *Getting My Act Together* had found itself a passionate audience. The show was selling out on word of mouth alone, and would go on to run for almost three years off-Broadway, one of the longest such runs in that era.

The success, though, meant that Mom's show and, because she starred in it, Mom were in demand around the country. She acquired a manager—well, *acquired* is not exactly accurate. *Getting My Act Together*'s lighting designer, an affable, bearded, beret-wearing mensch by the name of Marty Tudor, approached her one day and said, "Hey, can I be your manager?" Mom replied, "I don't know; I've never had a manager before." He replied, "That's cool; I've never been one before." Marty, who used to design light shows for concert acts like Barry Manilow and had done enough tours with megastar Meat Loaf to refer to him simply as "Meat," was tired of the rock-and-roll life and was ready for a career change. My mom was willing to take a chance.

Where money was concerned, there was finally some breathing room, but she was also away a lot: to Los Angeles to meet with interested movie people, to Chicago to star in the show for three months, then to other cities that wanted to run *Getting My Act Together*. When I look back on that stretch of my youth, when I was fifteen and Robin was seventeen, I never equated Mom's extensive traveling with the frowned-upon notion that as a parent she "wasn't around," or that she was being irresponsible. She was doing what any self-respecting, hardworking man or woman would do when the fruits of his or her labor met with success: They worked at growing it. If you were a playwright, the chance to see your play done all over the country was what you lived for. It's there in the title of her show, for Christ's sake—she took that act on the road!

It couldn't have been easy on her, leaving two kids alone while she got another child—her show—up on its feet. But as I said, in our building there was a sense of community, of neighbors looking out for neighbors. Then again, this wasn't always soothing to Mom. By the time she was off to Chicago, I was looking to make my own money, so I started working down the street at the Equity Library Theatre located in the Master Apartments building, one of New York's oldest theater companies and a union-sponsored house that specialized in revivals and showcases for young actors. I began as an usher, and for a fifteen-year-old kid with a burgeoning interest in acting, it was a great education in various plays and musicals. Well, an education in first acts, at least. By intermission I was officially off work, so I'd usually leave, which means that as far as I know, Willy Loman becomes salesman of the year and retires with a gold watch. I should really find out someday. Anyway, I liked the job and wanted to work more so I could have more money. So one day while Mom was in Chicago, I decided to plead for more hours from the theater's house manager, Russ. This conversation happened to take place on the sidewalk outside the theater, and apparently within earshot of a concerned twelfth-floor tenant.

The next morning, Mom was woken up early in Chicago by elderly Norma Vogelstein from upstairs, who related in her most judgmentally alarmed old person's quaver, "Dear, we're very worried about Jonny. He's been seen on the street begging for money and jobs."

That's right: To Norma Vogelstein's Depression-era ears, Gretchen Cryer's kids were abandoned, starving urchins, to the point where one was openly beseeching people on the street for sustenance. Naturally,

I soon got a call from my mortified mom, terror on the edges of her voice, wondering what was up with the public supplicating. I eased her fears, explaining that I was just asking for more hours, and that all was fine.

Robin, though, who was entering a rebellious phase of her independence, decided to quit high school while Mom was gone, which only deepened the guilt Mom occasionally felt about being in another city for work. But she had a sense of humor about it, too. During her stint in Chicago, she appeared on the *Phil Donahue Show*. At one point, a guy in the audience stood up and said, "How can you be a good mother when your children are in New York and you're working in Chicago?"

Rather than get defensive, Mom went the dark-humor route. She said, "Well, to tell you the truth, I just got a call that my son was begging for money and jobs in the street, and my daughter just quit high school."

Fortunately, TV's resident champion for women interceded, and stood up for Mom. Phil asked the guy if he'd ever say that to a man who had to go out of town for work to support his family. If Mom ever needed any more reasons to give voice to struggling women through her show, that asshole in Phil Donahue's audience was surely one of them.

Now, did great freedom at an impressionable age mean I was a responsible kid? Well, not always, if David Dennis was around. For an awkward lad lacking in perceived ability, and self-conscious to a fault, David was a bracing pal to have in one's corner. Blessed with a gregarious nature, oodles of charisma, and the ability to bend you to his wishes through sheer force of personality, David was dangerously fun. I was his conscience, but he was my excuse to be naughty. Whatever unsafe, time-wasting activity might be proposed, I could be counted on for a meek, "Are you sure we should do this?" But I never really meant it.

Enthusiasm was David's currency, and it didn't matter what the catalyst of the enthusiasm was—it could be hearing there was a guy dressed as a chicken in front of the Burger King, at which point David made running down to meet him and get his picture a worthwhile mission. The point was to care about something; it filled your life in a valuable way, I learned.

Nevertheless, our teenage years were chock-full of the kind of imaginatively stupid—but enthusiastic!—shenanigans that make me incredibly fearful now for my own children's adolescence. We did stuff that would curl your hair, especially when the third member of our posse, a Cuban-born charmer named Artie, was around. Artie was strikingly handsome, sporting a preposterous pompadour inspired by the Stray Cats, and a slight lisp that gave a winning cuddliness to anything profane or macho he said.

I always joke that the dynamic of our group was along the lines of Leopold and Loeb, but with the capacity to harm turned toward ourselves. Don't get me wrong: Kids in our neighborhood played all the wholesome-looking games that movies about New York have always depicted—stickball, handball, ringolevio—but our playtime often took a different turn. We had games like "Overzealous Security Detail," "Prison Snitch," "Careless Gas Station Attendant," and, one of my all-time faves, "Fraudulent Pot Bust." That last one goes like this: Two of us would pretend to be cops who, upon stopping the third in his tracks and rifling through his pockets, would stuff a plastic Baggie in his pocket, pull it out, and then growl, "What's this, *marijuana?*" and proceed to pummel him repeatedly. Pretty much all our "games" ended with someone getting pummeled, or merely tortured, or farted upon, or all of the above. Score was never kept.

Then there was the time our fondness for lighting fireworks-laden paper planes and throwing them out the window—a "game" I titled "Nightmare in MiG Alley"—went a bit awry. I know, I know. How is that possible? Well, David lit a firework, and as he was preparing to launch, it went off by his ear. He shrieked, because he was in pain. Artie and I laughed, because we were those kinds of friends.

David started screaming, "Do I *still have my fingers?*"

"Yes," I said.

"What?" said David.

"I said *YES!*"

"Do I still have my fingers?"

"YES!"

"WHAT?!"

At which point Artie or I probably checked to see if what David was missing was an ear. (He wasn't.)

One time David and I participated in a séance at the Equity Library Theatre, in the hopes of contacting the ghost of a dead Russian. The Master Apartments building, which then housed the Equity Library Theatre and still stands as a beautiful art deco monument on the Upper West Side, was built in 1929 in part as a showcase/haven/command center for a guy named Nicholas Roerich. He was a Russian-born artist who attracted a worldwide following to his brand of Eastern-influenced mysticism and philosophy. Roerich believed, for instance, that during the years of Jesus's life the Bible skips over, Jesus traveled to Asia and studied Buddhism. He was a controversial dude, to say the least, and the Master building had a museum dedicated to the guy's art. It was also thought that Roerich's ghost haunted the place.

Well, those of us who worked as ushers at the Equity Library Theatre—which used to host Roerich's lectures—had to find out. One night, we waited till everyone left after the show, and set up our spirit-calling circle of chairs onstage. Someone took down the portrait of Roerich from the lobby and put it in the center of the circle, his bald-headed, wizard-bearded mug staring into our souls as if he knew this day would come.

Shit got quiet. Then the chanting began. First his name.

"Nicholas Roerich . . . Nicholas Roerich . . . Nicholas Roerich . . ."

Not everyone knew exactly how to say it, so some pronounced it "Row-ritch," while others of us—the smart ones—said "Roarick."

Pretty soon we just started saying all kinds of weird stuff, just because we were in the mood. Some of us got up and moved around, the way you make fun of interpretive dance.

Then all the red lights in the theater turned on at the same time.

The simultaneous shriek that detonated from that group of thirteen- and fourteen-year-olds was like a hydrogen bomb of adolescent panic. It had to have burst an eardrum or two. The dash for the exits would have impressed a crack team of firefighters. David turned to me and kept saying, "Give me my cane! *Give me my cane! Give me my cane!*" As if he needed it, he was out of there so fucking fast.

My brain, meanwhile, went into shock, and then decided to update my reservoirs of accepted wisdom, as if adapting to the sudden proof that ghosts were real. Like a catastrophic data loss followed by a high-speed upload, I began believing in everything my supposedly rational teenage brain always thought wasn't true. Bigfoot? *Obviously.* Loch Ness Monster? *Of course.* UFOs? *Fuck, yeah. Close Encounters of the Third Kind? Documentary.* That money under my pillow when I was five? That *was* from a goddamn tooth fairy!

The sad part is that this was still coursing through my consciousness as we were all in the lobby catching our breath and house manager Russ emerged from a connecting door, laughing his ass off. He'd stayed behind to fuck with us, as anybody with a sense of humor would have, and must have loved the psych-out carnage on display. But it took the rest of the night for me to decompress, which was weird. It was like I had to personally shove each myth back into its hole in the newly revived skeptical part of my brain.

I grew up surrounded by the theater, which looked fun, but also seemed to me an oddly unattainable world, something beyond my reach. Perhaps this was because I surmised that stage performers needed to have an actual skill, like acting or singing or dancing, or all three, and I possessed not a one. I couldn't even do a card trick.

Television, on the other hand, was this warm, funny, comforting babysitter, and from around the age of about eight on, I was pretty obsessed with it—*The Carol Burnett Show*, *Barney Miller*, *The Dick Van Dyke Show*, *The Mary Tyler Moore Show*, *All in the Family*, *Maude*, *The Bob Newhart Show*, *Saturday Night Live*, *The Jeffersons*. I know the Golden Age of television is often referred to as the 1950s, but the 1970s were right up there in my opinion. I mean, *The Facts of Life*, people. You watched it. Don't deny it. You cared when Jo shed that rebel pose and let her soft side show. You loved it when Mrs. Garrett got off a zinger. And you knew, deep down inside, we are all Natalie. (If you are under thirty, I apologize for this series of words and names that make no sense. I hope in the future that you continue to think this book is "tight.")

But it never occurred to me that performing on the tube was something to aspire to, maybe because when I heard those immortal words "Live from Television City in Hollywood!" it sounded like television was a commuter destination or a tourist spot, not a magical land of art.

That's where movies came in. A darkened theater is where my showbiz aspirations really began.

I came of age in the dawn of the blockbuster, after all, when Steven Spielberg and George Lucas inspired moviegoers with their mixture of old-fashioned storytelling and eye-popping visuals. Event movies like *Jaws*, *Star Wars*, *Close Encounters of the Third Kind*, and *Raiders of the Lost Ark* were just about my favorite things on earth.

Unlike today's special-effects behemoths, the movies of that era couldn't be so overly hyped in advance. Back then, we didn't know what we were in for when we stepped inside the theater. When *Star Wars* first appeared at the Loews Astor Plaza in 1977, I remember going with my mother, her then-boyfriend Tony, and Tony's son, whom I got along well with, and while Tony's son and I were excited to see it, we weren't crazy-excited, because we'd seen only a couple of commercials. There was no Internet to tease and spoil the discovery of it. All we knew was that we thought it looked cool, so we gave it a chance.

For two unspoiled, blissfully unprepared sci-fi-loving kids, then, that first shot in *Star Wars* was a real declaration of wow. A tiny ship shoots into view from the top of the screen, taking fire from something, which we learn moments later is an enormous spaceship whose undercarriage (is there a better word for it?) hovers over our view ominously. It also seems to go on forever, the massiveness slowly dawning on everyone in the audience, and I recall Mom's boyfriend Tony bursting out laughing at the audacity of the movie's opening. As soon as that Imperial Star Destroyer passed by in full, showcasing its gigantic burners, Tony burst into applause and more laughter. Then I did, and so did nearly everyone else in that theater. Nobody had seen an establishing shot of grandeur like that before, and ever since, whenever a movie floors me with something completely unexpected and awe-inspiring, I hoot and clap. This is why we go to movies, no?

I had to be a part of moviemaking after that. It changed everything for me. At first I wanted to direct movies, as evidenced by the painstakingly crafted Super 8 films I made at home featuring the Japanese-originated line of toys sold in America as Micronauts. I would have been happy in any behind-the-scenes capacity, actually: special-effects technician, production designer, even an errand-running assistant. Whatever was going to get me close enough so I could observe cinematic brilliance as a Spielberg or a Scorsese creates that jaw-dropping moment that makes someone like me hoot and clap.

I had also grown to love the idea of "Hollywood," to the extent that when I was a grade schooler visiting my dad after he moved there to kickstart a movie career as an actor, I could stand on the Walk of Fame on Hollywood Boulevard completely starstruck by a name in brass on the ground and ignore what a disaster the neighborhood around it had become. I distinctly remember at nine years old idling on the sidewalk outside of C. C. Brown's (an old-school ice-cream parlor that had seen better days), staring at Mary Tyler Moore's name and imagining that if I waited long enough, I was sure to catch a glimpse of her as she stopped by regularly to properly care for her star, conscientiously scraping the gum off the charcoal terrazzo.

By then, the old Hollywood studio system lay in tatters, torn to shreds by filmmakers like Arthur Penn, John Schlesinger, and Robert Altman, who ushered in the modern era of adult-oriented drama, then later by the independent film world, which upended the studios' entire business models. None of the old rules seemed to apply. I was fascinated by showbiz news. I loved the often farcical stupidity of the town, the ridiculous, unnecessary drama, the myopic greed, the insane genius, the venality, the tasteless vulgarity, the wasted millions, the wasted actors, and the wasted lives. It was all wildly entertaining, often more so than the movies themselves.

David Dennis's brother Gary, who had an encyclopedic knowledge of film, showed me a copy of Kenneth Anger's groundbreaking pictorial history of tabloid Tinseltown, *Hollywood Babylon*. I was transfixed by its mix of real regard for the artistic accomplishments of its denizens as well as lurid interest in the unseen dark side of their personal lives.

The seventies had unleashed the sexual revolution on cinema as well as on the people who worked in it. And as I started to understand the concept of sex, it also occurred to me that this place I'd heard of called the Playboy Mansion was somewhere near this so-called Hollywood town. And that meant that, by extension, Bo Derek was nearby as well. Because I was sure she lived there.

I pictured the mansion as sort of the Pentagon of nooky, the world headquarters of this campaign of carnality, replete with scantily clad female generals gathered around glowing strategy tables planning indecence on a global scale.

Hollywood took on a patina of alluring decadence. If the theater was another planet, then Hollywood was a galaxy far, far away. But one where I hoped one day to live, preferably in a reasonably priced studio apartment. Near the Playboy Mansion.

Performing was certainly one way to dip my toe in the showbiz waters and get me closer to my celluloid dreams, so I made some tentative steps in that direction in my early teen years through the most convenient

venue: school. It started at Simon Baruch Junior High—commonly referred to as 104—where I had a chorus teacher named Bob Sharon, a
gifted musician and admirably stern taskmaster. (I picked chorus as an
elective not because I thought I could sing, but because my sister, Robin,
was in it.) Mr. Sharon expected a lot out of his kids, and therefore got a lot
from them. We were in a public school, but under his tutelage we might as
well have been in the most elite conservatory. He inspired devotion and
hard work to the extent that acceptance into the highest-level chorus—
called the madrigal society—earned you a goofy yellow hat that looked
like a four-cornered throw pillow on your head. It was a truly ugly piece
of headwear, and yet people strived for the privilege to wear it as if it
bestowed magical powers.

A plum assignment for a student in Mr. Sharon's chorus was performing at old-age homes, partly, of course, because it meant getting out of
school. My education in Jewish culture got a further boost because we had
to learn lots of Jewish folk songs. To this day I know a lot more of that
music than most Jews I know. During a play recently about an elderly Jewish woman, the character started singing "*Rozhinkes mit mandlen*," and I
instinctively turned to my wife and began whispering, "It means 'Raisins
and Almonds,' and she's singing how she'd give that as a gift, even though
they're very expensive. . . ." My wife was only somewhat surprised to discover that her husband had suddenly become a Talmudic scholar.

Though the only reason I was in chorus, as opposed to the drama
department or the art department, was because of Robin. When Mr. Sharon began casting the school's production of *West Side Story*, he plucked
me from the chorus, and I got a one-line role as a Jet known as Big Deal.
It was my first exposure to this great musical—that fantastic Leonard Ber-
nstein score, and Stephen Sondheim's witty, soaring lyrics—and to be a
part of it felt pretty cool. And because this was New York, we had actual
Puerto Ricans as Sharks, and truly white Jets.

Come showtime, facing an auditorium packed with hundreds of kids
and parents, I had my line down cold, and in my mind I was a pantherish

Russ Tamblyn type with a voice as booming as Ethel Merman's. Make way, everyone. The first act is about to go nuclear. . . .

"But the gym's neutral territory!"

I'd been a nervous wreck until my big moment halfway through the first act, and the sense of relief that washed over me after I brought the thunder is something I still remember. Now I could blend in with the chorus, and if I screwed up the choreography a bit, who would care, right? Only later, upon hearing the vinyl recording they made of the show—yes, vinyl, that's how elderly I am—and seeing a primitive video-tape of it, did I realize how I actually came off: as a distracted pudge ball with a vaguely disturbing zombie stare who got maybe half the choreography right, barely moved when I did the steps anyway, and whose big line had all the impact of a mouse sneeze.

"But the gym's neutral territory!"

And because this is a junior high school production, everybody else is screaming their lines at the top of their lungs with absolutely no variation. That aspect of the show was hilarious enough, but at least you heard them. Then I came along, sounding as if I'd been in a locked box off to the side of the stage. I can only imagine the epidemic of quizzical glances and utterings among the audience members.

"Something about a chimp?"

"Did they let a hamster onstage?"

"Is that little girl okay?"

Of course, at the time of the performance, I was blissfully unaware of all this. Being involved in that *West Side Story* was actually quite fun, and for a brief, shining moment made a nervous, timid boy with a suitcase full of anxieties feel connected. I felt a part of something artistic, even if it wasn't a movie, and I could sense a performance seed in me sprouting. Pursuing acting might just be worth my time, I realized, which made the summer looming ahead all the more intriguing.

Chapter 3
The Fish-in-a-Barrel Situation

Before *High School Musical* and *Glee* made ham-bone high schoolers breaking into anything other than pimples a cool thing, theater camp was definitely way down on the list of places you'd want to go to if you were a kid with confidence issues. Or if you were a kid who thought acting was fun, but *studying* to act sounded foolish. I was both: lacking in confidence, but suspicious of theatricality as a way to solve that problem. I loved movies, enjoyed theater, and had gotten a kick out of doing *West Side Story* in junior high. But a performing-arts camp sounded . . . odd. And yet, what convinced me at the naive and emotionally tender age of fourteen to spend my summer at one? My best buddy, David Dennis, was going, too. How could it not be fun with David?

The camp was called Stagedoor Manor, and it was located a few hours out of New York City in the Catskills Mountains. In 1979, my first year there, Stagedoor had been in operation only three years, but its reputation was growing as an arts-oriented summer camp for the age-ten-to-eighteen set. Calling it a camp, though, is probably an insult to people who actually pitch tents, urinate outdoors, fish for dinner, build fires, and don't scream like a bingo winner every time a fly buzzes their ear. Sure, I'd been on a few family trips to the state park on Fire Island during sweltering summers past—miserable, ill-advised excursions that tested my endurance levels for sun exposure. But I was already in the process of trying to erase those memories. Stagedoor Manor, on the other hand, was housed in a former Borscht Belt resort, and that meant staying in air-conditioned hotel rooms with real beds, functioning showers, and catered meals. It rapidly warped my view of camping. Years later, I dated a girl who wanted to show me a cabin she had in the mountains.

"You went to camp, right?" she said.

"Yes, I went to camp!"

"So you'll be fine."

We got there and I noticed that there were no windows on the cabin, just square holes in the walls.

"Where are the windows?" I asked.

"You said you went camping."

"Yeah, well, we had windows. And maid service."

Stagedoor may have been more civilized than the usual "camp" experience of roughing it, but there was no mistaking that you were entering another world: that of theater-geek subculture. This was where the schoolkids who had no hope of being popular in their everyday public schools could rise to the top of the food chain on talent and an encyclopedic command of the works of Stephen Sondheim alone. (Alumnus Todd Graff's 2003 movie *Camp*, which features a cameo by Sondheim, was inspired by his experiences there.)

Immersion starts immediately. If you take its legendary bus there, kids sing the entire way. It's a show-tunes rager for the entirety of the New York State thruway, so by the time the bus drops them off, the sheen of polite-society otherness is gone, and they're already like Shriners with secret handshakes in the form of two-part harmonies and knowledge of all the numbers cut from *Dreamgirls* during its Boston tryouts. Freak flags are at full mast.

Before you judge, though, consider the alumni: Robert Downey Jr., Natalie Portman, Zach Braff, Lea Michele, Amy Ryan, Jennifer Jason Leigh, Josh Charles, Mandy Moore, Michael Ian Black, and countless accomplished composers, writers, and directors. Nothing to sneeze at there.

In 1979, though, it was mostly just a place to spend the summer and maybe have some fun.

I wasn't privy to the traveling-chorus bus experience. My mother drove me to Stagedoor that first year, so it took arriving there to realize how ill prepared I was for the gung ho nature of it. I had an interest in acting, no doubt, but not enough to take seriously the clearly stated requirement that I have a song and monologue already prepared. The reason the camp holds auditions right off the bat—what, no orientation mixer with soft drinks and name tags?—is because there's no messing around at Stagedoor. Not only were your days filled with classes in everything from vocal technique and stage combat to movement and dance and seemingly anything related to theater, but afternoons and nights were rehearsal time for the many shows in the process of being staged. Back then, stints at Stagedoor were two months, composed of a pair of four-week sessions, with one show every two weeks. Sound intense? It was. Throw in the requisite festival-week production, and you had nine shows in eight weeks. (They eventually changed it to three three-week sessions, with one show per session, so it's infinitely more manageable than when I was there.)

In that respect, Stagedoor *is* camp: *boot* camp, for whipping a stage show into shape.

So auditioning that first day is really just to show the camp's directors what you've got so you can be placed in a show, since every attendee has to go somewhere. The kids who know this, and care about snagging plum roles—the ones with full-on stage dreams who sing cast recordings in their sleep—bring their A games. Nothing brought home more to my newbie eyes the seriousness of the venture for many campers than watching this kid named Michael crank up a vigorous *"Willkommen,"* the famous opening number from *Cabaret,* for his audition in the camp's Playhouse theater. Michael had his sheet music for the pianist. He had a top hat and cane. He had tap shoes. He also wore bright green Lycra dance pants—*interesting*—and sported noticeably big prescription glasses, which admittedly kind of undercut the flamboyant Weimar Republic decadence he was after.

I was impressed, puzzled, and appalled. What had I gotten myself into? I was there to hang with David, and indulge the acting thing a little. I didn't have anything like that ready, so I sang "Happy Birthday" and read from a book of monologues I hastily borrowed from a fellow camper. I was terrible, which I guess made me perfect as a nameless street urchin in the chorus of my first show that summer, *Oliver!*

When I started taking classes at Stagedoor, I initially bristled at the amount of deep study being applied to acting. It all seemed like a parody of thespianic pretension, and frankly it seemed a little dumb to me. Per the wishes of the camp's artistic director, Jack Romano, a man for whom digging deep was everything, the director of our *Oliver!* wanted everyone to come up with a backstory for the characters we played. I remember thinking this was a bit silly, especially for someone like me, who wasn't even officially a character in the show, just a lowly chorus member. But that was the idea: Everyone's important! The show works only if each person onstage is fully committed to being a flesh-and-blood person with a name and a past and a present.

It's the kind of exercise that naturally brings out the theatrical in some, so I watched as the urchin crowd around me morphed into a collection of humpbacked, one-legged, or one-eyed orphans. Everyone else's elaborate character work seemed to manifest itself in bodily injuries and deformities. Even Charles Dickens would have eyed this crowd and thought, *Yikes! Too much. I mean . . . um. Wow.* (For some reason, I picture Bob Newhart playing Dickens.) For my street ragamuffin, I chose the name Toby, and while I gave him a suitably grim history in which his parents died of cholera, I also made him able-bodied. It's the first time I can remember making a calculated acting choice based on setting myself apart: *Everyone's doing one thing, so I'll do something different.*

As the weeks went on, I was slowly warming to the idea that acting exercises were kind of interesting rather than ridiculous. Meanwhile my pal David Dennis, who roomed with me that first year (along with a boy named Billy Goldstein), continued to smirk at how seriously these singing/dancing/acting campers took everything. David preferred to hone his skills at decadence and rule breaking. For instance, David and Billy were adept at convincing camp counselors to buy us cheap Ernest & Julio Gallo jug wine. (This was the time of the comedy *Meatballs*, when your counselor just might be a who-gives-a-shit Bill Murray–esque college kid biding his time for school credit.) I'm sure the places I send my children for the summer are staffed only by future Rhodes Scholars and neurosurgeons.

David and Billy quickly became camp legends for their antics. They disappeared from camp once for an unsupervised walk into town, and nobody would ever have known if David's mom hadn't coincidentally called the camp that day to say hi. Increasingly worried-sounding PA announcements of, "David Dennis? David Dennis? Please go to the office now," in five-minute intervals were the only giveaway that something was up. (A counselor found the two in town, and their reappearance in the common area brought the whole room to a silent halt, as if famous outlaws had been captured.)

David and Billy were also notorious for "raiding": sneaking into the girls' rooms, or smuggling girls back to theirs. David's whole reason for going to Stagedoor, in fact, had to do with the girls-to-boys ratio. It didn't matter that in this pre-*Glee* era, theater camp was so spectacularly uncool. There were maybe forty boys to two hundred and thirty girls, and at least half those boys were gay. So if you were one of the twenty or so straight boys, it was the proverbial fish-in-a-barrel situation. I remember in my last year an eleven-year-old Josh Charles being constantly surrounded by adoring fourteen-year-old girls. Was he talented and charming? Sure. Did those odds help? Absolutely. That's what drew David back to Stagedoor. But it wasn't enough to keep him there, and that first summer of mine—his second—was also David's last.

I, meanwhile, was beginning to think I'd found the only thing that mattered to me, and I eventually came to wonder why Stagedoor couldn't last all year long. I didn't need David to enjoy Stagedoor, after all. My mother likes to tell people the moment she knew it was all over for me, when I'd found my calling and wouldn't want to do anything else. After *Oliver!* I was cast in a tiny role in an ecologically minded musical called *Earthlings.* Though it seemed Stagedoor was perfectly fine staging adult fare like the Nazi-era *Cabaret*, the French song revue *Jacques Brel Is Alive and Well and Living in Paris*, and the play *Equus*—about a boy sexually attracted to horses—I was stuck appearing in something that was aimed at bored schoolchildren who need a cheery lesson in preserving the planet. But I did my part. My character, a businessman, is introduced with the line, "Joe was a very rich man."

I walked forward and said, "I'm a *very* rich man."

Howls of laughter roared back at me, and Mom—who was there for that first performance—says she instantly detected a glint in my eye, a glint that distinctly signaled, "Must. Keep. Doing. This." After that, every laugh I got in the show was like another little hit of some amazing new drug, one that simultaneously reduced my regularly inflamed lack of confidence and bolstered my ego. Once I figured out that being funny onstage was what I was good at, I was officially hooked.

Suddenly Stagedoor Manor wasn't a mere summer holding pen for over-the-top kids with attention issues and dress-up complexes; it was a breeding ground for what I wanted to do in life. Acting-class exercises, like the one in which you lie onstage pretending to sleep, then wake up to discover you're in a crystal forest—which must be conveyed *without speaking*—felt indisputably necessary as a budding actor. Can't you see I'm leaning against a crystal tree? Can't you?! It's right here!

These and many other illustrious drills came from the skewed mind of artistic director Dr. Jack Romano, who was a key figure for me and many Stagedoor alumni. A Jewish Cuban émigré who had legendarily attended the Royal Academy of Dramatic Art in London, Jack was very outspoken and passionate about stagecraft. That ardor for acting occasionally resulted in a chair being thrown across a room, or—in the case of a one girl's less-than-satisfactory singing—pulling his hair and shouting, "You sound like a fart in a ballroom!" He could be cruel, but it never came off as true cruelty—it was always imbued with the feeling that he wanted you to be better. He also had a kind of built-in ridiculousness that undercut anything unkind he might say. With his Caesar haircut, thick accent (he pronounced *focus* as "fuck-us"), and impish grin, he was difficult to take offense to. He was a great, mesmerizing teacher you couldn't help but follow into the craziest corners of your imagination. He cared about it all, and he made you care about it.

Getting praise from Jack felt better than anything else, and one day I felt particularly inspired to knock him out. A favorite exercise of Jack's was something he called the subway improv, in which the edge of the stage represents the lip of a subway platform. The backstory is that there's a serial killer on the loose, a detail I gather was inspired by the notorious Son of Sam murders that had terrified New Yorkers only a few years prior. Everyone plays a citizen entering the subway, and without explicitly saying so, you had to make some kind of acting choice that communicates this citywide fear. Jack would then clap his hands to signify the train coming into the station, which would end the exercise.

The improv started, and I came in with a deliberate sense of playing up the weird and creepy. I whistled "Strangers in the Night," and self-consciously drew attention to myself as if I were, in fact, the serial killer himself. But then Jack started clapping, and as the imaginary train pulled in, I revealed that I wasn't the serial killer, but instead someone committing suicide. I jumped off the edge of the stage as the train approached, and with that, Jack's jaw dropped and he let out a horrified gasp.

"Nobody ever did that in this class! I've never seen that," he said, seemingly out of breath. This was from someone who'd taught quite a few acting classes by this point.

That was a good day.

Not so good was the day a few years ago when I discovered this story had morphed over time and become attributed to noteworthy Stagedoor Manor alumnus Robert Downey Jr. It's even been published as an invention of Robert's in Mickey Rapkin's entertaining book about Stagedoor Manor, *Theater Geek*. Well, I'm here now to correct a historical wrong through this memoir and say, I'm the one who jumped! I'm the gasp-inducing suicide! You know what Robert Downey Jr. was famous for? Getting care packages of pot from his counterculture filmmaker father! (A close friend of mine was Robert's roommate one year—Iron Man and I were never there at the same time.) I'm sure his acting was impressive, too, but let's set the record straight on who rocked the subway improv, of which my example was cited by Jack Romano in Stagedoor classes for years afterward.

Moving on.

After that first summer at Stagedoor, and getting swept up in the collaborative mojo that went into putting on a show, I went back to 104 for ninth grade feeling like a seasoned professional. It was still a nice surprise, though, to jump from chorus member in *West Side Story* the year prior to a more prominent role that year, playing fifties rock star Birdie in *Bye Bye Birdie*. I had been spoiled by the talent at Stagedoor, so I expected to be surrounded by plucky strivers and gifted performers. I discovered instead that all the good singers had graduated last year, and the kid hired to play the lead—Birdie's manager—was the exact opposite of the light-on-his-feet guy who originated the role, Dick Van Dyke. This kid couldn't move, or sing, or even speak without droning. Of course, the general lack of talent also explains why I landed a plum role, so I couldn't get too mad about it. *Birdie* ended up being a charmless show, and after my summer, I was already developing a haughty sense of what was good and what was amateur hour. In other words, all I could think was, *Get me back to Stagedoor.*

Don't get me wrong: Stagedoor Manor shows weren't all good. In fact, some were terrible. But Stagedoor productions, which I participated in over four glorious summers, were fascinating examples of the ups and downs of instinctive decision making and willed creativity. When there are only two weeks to put up a show, you have to do everything quickly, stick by the choices, and fly or fall based on them. The quality varied wildly, since the same pool of people was involved in every show. If an obviously going-places Natalie Portman is in your play, that's great, but she might be starring opposite a never-going-anywhere Joe Nobody. Sometimes it's an experimental idea that crashes and burns, like the all-female *Godspell* I saw, in which Jesus—played by my sister, Robin, who attended only one Stagedoor summer—is a theater director, the disciples are the cast of a show, and in the end Jesus is crucified by the stage manager. That metaphor didn't make sense on any level whatsoever, except (perhaps not surprisingly) to the production's director, but the spirit of experimentation was nonetheless exciting.

Sometimes the spirit of creativity and need to have an "experience" made for something memorable. I played Pilate in a psychedelic-inspired *Jesus Christ Superstar*, and that was especially insane. During the climactic crucifixion scene, Pilate sings, "I wash my hands of your demolition! Die if you want to, you innocent puppet!" as he cleans the blood off his hands. We decided it'd be cool if when he washed his hands, suddenly instead of their being clean, there was actually more blood on them ("You'll *never* be clean, Pilate!") We accomplished this by surreptitiously switching the water bowl with one filled with stage blood while the audience's attention was elsewhere. Well, that little effect just ignited dedicated drug-using camper Jenny and the fanatical shroom-taking contingent of friends that she had in the front row, and she started losing her shit and screaming as if it were a horror movie. This, in turn, ignited more screams from the whole audience until it got so out of hand, we had a real *Passion of the Christ* state of affairs on our hands. Truly weird for a camp full of Jews.

Technical issues sometimes made for creative if problematic fixes. At Stagedoor, four or five shows were going at all times, but the main productions were at either the fifties-style modern-designed playhouse theater—formerly a nightclub when the place was a Catskills resort—or in the barn, which was a terrible place to put on shows, because it was, well, a barn. A barn is not a place where you wanted to spend a lot of time during a muggy summer. Also, the makeshift stage in the barn had metal bars spanning its width, holding the "walls" of the stage up, which often created strange shadows when light was directed at the performers. Kids would be singing and then there'd be a long black shadow across their faces. It looked like those photos of illicit behavior in which people's eyes are blacked out by strips. Throw in the nagging sense that you were sitting in the firetrap theater, and the barn was hardly a beloved space. (The barn did burn down, ultimately, and a beautiful new legitimate theater there was built in its place.)

During my first summer there, *Equus* (the weird horses/boy psychodrama) was at the barn, and *The Sound of Music*—featuring Robin as one of the nuns—was being staged simultaneously at the playhouse. Both shows required rotating sets to change sceneries, with the young actors who were last onstage themselves physically pushing the sets around between scenes. But in the barn, the rollers weren't smooth enough and made a horrible noise. It was especially unfortunate, then, that Jon Luks, the talented choreographer who was directing *The Sound of Music*, managed to piss off his tech crew with some last-minute demands, because in the dead of night they took all the wheels off the *Sound of Music* sets and put them on the rotating *Equus* set. Great for *Equus*, whose set now rotated silently and with ease, disastrous for *The Sound of Music*. Great for me in the audience at the beloved musical, too, because I got to see:

My sister and two fourteen-year-old girls dressed in nuns' habits finish singing "How Do You Solve a Problem Like Maria?"

"How do you hold a moonbeam in your ha-a-a-a-nd . . ."

The lights go down.

Polite applause that dies down quickly.

In the darkness, the sounds of a scuffle. Urgent whispers.

As my eyes adjust, I can just barely make out the three nuns as they put their shoulders to the side of the abbey set, pushing with all their might, legs churning, huffing and puffing, struggling like the offensive line of the Atlanta Falcons to move the (now immobile) scenery.

They let out a collective, *"Uuuurrhhrhhhr!"*

And finally *screeeeeeaaaach*, as the abbey set grudgingly turns around and becomes Maria's bedroom. But only halfway. The nuns let out another tennis grunt: *"Hurrrrrnnnggggg!"* Another *screeeeeeeeek!* And the stage is set for Maria's entrance. Lights come up to catch three dog-tired nuns trudging stage left.

At least I was entertained.

Although Stagedoor's reputation now is such that there's a wait list, which guarantees any given class is studded with showbiz wannabes, when I went the vibe was still loose enough that there were invariably kids there who still didn't know how they fit in. It was somewhat of a dumping ground for kids nobody knew what to do with. I remember a lisping loner named Ellen who wore a Greek fisherman's hat and glasses, and who would sit on a rock in front of the main building and bark, "Leave me alone! I want to be by myshelf!" It rubbed people the wrong way, and when she had to deliver an S-studded line in a show—which came out as, "New York ish full of pot shmokers, shpeed, and L-ESH-D"—I saw the director stifling a giggle and realized, *Holy shit, giving her that line was deliberate.*

But it was fun to be surprised by people you'd written off as not made for this. One slightly overweight, frizzy-haired girl named Randy seemed particularly miserable, and liked to show people the dotted line she'd written in pen on her wrists. She wasn't a singer, but she was cast as one of the singing von Trapp children in *The Sound of Music*, only the joke—which Randy was in on—was that she was the one von Trapp child who couldn't carry a tune. They even put in a line to help set up the genuinely funny moment when she croaks out a monotone lyric. It proved that with ingenuity and effort and participation, there could be a place for everybody.

With the intensity of the place, and practically no time to do anything but eat, drink, breathe, sleep, and shit theater, it's not surprising that I learned a lot about performing at Stagedoor over my four summers there. I learned what I could do, and what I couldn't.

When they did *Chicago*, I really wanted to play a supporting part, Roxie Hart's ignored husband, Amos. I knew I was right for that, but I was pulled into playing the lead in the musical *Pippin*, an atrocious production in which I fully stank. It's also a strange memory for me in that during one scene, in which Pippin first experiences the pleasures of the flesh, the director had two twelve-year-old girls smear whipped cream on my arms and then lick it off. Top that, Charlie Sheen. Or rather, don't. Please don't.

Sometimes the sheer number of plays and musicals you could be exposed to amounted to an education in itself. Sometimes they'd unearth a lost treasure like the 1937 Rodgers and Hart musical *Babes in Arms* and knock it out of the park. Since nobody knew it, it would feel like new. I might be wrong about this, but I got the impression we were the first place to stage the musical *Working*—adapted from historian Studs Terkel's interviews with people about their jobs—after its short-lived 1978 Broadway run.

One of the key acting lessons I picked up was during my time on *Working*. I was cast in multiple roles—as was every other cast member, which was how it was done originally—and one of those characters was a Latino who sings a lamentation about migrant workers called *"Un Mejor Día Vendrá."* Before that, though, the character has a monologue about the incredible toil of grape picking, and during read-throughs I would deliver it with all the emotional weight I could muster for how crushing this guy's life must be.

But Jack Romano would always stop me and say, "No, you can't feel pity. You're living it. You have to be strong in spite of it. You can tell people about it, but nobody wants to see you pity yourself."

"Okay," I said, "but this guy has to pick until his fingers bleed, and then he's singing about a better life. How can I not convey that?"

Jack kept arguing. "You can't be this sad guy. That's you; that's not him."

Eventually he took the part away from me, and put in Gordon Greenberg, who performed it with some self-pity, but not nearly the amount I gave it. Ultimately I understood. We were a bunch of fairly well-off—and in some cases, quite rich—city kids who hadn't been exposed to the kinds of lives depicted in these plays. It helped me realize that just because Jon Cryer feels a certain way about a character, that isn't necessarily what the writer intended, or what an audience wants to see. People want to see others fight against their lousy circumstances, and what I was doing with the migrant workers was wallowing in them. I was also surprised that I didn't harbor any ill will toward my replacement, Gordon, who went on to have a storied directing career, incidentally. I understood that what I wanted wasn't what was best for the show, and that taking it personally would have been a waste of energy.

As it turns out, I'd have more than a few chances to put that mind-set into action as my career got going. But that's for later. (Don't you love foreshadowing?)

It was apparent to me after a couple of summers at Stagedoor that a handful of things were true: I was going to live forever, I was going to learn how to fly (high), I would feel it coming together, and people would see me and cry.

Clearly I would have to go to the New York High School of Performing Arts.

In 1980, just before my second summer at Stagedoor, the movie *Fame* came out, and made going to a high school geared toward the arts look like . . . well, pretty hellish, actually, a powder keg of pressure, ambition, and fated choices. But it sure was a glorious hell: hardworking, talented kids spilling their guts out to make it as an actor, singer, or dancer. Since I'd now decided that acting was my path in life, going so far as to take Jack Romano's winter classes in Manhattan at the Hotel Carter, I wanted to get into the *Fame* school, or the other noteworthy public school dedicated to art, Music & Art on West One Thirty-fifth Street. David Dennis, who'd always had a talent for drawing, was already in Music & Art, as was my singing sister, Robin. It seemed natural I would apply.

My mother had another idea, however. Though she expressed some misgivings at her son jumping into the same profession she'd struggled at for decades, she took my desire seriously enough to look ahead at post–high school. Since I would surely be applying to a college with an acting program, she suggested I approach high school as an opportunity to show a college how well-rounded I was. I'd already have numerous summers at Stagedoor, winter acting classes, and working at the Equity Library Theatre on my application.

"That part's taken care of," Mom said. "If you go to Bronx Science, a strong math/science school, colleges are going to be much more open to bringing in that guy, rather than the applicant who's all about the arts."

When Mom suggested this, there was no invisible hammer being swung down. It was still my choice. But her logic was sound, and I agreed. I applied to the Bronx High School of Science, one of America's top science magnet schools, and got in. It's not as if there wasn't an affinity in me for what the school had to offer. Space was especially interesting to me, ever since America had touched down on the moon when I was four. All that stuff enchanted me. I would write to NASA asking for autographs, and I'd get sent press packets with photos that I treated like gold. When Skylab got in trouble because one of its solar panels didn't open, and they had to jury-rig that big gold umbrella to keep it from overheating, that was some pins-and-needles shit! When other boys were trying to figure out how to lock lips with girls, I was marveling at how the *Apollo* hooked up to Russia's *Soyuz* spacecraft—they had different atmospheres, people! That was not a guaranteed match. How would we know it would last for those two?

The problem in going to Bronx Science, though, was running up against the wall that was the limit of my interest in math and science. I was an arts guy now. I had an outside outlet for it, so I never really cared that much about high school. Plus, it was instantly hard, and after always being a top student, I was now falling behind. I had to take classes like meteorology and oceanography. I failed my first class, mechanical drawing, necessitating my taking it again. Sure, now I can hand a furniture builder a sweet schematic for an armoire, or impress an architect with a detailed, dimensional representation of a guesthouse. But at the time I was flailing and thinking, *I'm not going to be an engineer, so why am I here again?* I was a nerd, yes, but for musical theater. These were much different nerds, budding tech wizards who dreamed of owning personal computers someday and treated punch-out cards the way I did a play script. Surely these people would never amount to anything!

Bronx Science was the kind of place in which school battles were Rubik's Cube challenges. Whispers would go through the hallways.

"It's Yin Fan versus Hwang Lee at four by the greenhouse!"

"Not those two guys!"

"Be there or be a rhombus!"

Then, at the appointed time, you'd see two students with those faddish 3-D gewgaws attached to key chains, facing off against each other. But the object wasn't making each side a different solid color. That would be too easy. These geeks were speed-turning to make elaborate, multicolored, predetermined patterns. It wouldn't surprise me if other contests involved blindfolding, tying one hand behind the back, and walking a rooftop ledge at the same time. These guys were hard-core. Bronx Science

Jon Cryer

had the questionable distinction of having the only Ultimate Frisbee team that, to a man, understood the aerodynamics of the Frisbee.

Creativity at Bronx Science was manifested in different ways, and occasionally I had to applaud. The school prank that involved releasing forty live lobsters on the second floor of the west wing was truly awe-inspiring. (How much could that have cost? How were they transported alive?) I even made a small contribution to the school's culture of discipline-appropriate antics when Senior Day arrived my junior year. Many seniors liked to fill their hands with shaving cream, creep up behind the new kids, and transfer that pile of foam to the head, neck, and back of the targets. I laughed, but also noticed the pitfalls. A mark might hear that distinctive airy gurgle of the Barbasol can discharging shaving cream. If he runs, who wants to see a senior with a sad face and a handful of cream and nobody to *blooosh*? Could the need for stealth be taken out of the equation?

I found the solution in the same toiletries aisle. I put an aerosol spray top over the can of Barbasol and voilà! You can coat somebody with shaving cream from a good four or five feet away, and by the time they hear the *sschhhh*, it's too late. Done and done. Yes, I brought this innovation to the Bronx High School of Science, but did they put up a picture of me in the hallway? No. Maybe this has something to do with the fact that I ate lunch alone the entire time I was there, and ignored plenty of kind requests from well-meaning nerds to engage with me socially. I just didn't care enough about school to be engaged at Bronx Science.

Much like that last year at junior high, my overriding thought was, *Get me back to Stagedoor.*

I made all kinds of great friends at Stagedoor. My best new friend at camp was a kid from Long Island named David Quinn. Like the other David in my life, this David was also outgoing, gregarious, and charismatic, but completely undeservedly to my teenage eyes. He was this bespectacled,

44

tubby Jewish kid who for fun would walk around shirtless, fold his nipple inward, and have it talk to people. This was his ventriloquist act, a nipple that sang the popular songs of the day ("All the boys think she's a spy; she's got . . . Bette DA-vis eyes!") And somehow, some way, he got more action than I ever did.

Mostly this was because David Quinn was the type of adolescent heterosexual male who had the balls to just walk up to girls he thought were beautiful and essentially proclaim, "Hey, we should make out!" Make those kinds of good-natured overtures often enough in a sea of two hundred and thirty girls, and eventually you'll close a deal. David was beloved everywhere at camp, and not just because he was a gifted performer who could sing and act. (While I was relegated to the background in *Oliver!*, he was winning over all as the Artful Dodger.) The owners, teachers, and counselors just loved him, so he could go anywhere he wanted. And though he and I were cordial passing acquaintances my first two summers there, once we roomed together beginning my third year, we became inseparable.

By the third year, you start to pick up on how to make life easier. David Quinn and I got to camp early our third year in order to switch out the crappy bunk beds in our room with the higher-quality bunk beds down the hall in one of the other rooms. We got ours moved out, and were halfway into our room with the better bunk beds when Jason, the guy who ran the camp, caught us. *Shit.*

"Uh, what are you two up to?" he asked.

I was about to fess up when Quinn spoke first. "We were going to move out these beds, because we didn't want bunk beds," he said. Smooth. What looked like going in could just as easily be going out.

"No," said Jason. "Put those back in your room."

Sure thing!

It felt like a good omen for the year, narrowly avoiding getting caught with our bed switch. That third year, David Quinn and I shared a room with another David—keep track, people—named David Bache, and a kid named Adam Warshofsky (it was a theater camp in upstate New York, folks; there were going to be a lot of Adams and Davids). Collectively we were known as the Boys of Room 116, and our particular specialty was performing in-room parodies of the camp's shows for whoever cared to see: counselors, campers, teachers. David Bache was always curious about who the gay students were at camp, even though he seemed categorically ignorant of the fact that Adam, the kid in the bunk above him, was translucently gay. Meanwhile, David Bache was throwing himself into his role in our drag-show version of *The Sound of Music*, which we literally held in our closet. He readily wore sweatpants on his head as Maria and stayed in the closet until we'd sing a line from "How Do You Solve a Problem Like Maria?" after which he'd click on the lightbulb and act out whatever it was: climbing a tree, scraping a knee ("Oh, *fuck!*" he'd shout hilariously), or displaying "curlers in her hair," which were toilet rolls.

Years later, when I'd heard David Bache had ended up marrying a lovely guy named Glenn, it occurred that perhaps he was asking who was gay because subconsciously he was just looking for members of his tribe.

David Quinn and I, meanwhile, had a list of that year's Stagedoor girls tacked to the inside of our closet, and we'd scratch off the names we weren't interested in. But while David Quinn was quietly going about methodically cutting a swath through the female campers, I was coming to the realization that it wasn't lack of opportunity that was holding me back, but unmitigated dread. I was still a romantic at heart, but I simply couldn't imagine a girl I was attracted to actually wanting to be with me in return. My sense of myself had by this time become completely infused with my staunchly held belief that I was deeply unattractive. So I was certain in every fiber of my being that no girl would ever refer to me as a "hunk," or "boss," or my favorite slang compliment of the 1970s, "foxy."

I did make out with a girl for the first time at camp. Her name was Teri Ryan, and she was a vision of early eighties teenage-gal hotness: a beautiful gum chewer from Long Island with Sasson jeans and a big pink plastic comb with the handle sticking out of her back pocket for easy care and feeding of her richly feathered hair. She smoked clove cigarettes, which lent her mouth a faintly sweet-and-sour taste when we kissed. I loved it. But the overriding emotion I felt at the time was one of astonishment that a girl that many people (not just me) thought of as attractive was willing, nay, actually interested in kissing me. We never had any kind of relationship after the aforementioned incident; nor did we even speak of it, so I attributed the kiss to a brief psychotic episode on her part.

By the end of my third year—David Quinn's fourth—he and I had the camp wired. We were killing it in our shows, routinely getting cast as leads, and coming home with armfuls of accolades at the season-ending awards show. Curfews were supposed to keep everyone in their rooms by ten p.m., but we'd routinely remove the medicine cabinet between rooms, which left a hole big enough to squeeze through for quick escapes. I also rigged a device with rope that could turn off the light in your room once the door to your room was opened from the outside. Thank you, nerd school! Then again, by a certain point, we simply defied curfews openly by hanging with the counselors, because they all knew us.

We stepped it up the fourth summer, our last, by scoring a room to ourselves—no third roomie to bring us down, man—and running the canteen, which used to be a bar off the playhouse but was now a place to sell candies, sodas, and frozen treats. Kids would hang out there during their free period between the last class after lunch and the start of afternoon rehearsals. David Quinn and I ran the canteen for the owners, and with that kind of responsibility, we might as well have been in charge of the Federal Reserve. As for whether all collected moneys at the canteen made their way into the camp's coffers, I don't remember so good. Who wants to know? Talk to my lawyer.

That fourth summer at Stagedoor, when I was seventeen, was also noteworthy, because I was there for only one four-week term. Not out of any dissatisfaction with Stagedoor, though. In fact, the camp had already helped me discover what I wanted to do, and now it had helped me take the next step. The previous year, with ambitions to learn as much as possible about acting, I asked Jack Romano, now a champion of mine, if he would write me a recommendation letter to the summer Shakespeare program at the Royal Academy of Dramatic Art in London. It was a big-deal program, something I felt I needed in my education as an actor, and I appealed to him as a graduate of the school to put in a good word for me. He said yes, and wrote a kindly letter attesting to my skills and commitment to the craft. It must have done the trick, because I was accepted to the program—thanks, Jack!—but it cast an interesting light on my time at Stagedoor that last year. Everyone at the camp knew I was heading to the Royal Academy after the first summer session. I was living the dream for a lot of the attendees, but the vibe I got from them wasn't jealousy. It was a mixture of eagerness and excitement for me.

My last show there was the classic fifties factory-strike musical *The Pajama Game*, directed by Jeanine Tesori, who would later go on to be a prominent composer/director. I was playing Sid Sorokin, the factory superintendent who falls for the pretty, feisty union head nicknamed Babe. After the last performance, I went backstage, shed my costume, put on my clothes, grabbed my packed bags, and headed to the car, where my mother awaited. What happened next, she and I differ over in terms of its meaning. As the car pulled out of the driveway, my days at Stagedoor officially behind me, campers ran after it yelling, "Jon! Jon!" Mom likes to think of them as groupies, because it's not a bad zero-to-hero narrative in her mind that the roly-poly, barely assertive, and showbiz-skeptical junior high kid with slumped shoulders she first dropped off years ago was now an ambitious, focused, beloved theater-camp alumnus awash in adulation from teenagers.

Okay, I'll cop to some adulation. David Quinn and I truly were unlikely rock stars that last year.

But in my heart of hearts, I know those kids were really just my ever-aspiring Stagedoor friends and colleagues, the outcasts and oddballs I'd gone on an already exciting journey with, and who were now excited that I was headed off on an adventure many of them could only hope to go on. They just wanted to wish me well. To which I give a heartfelt thanks.

And lastly, with regard to the bonkers, vivacious, theatrically nerdist, insanely creative, and life-changing experiences that were my summers at Stagedoor Manor, I say . . . remember, the suicide subway jump was *mine.*

Chapter 4
The Fat Man Sits in Row H

My Shakespeare summer at the Royal Academy of Dramatic Art in London was all about the technical approach to acting. After Stagedoor, where a cursing, wild-eyed, but caring Jack Romano scared the shit out of you until you found that deep thing inside you that could be externalized in a character, the Brits focused on the external, the ways your speech and body could bring a role to life. At RADA, the goal was to aspire to a character's dramatic heights, rather than let the character grow out of you.

A movement teacher named June Kemp taught us mask work, for instance, in which we'd wear classical masks with twisted expressions, and it was our job to inhabit that expression with our body. It came off as unnatural at times, but that seemed to be the point.

In prepping a monologue once, this director who smoked like a chimney and never flicked his ashes persuaded me to make some pretty theatrical choices.

"Okay," I said, "but that doesn't seem like reality."

"Why should an actor be stuck with mere reality?" he said. "We're all agreeing to pretend here, so why not?"

It was hard to argue with logic like that, even from a man with a lap full of fallen ashes. That time in London very much helped free me as an actor, especially the encouragement to embrace the outlandish.

On the weekends I'd venture to the West End, the center of theater culture in Britain, and see as many shows as I could afford. Once I'd come to an understanding of the differences of the British process, my enjoyment of theater took on a new dimension. I sat awestruck by performances like Rupert Everett's in *Another Country* at the Greenwich and Bob Hoskins in the National Theatre's production of *Guys and Dolls*. Huge acting choices coupled with real and raw emotion. I developed a reverence for the work that was going on in the West End, and hoped someday they'd let me tread the boards there.

But upon returning to New York, I concluded that Stagedoor and its adrenaline-driven program of study/work/experience taught me more, and had probably prepared me better for whatever lay ahead. Although for the moment, what lay ahead was a senior year at Bronx Science (ugh), working as an usher at the Equity Library Theatre (money), and going out on auditions (yay) that didn't yield anything (sigh). My mother's manager, Marty, even offered to help me find an agent.

Something would happen; I was sure of it. I just didn't know when.

It turns out the "when" was damn quick. A funny thing began happening as I'd escort people to their seats at the Equity. Occasionally patrons would smile and giggle at me, as if I'd said something amusing, and we all know how amusing, "Seats eleven and twelve are right here, ma'am," can be. Figuring these people were just eccentric theatergoers, I thought nothing of it. Then I'd get from the same giggling smiler: "You were wonderful in the show." This was often whispered conspiratorially, as if I were supposed to say the other half of some espionage go-code— "The fat man sits alone in row H"—and begin discussing a scheduled assassination.

Instead, I'd just reply, "Thank you? That's kind of you, but I'm not in the show."

When it happened a couple more times, I finally got more information.

"I loved you in *Torch Song Trilogy*!" someone said.

"Great!" I said. "I haven't seen it."

"What are you doing up here?" was what came back at me.

"No, you don't understand. I wasn't joking. I haven't seen it."

"You're not Matthew Broderick?"

Ah.

Do yourself a favor, before you think I'm overstating this. Check out the photo insert. In 1983, I looked like Matthew Broderick. Same rosy complexion, same dimply smile, same devastating handsomeness. Matthew was becoming the toast of Broadway, having followed a *New York Times*-noticed run as Harvey Fierstein's gay adopted son, David, in the off-Broadway production of *Torch Song Trilogy* with the lead role of Eugene in Neil Simon's soon-to-premiere play *Brighton Beach Memoirs*. He'd even made a couple of movies, *Max Dugan Returns* (also written by Simon) and an upcoming summer flick called *War Games*. I was jealous, of course, because everybody was saying this guy was amazing. I ran over to the Alvin Theatre, where *Brighton Beach* was set to open, stared at the big posters outside, and thought, "Okay, I get it now. He looks like me. Or I look like him. Or I need to talk to my mother about my birth. Or Matthew's mother. Or, if there's more of us out there, the CIA."

In any case, a ball started rolling. I was walking down One Hundred Fourth Street with my mother one day when we ran into an old friend of hers, an actor named Peter Ratray, who was then appearing in *Torch Song Trilogy*. He asked if I'd been going out on auditions, and I said I had, but with no bites.

He said, "Well, you should audition for *Torch Song*. There's a part you'd be perfect for."

Peter said he'd put in a good word for me if I'd get my agent to make a call. (And I now had one, thanks to Marty, who was also now my manager.) Then I could come in and audition, because they were getting ready to mount a tour of the show, and Fisher Stevens, who had taken over the role of David, wouldn't be going on the road with it.

I was riddled with nerves on the day I went to the Helen Hayes for my audition. So it was especially disconcerting to walk out onto the stage, ready to read, and be met with a guttural gasp from the seats that sounded like a dying vacuum cleaner, but was most discernibly frog-voiced actor/author Harvey Fierstein in a state of shock. After I went through the scene with the reader, Harvey introduced himself and apologized, saying, "I'm sorry. It's just that you look so much like Matthew Broderick, I honestly thought you were him for a minute." Although I was tempted to imagine elaborate pranks I could play on unsuspecting theater geeks with my gasp-inducing looks, I focused on my audition. I felt good about it, too. They were very nice to me afterward, and wanted to get to know me a little bit, which is a big indicator you've auditioned well.

On a high, I went that night to see *Brighton Beach Memoirs* and thought it was fantastic. It was a long play, but it had rich humor, great family dynamics, and wonderful performances, especially from Matthew, who was completely funny and engaging. He was a revelation, really, and though I got a few more pangs of jealousy, I was also motivated to be as good as he was. Well, somebody must have been able to read my mind, because the next day I got asked to audition for *Brighton Beach Memoirs*, too, to understudy Matthew. This was, to put it mildly, a lot of stuff happening very fast, but it was what I lived for.

The day after my audition for *Brighton Beach*, Marty called, and he had a sound in his voice I can only describe as insanely giddy.

"Jon," he said, "you got the *Torch Song* tour! They really want you!"

I could not believe this. My amazing week was getting more amazing-er. Amazeballs, the kids today might say. The blood was rushing to my face, and I was grinning wildly. "That's fantastic, Marty!" I yelled.

"But that's not all," he said. "The show you auditioned for yesterday?

Brighton Beach Memoirs? They just called. They want you to understudy for Matthew Broderick on Broadway."

Okay, you have to understand. My only performance experience at this point was Stagedoor Manor. I was still in high school at the time. I was an eighteen-year-old routinely met with dubious looks from Mrs. Tsaggos in social studies when I'd tell her I was going to miss her class because I had an audition. I had just gotten the phone call to end all thoughts of dubiousness.

I was speechless. Marty countered the silence by laying out my choices. "You could be the understudy to a lead on Broadway, with a shot at taking over for him when he's done, or you could go on tour with *Torch Song Trilogy.*"

Once I got over how incredible this day had become, I began seriously thinking about the options in front of me. *Torch Song* offered guaranteed performing; *Brighton Beach* was an offer to wait patiently in the wings. *Torch Song* was a supporting part; *Brighton Beach* was a lead. *Torch Song* meant dropping everything and leaving New York for new horizons but surely plenty of adventure, while *Brighton Beach* didn't necessarily have to disrupt my life at all, and I could finish high school, which I didn't want to leave.

But only one was Broadway, the Great White Way, the apex of the American theater world.

"Broadway," I told Marty.

When I told my mother the big news, she was proud and excited, and fully supportive. Gretchen Cryer was in no way one of those showbiz parents who dissuaded her kids from going into the family business. She knew how gung ho I was, how much enjoyment I got from acting. Her attitude was, "Well, of course they'd hire you!"

When I started prepping for Eugene, I fully expected to be nailing down the part in rehearsals with all the principals, the ones performing it night after night. I thought I'd be in the trenches every day with them.

After all, wasn't it most likely—if I ever had to jump into the role—that I'd be doing it with them? But the reality was that there were only two rehearsals a week, and they were with every other understudy, a sort of B-team get-together. For such a huge part, it didn't seem like a lot of time. Six weeks in, with only twelve actual rehearsal days, I was showing up still not knowing all the lines. In my defense, a lot of *Brighton Beach* is Eugene, and in monologue, and there's a lot of *Brighton Beach* to begin with—the show regularly ran two and a half hours.

I was feeling pretty good, though, the day director Gene Saks came in for a full-dress run-through with all the understudies. Afterward I waited patiently for feedback, but Gene had no notes for me. The other actors got notes—more this, less of that—but I was left alone, to which I surmised, "Nailed it!" I went home that day with visions of elated theatergoers exiting the Alvin on some future night, convinced they'd seen a new star being born as they clutched a little slip of crudely scissored paper that read, "Tonight, the role of Eugene will be played by Jon Cryer."

The next day I was heading out to go to rehearsal when my manager, Marty, called me. "Can you come to my office?" he said, his voice unusually scratchy.

"I'm supposed to go to rehearsal," I said.

"It's more important that you come to the office."

As I made my way there, I kept thinking, *Why did he sound like a school principal in disciplinary mode?* After I walked into his office, I thought, *Why is he crying?*

"They let you go," he managed to get out.

Marty was sweet that way. He was still new to the manager game. What hurt me hurt him. And yet right now I couldn't quite compute this data. "What?"

"They decided you weren't ready, and they're letting you go."

I was stunned. Stunned, and frankly pissed. But first stunned. "How is that possible? Why? What do you mean, I wasn't ready? I need to know why!"

Marty didn't have much more information than that, so I called Gene Saks directly. No matter that I'd barely had an interaction with the man, I wanted to know what happened. This storied theater director was gracious enough to take my call, and laid it out for me.

"Jon, you just didn't look like you were ready to do the part," he told me. "And you'd been there for six weeks already."

The only reaction I could possibly have was, He was right. I couldn't argue with him. He tried to lessen the blow by saying that they were bringing in a well-known name—Doug McKeon, who'd been in *On Golden Pond*—and that I shouldn't fret too much. What I never knew, and what nobody told me, was that I was expected to see the show as often as possible and be off-book, ready to go, on my own, in two weeks. The understudy rehearsals were really there to practice on my feet what I'd studiously picked up from watching the show night after night, and memorizing like gangbusters in the meantime. Had they told me this on day one, I would have worked my ass off to get ready, but at heart I had to agree with Gene: I wasn't ready.

I went home devastated, feeling punched out and dazed like an unprepared fighter. Plenty of tears were shed in the presence of my mom, and I have to say, this is when having parents in the business is an enormous advantage. They've seen it all, and they completely understand. One of my mother's closest friends is the wonderful actor/director Austin Pendleton, and he said something to me that greatly helped me feel better: "Jon, I don't respect anybody who hasn't been fired at least once." Phone calls and visits from Mom's theater friends were a welcome balm to my wounded ego.

Then I got another phone call from Marty. Considering the roller coaster his telecommunications typically engendered, I considered not picking up.

"Jon, we have good news," he said. "Forget *Brighton Beach*. *Torch Song* doesn't need somebody for the road now. They need somebody to take over for Fisher Stevens here. They're willing to offer it to you, so you're getting that rarity, kid: a second chance."

The sense of relief was overwhelming, the sense of gratitude just as strong. I was going to make this work. I ran down to the Helen Hayes that night to watch *Torch Song Trilogy*, and went backstage afterward to meet the cast. There was Estelle Getty, not yet a "Golden Girl" but already a stage legend, walking up to me and saying, "Hello-o-o-o, dahling!" as she gave me a big hug and kiss. Warmed by the sentiment, I said, "Estelle, it's so nice to meet you."

Her face went absolutely frozen, her eyes confounded. "Oh, oh!" she said. "I'm sorry; I thought you were somebody else." *Okay*, I thought, *let's turn this gig into an opportunity to let everyone know I'm not Matthew Broderick*. (In the good way, obviously. Not "I'm not as good as Matthew Broderick." As in . . . Oh, you know what I mean.)

I went in to rehearse the next day, and the vibe was good. I walked around, script in hand, casually working on the lines as they directed me through the blocking of the scenes. I'd write down the character's actions and movements in the margins next to the lines, all the while eager to get home and commit David to memory.

At home, another call from Marty. "Hey, Marty," I answered. "Thanks for checking in . . ."

"They're going to fire you."

"What?!"

He sounded exasperated. "They said you didn't know the lines!"

This was starting to get ridiculous. Was this some giant prank? My ire rising, I blurted back, "I didn't know I was expected to know the lines on the first fucking day!"

"All right, all right," he said. "I'm going to call them and ask them to give you another chance."

"Thank you!" I practically shouted. "Please!"

After I spent a few tense minutes alone near the phone, Marty finally called back. "They're going to give you another day," he said. "But learn that poem."

Those of you familiar with the old Little Rascals shorts will recognize

Marty's advice. It refers to the one in which Breezy cuts school because he doesn't want to recite a poem Miss Crabtree assigns him, and yet an internal voice keeps telling him, *Learn the poem. Learn the poem.* So I learned it. I crammed like, well, what I was, essentially: a high schooler before a big exam. Only this was something more than just an exam. I wanted people to know I could do this. You may think it a little draconian to expect a novice to memorize an entire part in a day, but if this was how the big leagues worked, I wasn't going to question it. I was going to do anything to give them a reason not to can my ass.

I went in to rehearsal the next day and was basically off-book. I screwed up some lines, but hey, I was in better shape after two days on *Torch Song Trilogy* than I was after six weeks on *Brighton Beach Memoirs*. Losing your job does have a beautiful way of sharpening your focus. Things went smoothly after that. I eventually replaced Fisher Stevens in the show, and it wasn't long before they asked me again if I wanted to go on tour with it. That took me to San Francisco and Los Angeles, where great reviews for the LA premiere of *Torch Song* led to my getting my first movie roles.

Years later, my mother and I were reminiscing about my first taste of professional acting, and she said something that really struck me. She said that while she knew from watching me at Stagedoor Manor that I had a talent for performing and making people laugh, and that from seeing me onstage in *Torch Song Trilogy* she knew I was going to make it, what really gave her the idea that I was cut out for acting as a career was how I dealt with the firing.

"Jon," she reminded me, "when they handed you your pink slip, what was wonderful about your reaction was that it was complete anger and outrage. You came home and said, 'I could have done it, Mom! They didn't give me the chance!' Rather than, 'Oh, poor me, I'm defeated. I'm never going to do this again.' You were a warrior, and I was so very proud of you."

Now that you've gotten the admittedly incongruous image of me as a warrior out of your head—was I in armor, perhaps? samurai-like? some shirtless, bloodied hulk in an MMA ring?—know that inside me I did discover a resilience and an urge to prove my worth that's stood me in good stead ever since. My life in show business would go on to be quite the amusement-park ride in terms of highs, lows, curves, and occasional screaming, but to have your first up/down stomach churner right off the bat was immensely valuable.

As for the Broderick thing, it's a fact of life that whatever helps you get a job in the acting world is ultimately a good thing. (Except maybe the casting couch, a piece of furniture I've fortunately never been invited to test out.) What I'm saying is, there's getting the gig, but then showing what you've got. Really, you're looking for what gets you to the latter. At the time, my physical similarities to Matthew Broderick were impossible to ignore, and I know that had they not existed, I would surely have not booked those two jobs in the same day. Besides, if I was going to look like another actor, genetics could have been a lot less kind to me. I doubt there would have been a market for an eighteen-year-old who looked like, let's say, post-boxing-career Mickey Rourke.

I make that incredibly vicious remark about the *Diner* star because of something that happened at a Gold's Gym in Los Angeles ten years ago. I was working out there with my personal trainer, Rich Guzman, when I noticed over in the corner on the weight machines a bulked-up figure with a battered but just-recognizable face.

"Is that Mickey Rourke?" I said incredulously. "Wow, what happened to him?"

"That's what he looks like now from all that boxing," Rich said.

I left after my session, and what I heard later was that Mickey Rourke came over to my trainer and inquired, "Hey, was that Jon Cryer?"

"Yes," Rich replied.

Mickey grimaced, then asked, "What happened to *him*?"

Around the time I was fifteen, my father moved back to the East Coast. He'd been offered the part of Juan Perón in the Andrew Lloyd Webber/

Tim Rice musical *Evita*, replacing the talented Bob Gunton, who originated the part on Broadway, and whom you probably know from playing
the warden in *The Shawshank Redemption*. Gunton was leaving, and David Cryer would be his replacement.

I hadn't seen much of my dad at all in the ten years or so since my
parents divorced. He and his new wife, Britt, had moved to Los Angeles,
where they started a family, and I'd visited only a couple of times. Dad had
tried his hand at acting in movies and on television, but the roles were few
and far between. He played the guard who hoses down Clint Eastwood in
Escape from Alcatraz and barks sadistically, "Welcome to Alcatraz!" He
was also in the midseventies roller-coaster disaster movie enigmatically
titled *Rollercoaster*, playing one half of a bickering married couple whose
parking-lot argument forces the bad guy to pause in his bomb assembly.
He was in an episode of *Wonder Woman*, which was actually a big fucking
deal to me, because I harbored a pulse-quickening crush on statuesque
Lynda Carter. He was also in *American Gigolo*, which mattered less, as
I did not have heart palpitations for Richard Gere.

This is by way of saying, I'd never really seen my dad do what he was
meant to do: act and sing onstage. When I was a wee 'un and he was performing on Broadway in *1776*, I had no understanding of what the show
was or what my dad did. My recollections were vague. I just knew he
played a serious guy who sang "Molasses to Rum." I didn't have an appreciation for his talents.

Seeing him in *Evita*, then, was a true lightning-bolt moment for me.
He was fantastic in it. And now that I'd had my own epiphany about my
calling in life, we had a portal to a new communication. Whether it was
him driving me up to Stagedoor, or hanging out backstage at *Evita*—
where I first got to meet the phenomenal Patti LuPone, who played opposite my dad for the last month of her run—or bouncing over to check
him out onstage after I got out of understudy rehearsals on *Brighton Beach
Memoirs*, it felt like this was a family thing. *We're the Cryers of Broadway!
This is what we do!* Even though my hopes were dashed after getting

fired from *Brighton*, it still felt like, "Hey, them's the breaks in this family business of ours! We act; we go home; then we act again somewhere else!"

My father and stepmother and their children even lived with us the first month he was back in town while they waited to move into a house in Teaneck, New Jersey. Not only was Mom and Dad's divorce amicable, but Gretchen and Britt became great friends. That time in the apartment with all of us under one roof was a special one, because it seemed to signal a new era for our families. I had a real rapprochement with my stepmother, Britt. There'd always been tension between us, and I know I'd been surly with her on visits to the West Coast. But now I was a miserable high schooler wishing I could just act and act and act and not spend most of my year failing classes. Summer at Stagedoor was the only time I was happy. I opened up about this to Britt—a talented dancer and actress who'd once been part of Paul Taylor's company—and she comforted me about the realities of following your dreams. We had our first connection as grown-ups. Ever since then, we've been close.

It felt as if the family had expanded, with everyone in an emotional place that felt older, wiser, and less stressed. We were all grateful to have one another around now for support. Mom got the time and space she needed to explore herself and become the artist she would become, and a financially secure one at that. Dad was able to try what he wanted to try, and then come back to that at which he was incredibly gifted: musical theater. Dad would go on to spend nineteen years performing in *Phantom of the Opera*, on Broadway and on the road.

That's a long time with one show, writes the guy who's been acting in a sitcom for twelve years. But it's a testament to his love for all of it: the show, the job, the atmosphere. He's been able to make the theater his life, and for an actor, you can't ask for much more than that.

Chapter 5
No Knob on the Gearshift

As heady as it was to land Broadway gigs like *Brighton Beach Memoirs* and *Torch Song Trilogy* with little experience, I still had my sights on the movies. Directing films continued to appeal to me, and now that I was getting my sea legs as an actor, getting a role in a movie sounded like the perfect job, one where I could observe what a director does from the other side of the camera. Act, then watch. Act, then watch. Rinse. Repeat.

So for a young film nerd and aspiring actor, the words "Bob Altman wants to meet you" are a pretty exciting thing to hear from a casting director. I was doing *Torch Song Trilogy* in New York at the time, and among the many auditions I was being sent on was one for a part in a comedy Altman was preparing to shoot in Arizona called *O.C. and Stiggs*. Though I hadn't seen all his major movies at this point, I knew this was a big, big deal, a golden opportunity made extra nerve-racking because of the talent behind it all. And now, after auditioning for the casting director, I was going to meet the man himself.

My nervousness was mitigated, though, by one element working in my favor: I was familiar with the film's source material, a series of stories in the humor magazine *National Lampoon* about a pair of antihero teenagers named O. C. Oglevey and Mark Stiggs, who got their mean-spirited kicks out of disrupting the stultifying suburbia around them. This was the 1980s, when hatred of yuppies and the prankish antics of young men (thanks greatly to the *Lampoon*'s own smash-hit movie *Animal House*) were—to use modern parlance—"a thing."

I knew and enjoyed the stories, and was led to believe they meant something to Altman, who had a famously irreverent sense of humor. (Before *Animal House*, after all, there was *MASH*.) I was sent to an expensive-looking apartment with a wonderfully casual disarray to it, which is a good description of Robert Altman in general: He was a big guy, tall, white-haired, and rumpled, but friendly and funny. He, his films, and seemingly his life were perfect examples of an appealing messiness. At any rate, he took his time getting around to reading me, partly because we were having such a good time talking, and he was impressed that I was familiar with the *Lampoon* stories. Before I knew it I was off to Arizona for two months to shoot my first movie, under the direction of a cinema god. Score!

It's a common perception that the theater is for intellectuals and movies are for everyone else. Although I don't believe that, I will say that after landing two stage roles playing very smart people—Eugene in *Brighton Beach Memoirs* and David in *Torch Song Trilogy*—I was to make my movie debut playing a full-on idiot. In the *Lampoon* stories, Randall is somewhat brain-damaged from, among other things, having a nail accidentally driven into his head during the installing of an acoustical tile ceiling. He also once tried to mow the family's garden, which is made of rocks. Hamlet he was not. I nonetheless decided to play Randall as if he were the *Brighton Beach Memoirs* character's intelligence-challenged cousin, in that I kept Eugene's Brooklyn Jewish accent while I said and did the stupid things required of me. Why such an accent would show up in

Phoenix, Arizona, in a WASP family, I have no idea. But hey, Bob liked it. So I kept doing it.

In fact, what I started to realize was that Robert Altman liked everything, which was why there was no real script, and once he gives everyone a basic idea of where a scene is going to go, the expectation is that you're going to just make up a bunch of stuff when the camera rolls. You knew your lines, but kept it loose. This was Bob's notorious way of working, a free-form jazz improvisation that feels like a party he's throwing that happens to involve several thirty-five-millimeter cameras. Every cast member is miked, so whichever way a scene goes within an established movie set, the experienced camera operators have a way to capture it. It's sort of like the way I imagine grouse hunting is among the aristocratic set in England: a scenario controlled just enough around an established perimeter so that the targets eventually make their way into a hoped-for range, ending with someone yelling, "Good shot!"

You never knew what would happen with Bob at the helm—see the dove-shit story at the beginning of this book—and as a matter of course, the structured-improv modus operandi of *O.C. and Stiggs* was quite fun, actually. But there are rules to dealing with such looseness. I learned the hard way when I had to shoot a scene in which Randall gets his hands on an Uzi at the big wedding. The two main characters give him the gun just to cause trouble, and—being a class-A nimrod—he fires it. But when the camera started rolling, on a take that Bob planned to shoot only once, the gun didn't work. I turned to the crew's weapons guy (I want to say his name was also Allen) and said, "Oh, it kind of jammed." Bob was incensed: He hadn't yelled, "Cut," and now the shot was unusable because I broke character the second I perceived something was wrong. What I should have done was played along, even if I'd said aloud something like, "Damn thing doesn't work," gnawed on it, playacted firing it, whatever. Ever since then, until I hear, "Cut!" I keep it in character.

That was the only time Bob got mad at me. For the most part, everything about *O.C. and Stiggs* was pretty enjoyable, from the filming, to watching the dailies with Bob making snarky comments, to the Friday night screenings he had of his movies, which amounted to a quick education in the strange variety of his oeuvre (*Brewster McCloud*, yes; *Popeye*, no; *3 Women*, huh?). In retrospect, I've realized what an honor it was to sit with Robert Altman and watch his work with him. I think what I took away from it was that his puckish sense of humor infuses every frame of his films, even the more somber ones. Yet it also hinted that the installment we were making might turn out to be an impenetrable in-joke. As in, fun for us but maybe not for an actual audience. It was starting to dawn on me that Bob's risk taking, while invigorating for an artist under his umbrella, might also make the whole thing go down in flames when put together.

As it turned out, *O.C. and Stiggs* wouldn't get released for another three years, long after I'd made a few other films and seen them open in theaters. Bob may have had it in mind to wring a few nasty chuckles at a certain clueless strata of moneyed America, but the final movie was too disdainful to get an audience to laugh along with it.

After shooting my first movie, I returned to the theater when I was asked to play David in the touring version of *Torch Song Trilogy*. That meant a run in San Francisco and a stint in Los Angeles. The reviews for *Torch Song* in Los Angeles were great, and now the auditions I went on meant occasionally getting to enter a real, bona fide movie studio. Hollywood dreams seemed closer than ever, especially when my agent sent me to the Burbank Studios—now known as the Warner Bros. lot, but then a facility Warner shared with Columbia—to audition for the lead in a teenage love story called *No Small Affair*.

Strolling past the massive soundstages, hoping to catch glimpses of movie stars in crazy costumes, I wondered, *How does anybody get jaded working here?* I tried to imagine a future in which it wouldn't be thrilling, and thought, *Impossible!* Walking by the office of powerful producer Ray Stark, who'd brought so many Barbra Streisand and Neil Simon movies to the screen, I realized there was no way I'd seem anything but wide-eyed and wowed at this audition, no matter how self-assured and nonchalant I may have wanted to come across.

No Small Affair was a little movie about a teenage photographer who falls for an older woman. As he tries to help her career, they fall in love, but come to the bittersweet conclusion that it won't work. This was the second start for the project, actually. Director Martin Ritt (*Hud*) had originally begun shooting it, but fell ill, necessitating a shutdown. His stars? Sally Field and . . . who else, Matthew Broderick. I'm sure I went in to read for new director Jerry Schatzberg and instantly mentioned that I'd understudied Matthew twice by this point. Hey, for all intents and purposes, with my doppelgänger's movie career now in full swing—*War Games* had come out the year before—I had no issue hinting that I'd be a much less expensive Matthew.

Jerry Schatzberg was a soft-spoken guy, known for low-key seventies dramas like *Panic in Needle Park* and *Scarecrow* with Al Pacino, and sophisticated adult fare like the political tale *The Seduction of Joe Tynan*. It seemed odd to me that he was doing a kind of teen romance like *No Small Affair*, but it wasn't a broad movie, and was meant to be in a minor key. Besides, Jerry started out as a professional photographer, which led me to believe the story might have personal resonance to him.

I did my first and only screen test in my career for Jerry, and it was the kind of experience that immediately clued me in to how unprepared I was for certain aspects of movie intimacy. The production was looking at Ellen Barkin to play Laura, the nightclub singer that young Charles the photographer falls for. At that time Barkin was riding a wave in Hollywood due to movies like *Diner*, which showcased her offbeat beauty and sultry toughness. She had a ferocious, tigerlike strength, and my character was this young, goofy kid. The scene they paired us up for was intended to show off any romantic pizzazz we might have.

I was terrified, as I generally am with any sexually tough lady, but hey, it worked for the part of Charles. She, meanwhile, must have thought she was doing a scene with a quivering rabbit. Put a tiger and a rabbit in a cage, and the rabbit is not going to last long. The scene ended with a kiss that, of course, she managed to make supersmoky because she's Ellen Fucking Barkin, and I managed to make look as smoke-free as a nicotine patch, because I'm Jon Niven Cryer. (Editor: fact-check Ellen Barkin's middle name.)

At any rate, after the kiss, we heard, "Cut!" and she looked away with a "What am I doing here?" expression, and I just assumed at that point that they'd go with her erotically charged Laura, and find another Charles, someone who wouldn't look like his costar might leap on him and tear out his throat. We went out to lunch afterward with Jerry, with the intention of getting to know each other as we embarked on this wonderful journey, but the prevailing mood at the table was that we had zero chemistry.

And yet . . . they kept me, and started looking for another Laura. I couldn't have been happier, not just because I got the part, but because among the next group of women I read with was a beautiful up-and-comer named Demi Moore. Fresh from a stint on *General Hospital* and her first big movie, the beach-set farce *Blame It on Rio*, Demi was unlike Ellen Barkin in that she mixed a palpably smoky sexiness with an incredible approachability. Our screen test worked, and we hit it off immediately.

I discovered that on top of her sex appeal and openness, she was an absolute goofball, which I quickly learned is a devastatingly attractive combination to me. She got the part, and very kindly offered to show me around town, as she knew that I was an innocent to Hollywood nightlife. That evening was a bit of a blur, probably because at one point she kissed me. And as there is simply no way to overstate my wonderment at this event, my mind still has difficulty processing it. Let's remember, I'm the guy who had a hard time understanding why the feathered-haired Stage-door gum chewer from Long Island wanted to make out with me, much less a woman who would later be regarded as one of the most alluring on planet Earth. I was flabbergasted at the intimate turn, and after that, performed that most graceless of noncognitive dives: the emotional belly flop. I fell for her hard.

As an inaugural Hollywood romance, Demi was a gas: fun, engaging, and stylish. She'd had a few more years on me in the business, and she had a great attitude about her experiences, which included everything from TV to movies to—she sheepishly admitted to me—being the woman on the iconic poster for the slasher film *I Spit on Your Grave*. (Do you know it? It's a yowza image of a woman in tattered clothing walking away with a knife in her hand. Yes, that famous ass is Demi's.)

She took me out to dinners and parties and introduced me to her crowd. She took me to the set of *General Hospital* while it was shooting and I got to meet John Stamos, a man whose overpowering star wattage engenders giggling in teenage girls and straight men alike. I, meanwhile, introduced her to my circle of friends, and through me she got to meet *Torch Song Trilogy* author and star, Harvey Fierstein, the only person with a voice more gravelly than her own. It was like introducing a food processor to a cement mixer.

She tooled around Los Angeles in this beat-up Honda Civic convertible that only added to her edgy-hot-girl charm, when being a passenger on such occasions didn't scare the bejesus out of me. The rearview mirror had fallen off, there was no knob on the gearshift, and the brakes didn't work anymore, so every stoplight approach—occasionally with an open beer in one of her hands—involved the long, screechy futility of a useless brake pedal followed by the bone-rattling yank of the emergency brake. Once at a standstill, I'd be grateful to be alive; then I'd look over at Demi's gorgeous mug offering a guilty smile and, well, be grateful to be alive!

I was nineteen, starring in a movie, and in love. What could be better? Calls back home to my best friend, David (Dennis), invariably involved many iterations of this piece of advice: "If you ever get the chance to fool around with a beautiful actress in a hot tub, do it, because it's incredibly fun."

Demi was cast fairly late in the process, so we had only three weeks to be together before the start of principal photography, but I was doing my best to cram many years' worth of relationship expectations into that concentrated period. I was certain what we had was the real thing, and that we would last.

So imagine my surprise when, mere days after we began filming, I started feeling this gorgeous wild child slip away from me. It started with the sense that perhaps she didn't view her downtime as first and foremost an opportunity to see me, or even let me know what she was doing. When the production moved to San Francisco for a few weeks, one night after shooting I returned to my hotel and thought, *I'll swing by her place!* Not fully cognizant that San Francisco is a series of paved and zoned cliff faces, I walked, or should I say climbed, up the hill to the house she was renting, which I began to envision had to be a mountaintop lair surrounded by goats.

In any case, with romantic visions of a canoodly overnight stay scored to the Thompson Twins' "Hold Me Now" (my Walkman accompaniment of choice that night), I reached the door and rang her bell. No answer. Ring, ring. More waiting. Ring, ring. Nothing. I was beginning to get an inkling that maybe she didn't think we were exclusive.

Then there were the days she seemed agitated on set, and I couldn't get through to her no matter what I said. I started to think about a seemingly innocuous piece of information she'd revealed to me once in a moment of honesty: that while shooting *Blame It on Rio* in Brazil, she'd tried cocaine and apparently found it enjoyable. At the time I twisted that admission of hers into something about my own feelings of being left out—why had she never offered me a snort? Sharing is caring. But I was now beginning to think something else. One of the makeup artists on *No Small Affair* even came up to me at one point and said, "I think maybe Demi's got a problem." Well, that must be it, I concluded. It felt weird to think that she'd opened up to me about the past, but not the present.

After the production moved back to Los Angeles, I had this idea that things would return to the way they were before shooting: laughs, love, near-death experiences in her car. *Wait until things are hunky-dory,* I thought, *to address what went wrong.*

I went over to her house on Willoughby Avenue one afternoon, rang her bell, and was greeted by her housekeeper.

"Is Demi around?" I asked hopefully.

"She's out with her boyfriend," she said through a thick Spanish accent.

I tentatively ventured, "But . . . *I'm* her boyfriend."

She bit her lip and, with a sad look in her eye, shook her head.

Later that night I went back to Demi's place to hash out what was going on in our relationship as well as my fears about her drug use. I tried to play it cool, as though I were a grown-up and it wasn't a big deal.

At a certain point I was helping her take off her boots—she's sitting on the bed; I'm standing, hands firmly pulling on her footwear as she uses her other foot to press on my back for leverage—when I brought up the more sensitive topic.

Had I called my friend David after that night with more advice, it would now have started with: "When you are helping your hot but troubled girlfriend off with her boots and your back is turned to her, don't suggest she has a drug problem." Demi sent me halfway across the room. I realized that whatever was going on with her, my intervention wasn't going to help it, and with that, we were officially broken up. Driving home in my rental car to my shithole hotel, the "Hold Me Now" of happier times was being replaced by a radio deejay's eerily cosmic playing of Michael Jackson's "She's out of My Life." (And no, movie geeks, I had not seen Albert Brooks's *Modern Romance* at that point.)

I was devastated, but we were still working together, even if we didn't have a whole lot left to shoot. Then it was decided during the last week of filming that the big finale we'd shot in a beautiful San Francisco loft with a gorgeous view of the city didn't work. Not only that but we couldn't get everyone back to the Bay Area, so they were going to rebuild an exact replica of the loft with a model San Francisco outside the window. In the movies, reality truly is warped into the shape you desire. The good news, though, was that the focus of the scene was going to shift from Demi's character to mine. I was going to get the big emotional moment, a challenge I was more than up for, and I suspected the reason the ending didn't work the first time we filmed it was because it had been one of Demi's irritable, off-her-game days. Though I was still smarting from the breakup, I took pride in the fact that if Demi hadn't picked me, in a way, the movies had.

On the moviemaking front, *No Small Affair* was a continued education for me. I realized that the way Robert Altman makes movies—do whatever you want!—isn't the way everybody makes movies. On *No Small Affair*, you learned your lines, said your lines, and didn't mess around. Whereas nobody on *O.C. and Stiggs* said one word to me about how to treat my costume, on *No Small Affair* I had to be taken aside by the wardrobe woman. "Don't just leave your costume in a ball," she said. "Don't expect that we're going to clean it. Take care of it. Respect that everybody on this crew is here to work." Believe me, I was grateful for being instructed on how to be part of a well-functioning team.

Another time, while we were in San Francisco, I contracted mono as well as a terrible throat infection, which you can actually hear in the movie. It sounds like I've got golf balls behind my tongue. At any rate, I was so sick that the production had to shut down for a week, which—if you're familiar with the ins and outs of filmmaking—is a near-calamitous interruption for such an expensive undertaking. But in my naïveté, I figured, *Hey, no big deal. Everybody flies back to LA and gets to see their families!* Uh, no. The bond company has to pay the studio for the time lost, and this doesn't make any of the money people happy. I'm not sure how I could have prevented getting so deathly ill, but I learned how much a movie depends on its lead actor or actress being healthy.

Some severe geeking out happened as well, when I learned before filming that our cinematographer would be Vilmos Zsigmond, the

Hungarian-born genius who won the Academy Award for Spielberg's *Close Encounters of the Third Kind*, one of my all-time favorite movies. (Need extra proof of Zsigmond's talent? How about *McCabe & Mrs. Miller*, *Deliverance*, *The Deer Hunter*, and *Blow Out*?) I was a little perplexed that someone so adept at epic images and big-canvas moments would take a small-scale adolescent romance, but he'd worked with Jerry Schatzberg before and probably thought it'd be a fun gig. It gave me the impression that even the greats don't always take jobs with the idea of doing something important. Besides, actors want to change things up all the time—why can't cinematographers? *No Small Affair* may not have been Zsigmond's most memorable work, but he was gracious and pleasant and indulged my questions about *Close Encounters*. I also remember that he had a grip in his employ named Dickie Deats, and when he would need an "inky"—which is a small spotlight—he'd say, "Deekee, geev me an eenkee!" No, I'm not above laughing at a masterful painter of light's thick Eastern European accent. He has an Oscar. He can take it.

Jerry, meanwhile, was a nice, soft-spoken director, but I didn't get close to him. You always felt you were intruding if you were having a conversation with him. Besides, he would never tell me how I was after a take was finished. He'd just say, "Cut," and move on to the next shot. At one point I asked him point-blank, "What did you think of it?" Slightly taken aback, he murmured in this tiny voice, "Oh, oh, it was wonderful, wonderful. . . ." It was as if I'd bullied him. That meager little "wonderful" was so underwhelming and forced out of him, it wasn't worth the effort. From then on, I assumed I was perfect in every take. (Surprisingly easy, actually.)

Truthfully, when I finally got to see myself on-screen in the finished film, which opened in November of 1984, I thought I was awful. For one thing, to my *Star Wars*–besotted eyes I looked nothing like Mark Hamill or Harrison Ford. I did sound like Yoda, however, in the throat-infection-afflicted scenes. As I watched myself, I recall that the overriding concern was, Why on earth would anybody want me to play somebody in their movie? Because it looked to me as if all the work I'd done internally came off as painfully obvious and clichéd, whereas the stuff other actors were doing was genuinely creative and interesting. Needless to say, back then my self-esteem wasn't a reliable source of positivity, and a still-percolating melancholy over Demi probably had something to do with that reaction. For all the ways I couldn't act jaded when I visited a big Hollywood studio to try out for *No Small Affair*, it was pretty easy now to return to New York—all of nineteen—and snarl to myself like a grizzled veteran, "Hollywood? Bah! All it does is chew ya up and spit ya out! Look at me; I'm a husk of a human being!" (Literally, too, according to the New York audience member I heard opening night who shouted out during a scene in which I had to take my shirt off, "Where's the beef?!")

There was closure with Demi, however. When she came through Manhattan the following year to do publicity for *St. Elmo's Fire*—during the shooting of which she'd apparently bottomed out and reportedly almost been fired—she came to a restaurant where I was hanging out with some friends to say hi. Although we hadn't worked out, I was glad to see her look as if she was in a different, better place in her life, newly sober and committed to making the most of her career, the results of which eventually proved to everyone how dedicated she was. For a brief, exciting period, though, Demi Moore was my first big Hollywood romance, and it stands as a mostly fond, fun memory.

By the way, do you think she ever watches Ashton and me on *Two and a Half Men* and thinks, *Well, there's a trajectory?*

Chapter 6
For Some Reason, a Trench Coat

Did you know I got to work with George Wendt on *No Small Affair*? You know, barfly Norm from the great show *Cheers*? Well, this story has almost nothing to do with George Wendt.

But it does start with him. One day on the set, a guy visited who sold earthquake kits. Being new to Los Angeles, and aware that occasionally the moving and shaking around town is literal and not figurative, I considered purchasing one. Then I saw George Wendt laying down cold, hard cash for a kit, and because of that, I did. (It's a little-known fact that I'll do anything George Wendt does.) The problem was, I didn't have my wallet on me, because I was in costume, which necessitated going back to my trailer to get it. I bought the kit and resumed filming, safe in the knowledge that the likelihood of my surviving the next jostling of the earth was considerably higher.

After I got home that day, though, I realized I'd left my wallet in the character's pants. I quickly called the costumer, told her that my wallet was in the pocket of my costume, and learned to my dismay that today, Friday, was when the production's clothes were sent out for dry cleaning.

Inconvenient, but fine, I thought. "I'll just swing by the lot and get them," I said, assuming that vast, seemingly fully functioning operations like studios had dry-cleaning plants on the premises. Probably next to the oil refineries and cattle pens.

"No, no, no," she said. "We send them to a place off the lot. The trucks pick up everything; they hit a few studios, then take it all to a dry cleaner's on Santa Monica Boulevard."

More inconvenient, but still fine. I'd simply go intercept the truck somehow. I figured the studios would be highly protective of their costumes, and therefore my pants would be easily retrievable once I tracked down where they were. I decided that waiting at the cleaner's was the simplest solution, so as nighttime hit I arrived at the shop, a mom-and-poppish place whose relative modesty surprised me, considering they handled the dry cleaning for the big studios. As I took a seat inside—having luckily arrived before the truck—I realized how much an industry like moviemaking really affects the economy of a city.

But then, as sweat began pouring down my face, I also realized that dry cleaners are virtual saunas if you spend more than five minutes in them. With no clear sense of when the truck would arrive, I told the woman behind the counter I would wait outside.

Ah, much better as I stepped onto the sidewalk. It was a warm night on Santa Monica Boulevard in West Hollywood, but not nearly as warm as being inside that place. There was nowhere to sit, so I leaned on a lamppost. So there I am, leaning on a lamppost. On Santa Monica Boulevard. In West Hollywood. In jeans and a T-shirt. On a Friday night. (You're ahead of me, right?)

"Hello-o-o-o!" I hear from a honking car slowly driving by.

"Hey, there," says a driver coming from the other direction, also well under the speed limit.

"How's it going?" say a couple of young guys walking past me, all smiles.

"It's going great!" I cheerfully chirp.

Wow, this is one really friendly town, I think. Why was I so nervous about getting acclimated? Here I am running a dumb errand and the citizens are making me feel like I'm one of them. Now here's a . . . well, okay, an older man, in glasses and—for some reason—a trench coat. And he also wants to know how it's going.

"Goin' good," I reply.

"Nice night."

"Yeah, it's great," I said. "Kind of hot, though."

"You look like you work out."

I burst out laughing. Come on, there's being friendly, and then there's just being ridiculous. I mean, seriously, even when I've exercised, when I've done triathlons, I don't *look* like I've worked out. Well, my laughter must have seemed rude, because the guy eyed me oddly, as in, Why are you laughing at me?

He said, "Well, look, if you need a place to stay tonight, I think I can help you out."

And with that, ladies and gentlemen, *lightbulb on.*

Very, very *on.*

"Oh! *Oh! Oh!* Um, no, thank you! No, thanks!"

I said that as I stumbled back inside the dry cleaner's, where I dutifully sat for another forty-five minutes, losing a tremendous amount of water weight in the process. Still, I figured, a better option than looking like an all-too-good-natured male prostitute with a penchant for giggling through transactions. The truck arrived, and I got my wallet and headed home.

When it comes to that particular goods-and-services section of Hollywood, it's probably difficult for passersby not to make certain judgmental assumptions about the people they see milling about. But because of my experience that eye-opening night, I've learned to take the optimistic view. To this day, if I ever find myself driving by that area, and I see young men with expectant eyes standing outside, I think only one thing: They're just waiting for their dry cleaning.

It gives me a certain solace.

Chapter 7
Jon? Jon!

Gretchen Cryer is a Tony Awards voter, so she gets free tickets to all the Broadway shows, and in the spring, close to nominations time, my mother is at the theater a lot. She takes her responsibilities as seriously as a UN inspector in a country possibly hiding nuclear weapons. One night in the spring of 1984 she took her seat at a show, and who should be next to her but director Gene Saks, the guy who fired me from *Brighton Beach Memoirs* the year before.

Mom is friends with Gene, but that didn't stop her from recalling how she wanted to pound him into the pavement twelve months prior. Being a lady, though, she kept her thoughts to herself; she simply turned and said, "Hello, Gene."

"Oh, hello, Gretchen," Gene replied. "Good to see you. How's Jonny doing?"

"Gene, he's doing *great*," she said, which was true. Mom cooled down a bit so she could play proud parent. "He opened *Torch Song Trilogy* in Los

Angeles, got great reviews, and then got cast opposite Demi Moore in a movie opening later this year. He's just doing great!"

"Wonderful," Gene said. "We always knew Jonny was going to be a star."

Mom kept her composure the rest of the evening, despite the fact that "Hey, asshole, if you thought he'd be a star, then why did you fire him?" was on the tip of her tongue all night. (As it turned out, she discovered many years later, the decision to can me was made soon after I was hired, but couldn't be acted upon until they'd secured a Matthew replacement for when he'd eventually leave the show. I was kept in rehearsals as a last resort. Which doesn't sound any better, but at least couches the whole thing as practical rather than deliberately cruel.)

So Mom stewed in her seat, her success-is-the-best-revenge news undercut by Gene's incongruous remark. And yet the next day, my manager, Marty, got a call from the office of Neil Simon's longtime producer Manny Azenberg, asking if I wanted—drumroll, please—to step into the role of Eugene in *Brighton Beach Memoirs. Boo-yah!* Now, we'll never know if Mom sitting next to Gene Saks and portraying my career as an unstoppable juggernaut of achievement got that ball rolling, but it sounds possible, no? That was a sweet phone call to get, let me tell you. I was filled with pride over being able to slay that dragon finally.

Once that euphoria died down, though, I was still left with the feeling that I had to prove myself, and erase the fact that I'd screwed up before. By that point the show had been up for a while. The mark Matthew had left was still apparent, because Doug McKeon—who went from understudy to replacement when Matthew ended his run—supposedly wasn't that well received. Well, that wasn't going to be me. I was going to be a more-than-worthy relief pitcher.

Relief pitcher is an apt metaphor, really, since *Brighton Beach Memoirs* opens with Eugene Jerome, teenage dreamer and fanatic for America's pastime, throwing a baseball and delivering a long monologue about the sport. The scene required me to throw the baseball twenty-five feet or so, and the way the production had it set up, it'd hit a corrugated-metal sheet and angle offstage into the wings. Well, I practiced that throw religiously up in the chorus dressing room. That long space, filled with mirrored tables and cots for sacking out, was where I used to warm up during my brief time as an understudy. During that period, though, I was always in street clothes, because Matthew Broderick was never a no-show.

But now I was warming up dressed for the part, thinking, *This is it; you did it; you're here.* And being infinitely reminded of such because all those mirrors were reflecting back at me a made-up, outfitted Eugene Jerome, and it wasn't Matthew Broderick. (I've never looked in a mirror, incidentally, and gotten confused—just so we're clear on that.)

That first show I was so in my head and on autopilot—spitting out the words, terrified about missing a single one—that I couldn't enjoy any of it. The goal simply was, *Get through it alive. If I say all the words correctly, audibly, and in the right order, to the right people, and at the appointed time, then it will be over.* Over for that night's show, that is. Then there was the next night. Shooting a movie is the province of "only once." That's all you need; then you move on to a new scene. Theater is eight times a week.

The late Meshach Taylor told a story about playing Lumière in *Beauty and the Beast* on Broadway after the show *Designing Women* ended. In the wake of the cushy, a-few-lines-a-week sitcom job, performing night after night as a singing candelabra was a workload shocker. One night, he sneaked a break to get a much-needed breather in the alley, only to discover the actress playing Wardrobe, still dressed as an armoire, taking a moment for a smoke. "Man, this eight-shows-a-week gig is kicking my ass," he said. His cabinet-clad colleague took a puff and snorted derisively.

"Broadway ain't for pussies."

It isn't, I learned. And I've never even had to dress like a piece of furniture. As you keep doing it, however, your attitude about it shifts, priorities become apparent, and a certain ingrained efficiency takes over. This was a bona fide Broadway hit I was in, but unlike *Torch Song*

Trilogy, in which fifteen-year-old David is a third-act character accent bouncing off whoever plays the lead, Eugene drives *Brighton Beach* from beginning to end. He's the engine, the person playing him needs to be a star, and if I ever needed a reminder of that, the guy who originated it won a Tony Award for Best Actor. Good luck, kid! Getting my sea legs those first weeks was the first time I felt like a professional in show business.

But that fucking baseball throw, for Christ's sake. I've mentioned that I'm not athletic, so naturally the first thing I have to do in my debut as a Broadway lead is get a ball from my hand to a designated area—not even a spot, an *area*—just offstage. This proved problematic on a regular basis. I managed to miss that target in every possible way, until once the baseball shot back out across the stage and into the audience, where a guy in the front row ducked and let it hit his female companion full in the face. Much more shocking than the fact that I'd thrown another errant pitch was the fact that chivalry was apparently now dead. I had to ask the poor woman for it back, but fortunately—perhaps with visions of further airborne dangers in her mind—she handed it over instead of throwing it.

Other pitfalls arose out of becoming comfortable with the show. Speakers backstage allow everyone—wherever you are—to hear the show, so you can know when to get ready. I got a little too cozy once during some downtime, and when I heard the speaker go silent, I thought, *You know, that's not a dead speaker. That's the sound of* nobody delivering my lines onstage. There's nothing like missing an entrance that sends adrenaline through you so fast and hard you fear it'll seep out of your eyeballs.

"Going up on your lines" is the term for forgetting them, and those are the moments when you find out just how awesome your fellow actors are. Joe Breen (who went by Patrick) played Eugene's older brother, Stanley, when I was in the show, and he saved my ass at least three times when I (figuratively) dropped the ball onstage. One particularly memorable instance happened during a scene that required me to lie down on a comfy twin bed and feign sleep, until the moment I had to get back up. I lay down—and promptly fell asleep. Joe was the one who woke me up, because he was supposed to be asleep in the next bed.

Suddenly I hear this hushed, "Jon? Jon!"

"Hmmm, yeah?" [Slight yawn.] "What's up?" [Dawning realization.] *"Shit."*

Believe me, the one time I got to help Joe out when he went up on his lines, I was grateful to be able to return the favor.

When Stanley Tucci—who'd been understudying Joe—eventually replaced him, Stanley's performance was a learning experience for me, because he was completely different from Joe, but no less powerful. With my role, I was essentially doing a Matthew Broderick performance, with changes here and there, because Matthew's had been such a master class that I didn't want to throw it off too much. I wanted to crescendo in the same places, stress some of the same points. But Stanley showed me how valuable committing to a completely different approach and making *that* work was. It certainly helped keep the show fresh for me each night.

The other fond memory of *Brighton Beach Memoirs* was my dressing roommate, Anita Gillette, who played my aunt. I was starstruck because not only had I seen her on Broadway a handful of times, but she had played Jack Klugman's wife on *Quincy.* So I was beside myself. But two things helped bring that down to earth: how completely encouraging and nice she was, telling me great stories about how long she'd been in the trenches, and the fact that this beautiful woman would change right in front of me. My keyhole days with Shelly were definitely behind me. At any rate, Anita's friendship meant a great deal to a nervous, eager lad such as myself.

By the time my run in *Brighton Beach Memoirs* was over half a year later, it was long enough to feel like a genuinely maturing experience. It also felt as if it was ending too soon. It was a highly rewarding show to be part of. Neil Simon's play was just the kind of crowd-pleasing hit that makes any hardworking stage actor feel great by the end, because the audience rapport with that show is phenomenal. They're with you all the way through, and it's an energy that's a pleasure to feed off of.

I'd also successfully erased the bad memory of getting fired by shepherding the role of Eugene in this beloved show through another stretch of performances, and handing it off to someone else. (Nobody wants to be the actor who's there when the show closes.) The clincher, though, to my satisfaction, was that I got asked to pitch in on Simon's follow-up, *Biloxi Blues*, which had opened during my tenure in *Brighton Beach*.

In a scenario I was eerily familiar with, *Biloxi* was having troubles with their Matthew Broderick understudy. They wanted me to be Matthew's fill-in, but still perform in *Brighton Beach*, so that meant if Matthew couldn't go on uptown, I'd literally have to take off my knee pants at the 46th Street Theatre, run up Eighth Avenue, and put on army fatigues at the Neil Simon Theatre on Fifty-second Street to do *Biloxi*. And my understudy would go on that night in *Brighton*. If that isn't a vote of confidence, I don't know what is.

I said no. It was looking like it was time to move on from playing Eugene Jerome, and something else had come along that proved too impossibly good to pass up.

Chapter 8
This Is Just How We Are!

It's fitting that awkwardness has been a keystone to a lot of the comedic roles I've played over the years. I am, to put it mildly, not inherently comfortable with my body, especially regarding its many signals and uses in social interactions.

For instance, I'm genuinely flummoxed by the high five. If someone in my vicinity extends a palm up, out, and above the head in anticipation of a celebratory slap, they might as well have handed me a bow and arrow and told me to pierce the apple on top of a boy's head. I can't high-five. Where gregarious, friendly types see an extension of natural camaraderie with that gesture, I see a test of coordination and accuracy. I wasn't good at sports in school! Why do I have to let everyone know that when my fumbled fling of the arm produces not a confident *thwack* but a noiseless graze of the outer fingers? Call it a high two-to-five and I can maybe perform.

There are those with innate facility for these types of things. I require advanced planning. I didn't just make up that "Try a Little Tenderness" dance in *Pretty in Pink* when the cameras rolled. That was hard, choreo-graphed, practiced work. Same with high fives. I now know that the trick to a good high five is to look at the other person's elbow. Line up the el-bows, and you will hit the hand. And yet, I am so much more grateful for the friends with whom our greetings are established, well-practiced forms of contact with wide margins for accuracy. Hugs, for instance. I'm good with hugs.

My discomfort with my body stems mostly from a sense growing up that I wasn't manly enough. I equated strength with masculinity as a kid, and while I wasn't really that aware of gay culture in my preteen years, junior high is when certain ugly epithets bubble up like noxious gases and create a standard-bearer for your sense of self-worth. I wasn't worried I was gay—I knew I liked girls—but I certainly became concerned with the message I was sending out in mixed company.

How I sat, for example. In junior high, I got this creeping sense that the way I parked myself in a chair was not testosterone-appropriate. Un-guarded, without thinking, I sit with my legs crossed at the knee, arms crossed and resting on top, and both wrists in full limp.

And when I do this, I look very relaxed. For a nineteenth-century English fop. Or a PBS talk-show host. Or, if you're a heathen bully, a *girl*. So whenever I was among my peers—girls who invariably sat the same way, and boys unafraid to splay themselves across any piece of furniture with their crotch as a focal point—I began to worry that my default sit might be a serious impediment to how I was perceived. It triggered a hyperawareness in social situations: I would sit my usual way, stop cold, then quickly untangle my limbs and try to look, for lack of a better word, butchier. What I must have looked like, however, is an incredibly antsy person.

Then one day my mother unearthed a picture of my dad and showed it to me. It was taken at a rehearsal for some play, and the frame was filled with theater folk, some midpose, others at rest, males, females, all sexualities and stripes probably. But there in the corner is my father, sitting with his legs and arms and draped hands crossed in exactly the same way, and damned if he wasn't the coolest motherfucker in the room.

It was an epiphany. "This is just how we are!" I thought. I got it from my dad, and if he could make not caring about it into an expression of confidence, there was hope. Ever since, I've owned my admittedly effeminate-looking mode of sitting.

Years later, I was at my son's school basketball game when I noticed something significant. He was sitting on the bench—because that's where us Cryers live at the basketball game—and it was in the familiar way I had fully come to expect from the males in our family. But then he suddenly snapped out of it and affected a more macho, athletic posture, more the way his teammates were sitting. I recognized that self-consciousness, and I flagged that moment in my brain.

A few days later, he saw me sitting the way I do, and he made fun of it.

"You know," I told him, "I always used to think I shouldn't sit like this. But then I realized, You know what? This is what it looks like. It's what makes me feel comfortable. Now I own it."

I could see a glimmer of recognition in his eyes. "Yeah!" he said. "That's how I sit, too!"

And with that, we had a genuinely nice bonding moment over our initial shame about how we sit, and how pointless it was to feel that way. Genetics aren't always something we have to fight. In fact, had my mother handed me off at birth to be raised in the wild by a band of gorillas, then discovered by naturists and painstakingly reintroduced into polite society, I would still sit like this. And if you said anything negative about it, I would snarl and try to rip your face off, because I'm a gorilla in this scenario, remember.

Chapter 9
And Another. And Another.

Like many movie-mad youngsters in 1984, I saw *Sixteen Candles* and found it really funny and perceptive about teenagers like myself. On one level it was no surprise to me, though, because its writer/director, John Hughes, was someone whose work I'd admired for years in *National Lampoon*, the magazine that also originated the "O.C. and Stiggs" stories.

The *Lampoon* was a truly special monthly journal for a horny teenage boy who liked to laugh at naughtiness—the pieces were irreverently funny, and occasionally a page was augmented by photographs of women with exposed breasts. This made-for-adults publication talked of sexual practices I couldn't begin to comprehend, and bodily fluids with which I had maybe only nominal knowledge. There was a big decision to make when I held a *National Lampoon* in my grubby teenage hands with my filthy teenage mind—*Am I in the mood to laugh? Or jerk off?*

"Why can't it be both?" I proudly declared.

John Hughes's stories were more of the laughworthy kind, but one in particular was an adolescent boy's fantasy come true: a hilarious, darkly comic yarn called "The Spy Who Wore Nothing," about a kid who wakes up in the middle of the night when a gorgeous woman climbs through his window. She informs him he's actually a deep-cover secret agent, and they have a wacky adventure during which she's naked. Let me clarify: It was *this* adolescent boy's fantasy come true. I can't speak for the rest of them.

Anyway, when the script for *Pretty in Pink* came my way, with Hughes on the ascendancy as a filmmaker to watch—he'd also written the movie *National Lampoon's Vacation*—I was thrilled. Here was a guy who'd just hit one out of the park with *Sixteen Candles* and had an eagerly anticipated movie ready to come out (*The Breakfast Club*), and I had a shot at the next one in the pipeline. That's an exciting feeling for an up-and-coming actor, the sense that you're now in the mix when it comes to what's new and hot.

Expecting something broadly comic like *Sixteen Candles*, I was surprised to discover that *Pretty in Pink* was closer to a tightly focused, small-scale drama with moments of humor. Hughes's teenage muse and new "it" girl, Molly Ringwald, was set to play Andie, a working-class high schooler who has an emotionally fraught crush on sensitive rich kid Blane, and a loyal friend and torchbearer in one Philip "Duckie" Dale.

I read the script and immediately loved Duckie, who countered his more pathetic turns of personality with a supreme swagger and biting wit. Basically, he was the guy I wanted to be in high school. Even in a school full of nerds, I was the outsider nerd—a lonely theater geek in a den of science geeks. Likewise, Duckie finds himself on the perimeter of his own group of friends when his unrequited love for Andie is threatened by her attempt at upwardly mobile romance.

This was somebody I could live inside. This part was mine.

I prepared like crazy for the audition: working the lines, working the lines, working the lines. I had two scenes ready to go. I headed over to the Gulf & Western Building and met director Howard Deutch, and was quickly reminded that he had a passing acquaintance with my family. He used to vacation on Fire Island, where my mom would rent a house every summer. That was a miserable stretch for a pudgy, nonathletic kid who'd rather spend time in movie theaters than sit on a beach and stare at the Atlantic. I didn't love being in the ocean—it's salty and wet. And sand—ugh, it's so . . . sandy. But lo these many years later it was nice to feel an instant rapport with a movie director over shared memories. Besides, Howie is an amiable, friendly guy anyway, and I would have felt comfortable in that audition had we not had anything in common.

As for what I wore, I opted not to dress the way I thought Duckie would look. Audition wardrobe is a tricky proposition. It's one thing if you're reading for the part of a lawyer—then it's usually a good idea to wear a suit, because it does grant you some authority. But for this I went in my standard audition wear: button-down shirt and jeans. Choosing a costume before the filmmakers even know what they want is a risk. Let them be inspired to imagine a costume on you based on the thrill of your performance, I say.

I read the first Duckie scene for him, and Howie really liked it. Then he asked me to read the second scene. Always a good sign when you get to read a second scene instead of getting a "Thank you!" or "Do you need us to validate your parking?"

Then he asked for another scene.

And another.

And another.

Each time, he'd say, "Can you read this next one?" And I'd answer, "Sure!" (What am I going to say? "Sorry, no. I have a crossword puzzle I need to finish"?) Then I'd go out into the hallway with the other actors—none of whom I recognized—and learn the next scene, while the others would go in one by one the first time. Usually, returning to the waiting area with all the eager aspirants is a vaguely dispiriting experience, even if you've had a good audition. It's like a cold reminder of the odds. But I was going out, going in, going out, going in, and that gave me this surging confidence that I had a really good hand in this particular round. As an actor, this kind of experience has been known to mentally transform the other hopefuls in the hallway from plucky equals into a class of performer beneath you. This is a supremely uncharitable attitude, and it feels *great*.

By the end of my hour or so there—a long time for an audition—I had read practically every Duckie scene in the movie. Would we now move on to Andie's lines? Blane's dialogue? Could they be thinking of making *Pretty in Pink* a one-man show? Of course not, but when you're this high you let yourself think silly shit. At any rate, I left the building filled with the vaulting hubris of someone who believes they've utterly, truly nailed it. It was a belief reinforced by hearing that I was being called back, this time to read with Molly Ringwald, and for John Hughes. Howie also talked to me about Duckie's big lip-sync number in the record store where Andie and her friend Iona work, and did I have any ideas?

Why, I did. Mick Jagger. "All my friends love my Mick Jagger!" I said. "I'll do 'Start Me Up'!" Howie okayed it. Now, my Mick Jagger is less an impression of the Rolling Stones singer than it is an approximation of Al Franken's famously uncanny impersonation of him. An homage to an homage, really, but a sure hit of mine at parties: rooster walk, hip undulating, lippy flamboyance and all. But now I was working on it like the most eager of hoofers, preparing my music cues, props (funky sunglasses), and moves instead of counting on something spontaneous to happen.

When I went for the callback, the vibe was a little more intense, since Molly and John were there. In person, Molly came off as both more stylish and sexier than the image I had of her from *Sixteen Candles*. This was partially because she's taller than you think she is. She had a good inch or two on me in height. She might have been wearing heels, though. And taken out of the context of movie scenarios, she had a calmly alluring vibe, an attractive confidence for someone only seventeen. Meeting her, I found Molly was polite but noncommittal, which is understandable in an audition situation. The filmmakers are looking at several people, so she doesn't want to instantly act all best friend-y and have the auditioner walk out thinking, "I'm in; I'm Molly's best friend!" only to not get the part and recede emotionally into "Fuck you, Molly! You led me on!" It's a fine line, so while she was well mannered, she was also pretty reserved. John Hughes was also civil yet remote, a quiet figure in owlish glasses and eighties-coiffed hair. I started to miss the instant friendliness of the first audition with Howie. *I know we're all professionals here, but does it have to be so serious?*

There was no small talk. It was all business. I read with Molly, and I felt that the scenes didn't go as swimmingly as they had when Howie was reading opposite me. (Was I more nervous with Molly and John? Perhaps.) Howie didn't ask me to do my Mick Jagger, either, which I was initially disappointed by, but then relieved about.

It was all over pretty fast, and suddenly I was leaving the room. But then John Hughes decided to accompany me to the elevator, and the callback ended on a nice, collegial note. I complimented him on *Sixteen Candles,* and he sounded surprised that I was familiar with his *Lampoon* writings. John even said that he'd taken a crack at turning that secret-agent story into a screenplay. At that moment, I appreciated the fact that John didn't treat me like a wannabe actor but instead like a coworker. He seemed to be breaking the unspoken hierarchy of the audition—the rule that discourages getting too chummy with those trying out for fear of sending someone out with unmanageable expectations or false hope. He didn't have that usual aloofness. He was open and friendly and I left feeling good. (Between Robert Altman's love of *National Lampoon* and John Hughes having written for it, I must say that my favorite teenage jerkoff rag really stood me in good stead as an icebreaker when meeting major filmmakers.)

But then I didn't hear anything for a while. Usually you'll get word of a decision within a few days, but a week went by and nothing. Then another week. My agent had no news. I was still doing *Brighton Beach Memoirs,* so I was busy with eight shows a week, not to mention other auditions.

I went up for a play that was going to star Kevin Spacey. Well, "star" isn't quite the right word, since no one had heard of him at that time. He was already considered an actor of great skill and charisma, though, and I was excited about the opportunity. I'd met him years earlier, when he'd done a play with a British actor named Greg Martyn, who just happened to be my mother's boyfriend at the time.

Greg was memorable due to his odd habit of wandering around our apartment nude when we had company over. I remember a time when he walked through the living room while David Dennis and I were watching TV. A few moments passed and then David turned to me, nonplussed, and said, "You know there's a naked British man in your house, right?" I nodded and we continued to watch TV.

The role I tried out for required a British accent, and I recall Spacey's being so amazing in the audition—and mine so Dick Van Dyke in *Mary Poppins*—that I literally paused midscene and said aloud, "I'm not going to get this, since this guy is so fucking good." Kevin was a pleasure to audition with, though: funny, charming, and devoid of actor bullshit.

To complicate matters, *Brighton Beach Memoirs* wanted me to re-up for another six months in the role of Eugene. But in the back of my mind the whole time was, *Why haven't I heard about the John Hughes movie?* It was disconcerting, like being interrupted midfilm and told you have to wait for the final reel to show up. And I use a movie metaphor, because movies were where I ultimately saw myself going as an actor. It was the medium that excited me the most. *Pretty in Pink* was my best shot yet at really establishing a movie career for myself, at making something that, unlike *No Small Affair*, would resonate with audiences in that way the best movies do.

Finally, after three weeks of silence, I called manager Marty and said, "Can you find out what's going on?" He paged me later, and I called him from a phone booth on Fifty-fourth Street and Seventh Avenue.

"You got it!" he said.

It had been touch-and-go, though. Instead of calling the casting people, he had called producer Lauren Shuler directly, who told him that they were definitely interested in me, but that there were other factors that were holding off the decision-making process on Duckie.

So Marty played the trump card: "*Brighton Beach* wants Jon for another six months, so shit or get off the pot." And they said, "We'll shit." And by "shit," they meant "hire your client."

I got off the phone with Marty and felt like I was on air. It was the kind of news one celebrates by taking a cab home instead of a bus. That's right, living large.

Soon after, Hughes's second directorial effort came out, *The Breakfast Club*—about five high schoolers from different walks of life enduring a soul-baring, daylong detention—and I rushed over to the Guild Theater on Fifty-ninth Street to see it. That was an exhilarating and strange experience. I remember enjoying it but also thinking during some of the heavier parts, *Well, these kids are taking themselves a bit seriously.* Nevertheless I still laughed with it, and experienced the tension of these archetypal teenagers feeling one another out and wondering if their shared humanity is enough to break the barriers of cliquedom. Everyone was memorable—Molly, Judd Nelson, Anthony Michael Hall, Ally Sheedy, Emilio Estevez—and at the very end, when Judd's brooding antihero is on the football field and raises his fist as Simple Minds' "Don't You Forget About Me" swells on the sound track, the audience erupted and I thought to myself, *Oh, my goodness, I'm actually in the next one of these.*

I was now in that pretty exclusive club myself, and I couldn't wait to activate my membership.

Chapter 10
But Now I Have to Shoot It

On the plane to Los Angeles to film *Pretty in Pink*, I thought, *Am I really now one of the cool kids?* I was going to shoot a movie about high school, but I was going through all the feelings one experiences right before heading off to the real thing. *Am I too weird? Am I going to fit in? Am I going to have any friends?*

It was a strange feeling to have, considering a solid two decades of outsiderdom, and all permutations of nerd: space nerd, musical theater nerd, Carol Burnett nerd, Marvel Comics nerd, *Star Wars* nerd, *Star Trek* nerd, *Little Rascals* nerd, *Twilight Zone* nerd, Looney Tunes nerd. . . . I could explode with facts and quotes from any of these at a moment's notice. But would I have to quell that to be accepted in this rarefied air of top-tier studio moviemaking, and this burgeoning genre populated by very serious, attractive teen thespians? And would anyone sit with me at lunch?

I decided to trust that the process of making the movie would give me the tools to feel connected to my fellow actors. Namely, rehearsal. Lots and lots of rehearsal.

Ever wonder why certain movies get slice-of-life and character inter-actions more naturally and effortlessly than others? They probably had rehearsal time. Ideally, instead of taking actors who are supposed to play family members, lifelong friends, chummy coworkers, or biweekly bond-age partners, and barely allowing them to say, "Nice to meet you," before throwing them in front of cameras for scenes of stark intimacy, a sensible movie production lets camaraderie and familiarity emerge by putting its cast through a rehearsal process.

Fortunately, this was the case with *Pretty in Pink*, as I happily discov-ered upon arriving in Los Angeles to begin preproduction. It was an in-credibly organic, slow-paced process—a lot like theater—and it allowed us to really get to know who we were playing, and who we were playing opposite. I met Andrew McCarthy, who was set to play Blane, and though I hadn't seen his breakout movie, *Class*, he was somebody I'd run into occasionally at auditions and who I knew had all the recommended daily allowance of prep-school handsome required for the part. I also remet Molly, and the three of us sat down with Howie and talked about our characters before starting to methodically work on scenes.

While I loved the *Pretty in Pink* rehearsals for the time they gave me to get a bead on Duckie, I was also thrown a little bit by the social dy-namic. Molly and Andrew held so much in check personally that I won-dered when we'd get to the hanging-out part. At work, all went well. But attempts to socialize never felt that comfortable—Molly would meet my verbal parries with awkward silences. We just didn't flow. Trying to be-friend Andrew was so tough it sent me in the other direction: as in, I adopted a low-boil dislike toward him. It was as if the pair of them was computers with an internal barometer that indicated exactly when we'd all have enough chemistry to look realistic on film, and once that was reached, they could switch off and go into sleep mode.

That being said, it was a tension that worked on-screen, and, as I found out later (among other things), was the point behind our casting.

"It wasn't supposed to be the three of you as friends," Howie told me recently over lunch. "It's an uncomfortable three-way relationship."

Okay, but it would have been nice to know I was on a Sisyphean mission trying to buddy up to those ice cubes. See, I'm a theater guy, and actors who grew out of the stage have a certain "we're all in this together" thing that bolsters and inspires, because you're going through a trial by fire as a team. You're in an instant family, with all the attendant highs and lows of close-quarters interaction, but it always gives you strength. The give-and-take interconnectedness of a theater enterprise is ever-apparent, since you're always in the same space every day with the cast and crew, until the show ends. That kind of daily cooperation and nurturing camaraderie, however, isn't always required of a film actor, who in many circumstances needs only to get it right between "Action!" and "Cut!" once for the thing to work, before holing up in a trailer the rest of the time if that is his or her wont.

In Andrew's interview about *Pretty in Pink* for the twenty-fifth-anniversary DVD edition, he remembered me as "just so needy." Setting aside the fact that under the guise of a supposedly objective comment about my behavior, this is really just a pithy euphemism for "could he have been more annoying?" I will take the observation at face value and say, Well, of course, why wouldn't I be needy? I was acting opposite two people who'd had success in films already, which was intimidating to say the least. (*No Small Affair* didn't exactly set box office charts on fire.) This was my first truly high-profile movie, I cared about the script, and its level of anticipation in the film world in the wake of *Sixteen Candles* and *The Breakfast Club* was sort of equivalent to Quentin Tarantino calling you to be in his next thing after *Pulp Fiction*. To put it bluntly, I was excited, nervous, committed, and hungry. I wanted it to work, I wanted it to be fun, and I wanted to not feel like an outcast for once. That's "needy," all right. That's also how showbiz should be, as far as I'm concerned. I want to see everyone's desire to engage, whether you're the new kid or the veteran. I find it invigorating. (Remember, just don't high-five me.)

I was also, I might add, playing an occasionally pushy dork with attention issues. This is not a job for the faint of heart, or voice, or chutz-pah. I needed "needy" as a way into the character. Molly and Andrew, on the other hand, weren't there to wring laughs from the audience or juice the movie's energy, two of Duckie's more entertainment-related responsi-bilities. They were hired to turn their easily available reserve into heart-breaking moodiness. Actually, one of the great things about Molly as an actress is what she doesn't give you. Whatever frustrations I may have had with Molly off-camera when it came to her fraternizing skills, that less-is-more acting style—already honed at seventeen—was made for the movies. Coming from the theater, I knew how to work an audience, but was still nailing down how to translate my craft to a medium in which I played to a camera, not a crowd.

Since Duckie was no wallflower, I knew his look would go a long way toward ramping me up to embody him each day of shooting. An actor can get a lot out of the costume—it's the building blocks of a persona, really—and if the clothes are already different from who you really are, all the better. My idea, then, was to dress Duckie in the manner of my good friend and rockabilly fan Artie, who managed to pull off his pompadour with a great sense of personal style. Girls went crazy for it. Although Duckie wasn't supposed to be a chick magnet, I wanted Duckie to have that aggressively fifties-tinged look of cool: a prow of teased-and-greased coif on top, augmented by rolled-up sleeves, a leather jacket perhaps, and blue jeans. Maybe loafers. No, wait: biker boots!

It was with visions of rockabilly Duckie dancing in my head that I went into my first fitting with costume designer Marilyn Vance, who had worked on *Sixteen Candles* and *The Breakfast Club*. She knew her teen togs. But the first thing she did was put me in a paisley shirt, and over that a plaid vest. *Okay*, I thought, *I'm not exactly sure where this is going.*

Then she added another item with a left turn in the pattern department. Then another. Then she stood back and took a moment to think.

"Maybe his thing is that *nothing* matches," she said.

My face fell. *That's not a thing*, I thought. *That's early-onset dementia*.

Of course, in retrospect, Marilyn was a hundred percent right in how she envisioned Duckie. Since the character is more complicated than the average nerd, the mismatched layers and prints suggested the right amount of collision-course personality. If I couldn't *be* the Clash, I could at least, well, clash.

The height of youth fashion at the time in Los Angeles was centered on Melrose Avenue, so we hit the eye-popping street's thrift stores and clothing shops and slowly began putting together the traffic pileup of textures, hues, and patterns that became Duckiewear: oversize blazers with sleeves ripe for rolling up, optical-illusion vests, flowery shirts that best showed off bolo neckwear, and a galaxy of accessories to make sure your eyes never quite knew where to focus. We got pins! Pins! Pins! Supercheap circular wire-rim glasses, too, to ground it all in something resembling Lennon-esque new wave. Then the porkpie hat for that touch of jazz-sideman insouciance.

The shoes, meanwhile, came from a true clothing-curiosity emporium called Aardvark's Odd Ark: dirty white crocodile creepers that suggested serious retro flash. The problem was that there weren't enough of them in my size, however, and I kept ripping out of them. I have massive feet (that's right, ladies). The shoes have vanished, incidentally. I have photographic evidence of me lending them to New York's Planet Hollywood, where they were promptly lost. I suppose I should never have entrusted revered Hollywood pop-culture artifacts to a place that served coconut shrimp.

I was asked once what made an article of clothing unsuitable for Duckie. I answered, "If it's tasteful or matches." It was not easy convincing me to sign on to Duckie's clothes. I was Irene Cara reduced to stripping in that scene in *Fame*, only instead barely suppressing a sob because of what I had to put *on*. I'll admit, every day I'd come to my trailer, take one look at the day's wardrobe, and mutter out loud, "Really?"

But it's to the credit of Marilyn's unerring sense of character-centric clothing that her ideas defined Duckie's sense of individuality for so many, and in the boldest of visual ways. And years later, when the Costume Designers Guild gave her a lifetime achievement award, I had the privilege of presenting it to her at the ceremony. I did not, however, dress as Duckie. Let's make that perfectly clear.

As for Duckie's hair, I again had my ideas in the run-up to filming.

"Give me a pompadour . . ." I told the hairstylist.

"You bet," he said.

". . . with a weird little ponytail!"

"Huh?"

Hey, the guy tried. Although I had enough hair back then for the pomp, I did not have enough for the extra appendage. We tried tying one on, but it just looked too weird. (And for Duckie, that was saying something.) So we just went with the pomp, which I want to say took a fair amount of work every day, between teasing my very fine hair into a properly bulbous ridge, then spraying it into place. My rough estimate is that two tanker trucks of spray were depleted throughout the course of the shoot on Duckie's look alone. I was just not used to spending a lot of time in a hair-and-makeup chair, and it has ever since given me new appreciation for the hours actresses spend in them on shoots, sometimes just to look as if they haven't been in them at all. One thing about being in that chair that was exciting, however: The makeup artist was Tommy Cole, who had been a Mouseketeer in the 1950s. I thought that was unbelievably fucking wonderful, that I was getting made up by *Tommy*!

My first day of shooting was at the record store Trax, where Annie Potts's character, Iona, worked. The location was in what is now the vivacious, consumer-hopping Third Street Promenade in Santa Monica, but what was then a depressed, little-trafficked retail strip down the street from the mall where they filmed *Fast Times at Ridgemont High.*

The scenes with Annie and Molly that day were dialogue scenes, and they went well. I loved Annie and her nutty costumes. She had psycho hair and a rubber dress, and God help me, she was hot. Fun, warm, friendly, and hot. I was experiencing a distinct lack of confidence, though, because I was slightly overwhelmed by the situation, even after a few weeks of rehearsal. I also knew what was coming up on day two: Duckie's record-store solo. I had been given the news during rehearsal that there was no way I could do Mick Jagger, because it was too expensive to get the rights to a Rolling Stones song. (This was before artists sold songs at the drop of a hat for use selling cars or toothpaste.)

Howie's idea was to do a song that suggested something about the relationship between Duckie and Andie. He asked if I liked Otis Redding, and I said, "Sure," but all I really knew was "(Sittin' on) The Dock of the Bay," which I didn't think sounded like a fun number to mime, or said something about our characters. But Howie gave me a tape of Redding's version of "Try a Little Tenderness," with its sweet, soulful escalation in tone and emotion, and my first impression was that it was a really long song, and would take up a lot of screen time. But Howie assured me they'd cut it down to a manageable length.

That first day on set, Howie played me the edit, which was considerably shorter and cut out a whole chunk of the beginning. Then he introduced me to Kenny Ortega, a theater choreographer with a few movie credits at the time (*Xanadu*) who was going to teach me Duckie's moves. Kenny was really friendly and open, and I was in heaven, because I was now with my people: theater folk! We're puttin' on a show!

When shooting ended for the day, I headed over to the rehearsal studio, where Kenny met me with a casually inquisitive, "So, do you dance?"

Flashing mental images of self-conscious boogieing at parties or clubs inspired a meek, "No, not really."

He said, "Well, let's just try a few things and see how you move."

I took a stab at jolting my body into something resembling rhythmic swaying and shaking, and God bless him, if he was at all disappointed, he did not show it. He'd smile, laugh, and say, "Hey, you're a mover! You're a real mover!" I know it was his way of saying, "Hey, you can (sort of) dance!" but it made me believe we could put together something really fun. A professional choreographer isn't going to insist a neophyte graduate instantly to Astaire-like levels of footwork. I realized he was taking in what I did naturally and thinking about how to translate that into a punchy little bit of personal expression.

Kenny and I spent the next four to five hours coming up with the dance. We knew we didn't want to just throw some random moves together. We wanted it to be theatrical, even tell a story almost, but most important, get the audience on the Duckman's side. It should start small, with a slide and some up-close lip-syncing, then build to ever more ridiculous choreography of the white-kid-soul-posturing kind. At one point I slapped the ground, then stood back up, and Kenny said, "You know, you start to really like how this kid is dancing!" I was just in that zone of letting loose and trying anything, but he seemed to grasp even in rehearsal that there's a point when your commitment to being a fool carries over into weird endearment.

After a nervous day of shooting, the evening's sense of invention and hard work made me cautiously optimistic. Mind you, I was still reeling a bit from having my rockabilly look nixed in favor of the hipster-explosion choice. But I was also smart enough at the time to understand that I was in the hands of people who knew what they were doing. We ended the night with two minutes of Grade A, vitamin-fortified, not-from-concentrate, organic Duckie Dale that I was now eager to showcase the next day.

Even though my job description was film actor, I went in to work the following morning feeling like a theater actor ready to perform for an audience. I wanted everyone to see the dance, and I wanted a reaction. Because when you're putting it all out there the way I was, the way Duckie was, you expect to end with feedback. You're gasping for breath, frozen in your final pose, ready for applause, boos, dollar bills in your G-string, whatever. So I did the dance for Howie and producer Lauren Shuler, gave it my all, and at the end, there I was panting like I'd just finished a performance of *Riverdance* and . . . silence. Absolute silence. The crew isn't applauding. The makeup people don't seem to give a shit. Was anybody even paying attention?

"What did you think?" I said to Howie.

More silence. And then . . . muttering. Howie muttered to Lauren. Lauren muttered to Howie. I'm still catching my breath, looking around like, *What the . . . ?*

I tried again. "Howie, what did you think of it?"

He turned to me as if suddenly remembering I was in the record store. "Oh, it was great, Jon. But now I have to shoot it." I'm not kidding when I say he sounded actually regretful.

If I needed any more proof that theater and film are different, this was it. Howie's perspective as a director trying to stay on schedule was essentially, "Well, now I'm going to need camera setups here, here, and here. How the fuck am I going to shoot this in the half day I have allotted?" My perspective as a needy actor was, "I just gave you a balls-out final-dress-rehearsal performance, and you can't at least say, 'Great job!' or clap or throw a piece of fruit?" I was really going to have to get acclimated to this filmmaking stuff.

As it turned out, we needed the whole day to film "Try a Little Tenderness." It was tiring having to do the dance over and over and over, from this angle and that angle. The record-store floor was such a mess that for me to slide properly they had to put a sheet of Lexan down, and I slid in socks. Everyone was supportive, which felt great, and by the end I was beat. Filming the dance did put us behind—there was no time to shoot dialogue scenes scheduled for the second half of the day—and Howie had to fight to get on schedule for the rest of the shoot. Mind you, this was only our second day. But Howie also knew that he had a potentially great scene on his hands, something people would talk about, and which set a tone for the movie and the dynamic between Andie and Duckie.

Howie and I were also not above assessing Duckie's level of devotion toward Andie in slightly cruder terms. During rehearsal Howie came up with what he called the Boner-meter as a way of letting me know how much to dial up or dial down Duckie's attraction to Andie at any given moment. When Duckie was over the moon—say, in that record store— that was a ten, a raging hard-on. But as soon as Andrew's Blane shows up, that took the Boner-meter down to a limp and flaccid three. Wince all you want—I'm sure Stanislavsky would have approved.

One of the fun parts of *Pretty in Pink* was getting to improvise. From early on, Howie would do one take as written; then he'd say "Jon, come up with something." The "Blane? His name is Blane?! That's not a name; it's a major appliance" joke was an ad lib of mine, and the scene in the girls' bathroom was me riffing on an observation I'd made once in junior high school when I stayed after class. I sneaked into the girls' room out of sheer curiosity, since nobody was around, and marveled at how much nicer it was than the boys'. And yes, I did think the tampon machine was a candy dispenser. Howie really encouraged the improvising, and he did so with James Spader, too, who I believe came up with sleazy Steff's great line, "The girl was, is, and will always be *nada*."

Where Molly and Andrew were tough nuts to crack socially, Jimmy was approachable, and we hung out a lot. I'd go to his trailer and we'd talk about life, the business, and all manner of stuff. We talked about how much we enjoyed having input into our characters. He certainly had a grasp of his particular niche. I remember him telling me in his Thurston Howell–on-mescaline drawl, "I think I pretty much have a lock on these teenage asshole characters." That certainly proved true. He was so good at it, in fact, that Howie didn't originally want him, figuring him to be an asshole in real life. James could be odd, for sure, but he was always friendly to me.

Our only real scene together was the fight, and I recall he and I were adamant that it not look like a movie fight. We wanted it to look like a real high school scrap, in which it's generally sloppy and nobody lands good punches—just flailing grabs and yanks—and you fall at weird times, and sometimes you're just wrestling. We worked on it hard, and our goal was to have this formless set-to with no clear winner before the teacher breaks it up. Of course, what was funny about eventually shooting it was that Jimmy was in such better shape than I was that it was clear he was really trying not to hurt me. So I will always be grateful a) that we got to film it the way we wanted, and b) that I didn't get punched in the face. I remember at the end, when Jimmy ad-libbed a snarling spit onto the school grounds, it was so badass I thought, "Wow, he's just the shit."

Pretty in Pink also marked an early movie appearance of Andrew Dice Clay in his "Diceman" persona, playing the club bouncer who won't let Duckie in. (Another scene we got to ad-lib.) Music was a good way to get Molly talking, and one night she, her friend Moon Zappa, and I went to see the Rave-Ups, with Andrew Dice Clay opening for them at the Palomino in North Hollywood. This was before Dice was a phenomenon, when he could still count on shocking a crowd into laughter by opening with the Little Miss Muffet/"What's in the bowl, bitch?" joke, then segue into various ribald variations on the fate of poor Mother Goose characters.

And yet, that night he bombed in a way I'd never seen a comedian experience, and haven't seen since. I know what was in that bowl, Miss Muffet: a man drenched in sweat, and not just because of his climate-inappropriate leather jacket. Dice was an odd character—nice, but odd. With him it always felt like a performance. It was hard to get to know the person underneath the leather-jacketed bluster. But hey, he kept at it to the tune of sold-out Madison Square Garden shows only a few years later, a level of commitment to an act I respected on a certain level.

I didn't do a lot of after-work socializing, usually because I was simply too tired, but also because for me, trying to get into the club of the moment often involved a humiliating amount of begging, cajoling, waiting, and bribery, and then would, more often than not, end with a dispiriting cab ride home.

On occasion Molly's friend Angie would attempt to coax me out to the latest trendy Hollywood spot. One evening it was a club called the Boss, which in 1985 could mean only one thing: a nightspot devoted to the music of Bruce Springsteen. As I stood outside waiting to get in, I began making small talk to a beautiful brunette—sweet!—and as we chatted, I could swear I knew her from somewhere. It was really bugging me, and then it hit me, and then it left my mouth: "Hey, you're the girl from that tampon commercial!"

She was. I was technically right. She had starred in a Tampax ad that was all over television. But when you consider the other thing she was known for—the girl who's chosen by Bruce Springsteen to dance with him onstage in his "Dancing in the Dark" video—you could say I picked the exact wrong thing by which to recognize a hot actress named Courteney Cox when you're hitting it off with her outside of a *Bruce Springsteen–themed club*. She never spoke to me the rest of the night. I knew there was a reason I didn't go to clubs.

Fortunately, back at work (where, let's face it, I was not as apt to embarrass myself), Harry Dean Stanton hadn't done any tampon commercials to cloud my sense of his illustrious career. Stanton, who played Andie's father, was like a worn but comfy piece of used furniture. I thought he was supercool because he'd been in *Alien*, and was looking forward to working with him. But as grizzled and genial as he was, it was also quite clear he enjoyed his cannabis. When we were ready to shoot our scene, I remember the first assistant director going to his trailer.

Knock, knock, knock. "Harry?" Waiting.

Knock, knock, knock. "Harry?" Waiting.

Knock, knock, knock. "Harry?"

At this point, the crackle of walkie-talkie communication filled the air, mostly distorted, but I could hear, "Door's not opening."

More knocks. "Harry? Mr. Stanton?" Then the first AD just opened the door, and it was like something you'd see in a cartoon: A curling waft of distinctively odored smoke emerged. A couple of guys walked in, and a minute later walked out with Harry Dean Stanton. He was so laid-back for our scene it was hard for us to generate any comedic tension. Howie kept trying to coax some energy out of Harry, but nothing was working, take after take after take. Then Howie got up close to the veteran actor and started talking some kind of gibberish to him, and finally Harry started perking up, and we got the scene.

I only found out recently over lunch with Howie what got Harry motivated.

"Harry only responded to basketball metaphors," Howie told me. "So I had to tell him, 'Look, we're not trying to slow the tempo and play our own game here. We're on a fast break; it's time to shoot and score!'"

Wow, whatever works, right?

As for Molly, the smallness of her acting choices took some getting used to. I kept wondering, *Is this even registering on film?* I was over here making these big gestures, and she was just being real. I'd ask Howie about how our scenes looked, and he'd say, "Dailies look great!" I'd scratch my head, because it seemed to me that there wasn't a perceptible difference between how she acted off-camera and on-camera. But that was because ultimately she wasn't playing somebody that different from herself. She was a brave poor girl, and that was about it. I was in a different boat: playing someone I wished I'd been in high school, so I bit into Duckie's swagger and chewed with vigor.

Molly was impressively self-assured for someone only seventeen years old. She knew what she wanted when it came to the movie, and she knew what she didn't like. She was also at home making people aware of it, most famously the man who put her on the map, John Hughes, since after *Pretty in Pink* she didn't make another movie with him. He'd wanted her for his reverse *Pretty in Pink* follow-up, *Some Kind of Wonderful*, but Molly was ready to move on from his brand of high school movie, and said no. It's often said that this was the reason John Hughes quit writing about teenagers altogether: that if his muse was out, so was he. The record certainly reflects some kind of conscious break John made with the subject of adolescence—after *Some Kind of Wonderful* in 1987, it was all John Candy and precocious moppets, save for the little-seen *Career Opportunities*.

John was not a regular presence during the shooting of *Pretty in Pink*. He saw me do the record-store dance, and he'd be there for the occasional scene, but he was mostly occupied with the movies he was directing. *Weird Science* was released while we were shooting, and all I'd heard was how great Anthony Michael Hall was. Going to the *Weird Science* premiere, I remember the fleeting feeling that I was part of a cool group of young actors. I met Anthony, but didn't get a chance to really hang out with him. It was quick and cordial, not like two Hughesean nerds sizing each other up—he wouldn't have been threatened by me anyway, since he'd turned down the role of Duckie before I ever got involved. (It seems Anthony, like Molly, was ready to break free as well.)

Then, toward the end of shooting, John began getting all excited about directing *Ferris Bueller's Day Off* with that look-alike dude who keeps following me around. Joking aside, I was secretly thrilled that for once I was in on something ahead of Matthew Broderick. I got to John Hughes first! Then again, there was also this nagging little feeling that our dad had moved on to be with his new family. It was suddenly, "Hey, (don't you) forget about us! We're still here, holding down the fort! Okay, okay, we get it. Ice cream sometime? A little catch, maybe? Will we see you over the holidays?"

But John wasn't totally gone for good on *Pretty in Pink*, as was soon to be apparent.

Chapter 11
My *Breakfast Club* Fist Moment

Beginnings are easy.

See how I did that? I began the chapter with a statement about beginnings. This book has layers! Being an author is a cinch! In your face, Herman Melville!

Endings, however, are a pain in the ass. And they are kind of important to a good movie.

Think about it. If a movie doesn't begin well, it has plenty of time to recover. Even if a movie sags halfway through, it can rally in plenty of time to leave everyone satisfied.

But if your ending doesn't work, you've just left a theater full of moviegoers feeling cheated. It's the last part of your movie, but the thing front and center on the audience's mind as they're walking out. If they liked it all except the ending, then chances are they're going to say they didn't like any of it.

Take *The Godfather*, and that final shot of the door literally and metaphorically shutting and visually wiping Diane Keaton's worried face from the screen, a truly profound and portentous ending suggesting the depth of Michael Corleone's corruption. What if after that, you added a scene in which Al Pacino opens it back up again and says, "Sorry. This thing just closes by itself—come on in, Kay, and tell us if you think the family should get into retail." Then you've just ruined *The Godfather.*

If Bruce Willis bails on those pretty shitty odds in the final act of *Die Hard* and quietly leaves the building for a late-night spa treatment in Koreatown, *Die Hard* is ruined.

If Rocky wins the fight in *Rocky*, is it still really, truly *Rocky*?

I'm not saying *Pretty in Pink* is in league with those classics, but it had an ending problem, it turned out.

The day we shot the prom scene at the Biltmore Hotel in downtown Los Angeles, I was in a good mood. My dashed wardrobe hopes for Duckie were given a generous parting gift: I was okayed to wear a snappy rockabilly-tinged tuxedo ensemble for the finale. Molly, however, wasn't feeling well. She had a stomach flu of some kind, and there was a lot to get done that day. There was Andie showing up all nervous, then Duckie making his appearance, and then the two entering the prom, the whole room stopping to gaze in utter shock, and then our characters stepping out onto the floor, where a spotlight hits us as we spin and spin and spin to David Bowie's "Heroes" as the whole of the high school looks on with the relieved sense that the world has righted itself. Andie and Duckie, together forever! Cue the freeze frame—my *Breakfast Club* fist-in-the-air moment had arrived!

What is that? You don't remember it that way? That's because *Pretty in Pink* originally ended with Duckie winning Andie. Or Andie winning Duckie. Or the two of us cowinners in the lotto of love. Long live the outcasts!

As we filmed it that day, though, it never felt like we really nailed the scene as a true romantic crescendo. Molly was remote again, more so than usual, but I just chalked that up to her being under the weather, and it was soon apparent to everybody how she was feeling. When we got to the part where we were spinning on the dance floor, she actually collapsed in my arms and fainted, she was so sick. People rushed up to help her, and though she quickly came back to consciousness, she was escorted off the set for a long break.

I said to Howie, "Should we wait it out? Come back and shoot tomorrow?" (If you recall from my *No Small Affair* illness, my view of leading-actor incapacitation didn't take into account such pressing matters as production overruns—the Biltmore ain't cheap.)

"No, no," Howie replied. "You know, I think we got it. We're not going to come back."

Fine, I thought. *I trust these people now.* Something seemed off, but hey, maybe it looked great in dailies.

The rest of the shoot went smoothly, and after *Pretty in Pink* wrapped I went straight to Virginia to shoot my next movie, a dark comedy called *Home Front*, about a neglected teen who decides to sabotage his absent dad's senate campaign. It was a funny script, and I would be the lead, so I leaped at it. I landed in something very different, however: The director was fired and replaced after a week, the production shut down for a month, and when everyone came back we had a new script that was being re-written further on a daily basis. It was painful to watch everything that was good in the original screenplay be slowly drained and replaced by mediocrity, but I was stuck.

I was in the middle of this sinking production when I got a call from manager Marty.

"Hey, Jon," he said. "So it looks like they need to reshoot the *Pretty in Pink* ending."

Bingo. "You know, Marty, I saw this one coming. Molly was pretty out-of-it that day."

"Well, they'll get you the pages," he said. "Oh, and they're going to change it so she ends up with Andrew McCarthy at the end."

I froze.

Wow, okay.

"I told you so" had suddenly become "I didn't know *that!*" But in receiving the blow that Duckie wouldn't get his big romantic sendoff with the girl of his dreams, something in me instinctively knew that I had to be a good soldier and accept it. And I did, just as Duckie invariably would when I played it. *This is how it works,* I figured. *Movies change. Reshoots happen all the time.* Don't get me wrong: I was crestfallen, and quick to blame myself for not generating whatever was needed in the scene for it to work. But I was going to do what was required for the good of the John Hughes brand.

It turned out Paramount needed me for a couple of days in Los Angeles for the reshoots, but that apparently was a problem for the *Home Front* producer, who turned into a prick and wouldn't let me leave for any length of time unless he got a ton of money. He was essentially holding me hostage, so Paramount opted to work around him. My schedule gave me one day off—Sunday—and there were no direct flights to LA, so the studio okayed making the corporate jet available. The solution was, I'd finish Saturday's *Home Front* filming (which always went past sundown), jet to LA that night, cram in all the *Pretty in Pink* reshoots that Sunday, and fly back in time to be at *Home Front* for my six a.m. Monday call time. It would be physically grueling for me, a brutal exploitation of the miracle of modern travel, but I was ready to make it work.

Then things got belabored. Andrew McCarthy's manager, Mary Goldberg, got the word that Paramount was sending me the jet, so she insisted it swing by New York and pick her up as well as Andrew, who was performing in a play there. This despite the fact that commercial flights were plentiful from New York City. Marty, hearing that Mary was getting a seat on the jet, now insisted on flying to Virginia so he could be on it, too. I thought, *Is he expecting a fight to go down and feels he needs to be my in-air cornerman?* No, apparently this is just the politics of perks in Hollywood. Never mind that this actually increased the amount of travel time, reduced the time on the ground in LA to make the reshoots happen, and would invariably tire us all out.

As it turned out, the Paramount jet was a tiny thing, and hardly designed for multiple posses. You could certainly sense from Andrew and Mary as they crawled onto the plane that it was smaller than they'd imagined. Mary's enormous head of frizzy hair was practically another passenger in that constrained cabin space. The extra stop also meant refueling halfway across the country, too, so it quickly began to seem like a needlessly lengthy travel experience just to get two actors to Los Angeles with their status levels intact. I did get a little bit of vengeful enjoyment later when Andrew—whose hair was now cropped because of the play he was in—needed to be fitted with a short-notice Blane coif that had to be one of the least convincing cinematic wigs ever. I, meanwhile, was still in possession of my locks, which were blown into my luxuriously snazzy pompadour. I took every opportunity to smirk at his goofy hairpiece.

It was good to see Howie again, but I had to inquire about the ending change.

"What happened?" I asked.

"We did testing, and audiences just didn't go for it," he said, as if this were no big deal. "Besides, the movie is about bridging the class divide, and John felt that had he gone with the original ending, it would have been like saying, 'You can't do it. Don't even bother falling in love with rich people—'"

I couldn't help it. I interrupted: "And John doesn't want audiences to come away feeling there was no hope for them to have rich people in their lives."

Howie shot me a look, but I just smiled at my snarky joke and went back to work. And let's face it: John Hughes did come up with a way to solve the ending and not completely cut Duckie off at the knees. Howie said that John was pretty despondent about the audience reaction to the ending, and just disappeared for three weeks, as if it never happened. But Howie had kept pushing John—who was by then deep into *Ferris Bueller*—and eventually John showed up at Howie's, sat on the floor, and said, "I've got it. Andrew's character has to show up at prom alone, and Duckie has to be the one to notice he's there alone. Then Duckie has to let Andie know that Blane's the guy for her." John solved it by making Duckie the romantic martyr, the one who recognizes when he's been bested by true love, and the one who instigates the moment that makes two and two four. (Or in this case, one and one two.)

I was comfortable enough with it that day. A little hurt, yes. Too tired to fight? Sure. But it was something to play dramatically, which is all you can ask for as an actor. We shot the scene, and when it came to the consolation-prize moment in which Kristy Swanson's flirty pink vision nods suggestively at Duckie, I must admit I felt mystified by it.

"It's so patently ridiculous," I said to Howie. "She's never seen him before, but all of a sudden she's into him?"

"Look, the audience really loves Duckie," he said, "and I just want to open a door for him."

How could I argue with that? During the rehearsal take, I got playful and chose to turn Duckie's reaction to this hot girl's leer into a self-conscious "can you believe this?" joke in which I looked straight into the camera—what they call "breaking the fourth wall," or shattering the illusion that there's a barrier between characters and audience. I knew it was weird, and not exactly appropriate for a slice-of-life teen movie. I was probably feeling a little loopy by that point, and maybe thinking about how well Eddie Murphy's hilariously deadpan turn to the camera worked in *Trading Places*. But I never thought Howie would love it as much as he did. He insisted I do it for the real take, too. Although we also shot one without it, Howie kept the one with my cheeky nod to the audience.

I got the main shots completed, but there was little time for insert shots if I was going to make the flight, so for the close-up of Duckie's hand in Andie's, they inexplicably picked a crew member much older than me, and now that shot in the finished movie looks like a wizened claw is suddenly clutching our heroine's hand. Whatever.

I was now headed back on the jet so I could make my Monday morning call time on the *Home Front* set. It occurred to me that I'd come away from my filmed high school experience much the same as I left my actual high school: saddened that I never felt accepted as a part of the in crowd, but all the wiser for it. And as *Home Front* continued to spiral out of control, looking more and more like a ready-made dud, I took comfort in knowing that in the can was something good, something people would have an interest in seeing, and a project that would show the world what I had to offer.

That sense of accomplishment really hit home when on opening day I rented a limo and took some friends as we hit various theaters to celebrate the moment. One of those theaters was the Loews Astor, where years prior I'd sat in wonder at *Star Wars*, and my hoot-and-clap policy of acknowledging movie magic began. We arrived after it had started, but I hightailed it to the front row and sat down just in time to catch "Try a Little Tenderness." It was still a little surreal to see myself so uninhibited on-screen, but I was proud of it. When my dance was finished, however, I heard it: hooting and clapping.

It remains indisputably one of the happiest moments of my life.

Chapter 12
People Actually Booed

Boy, you think you know a film you starred in when you were twenty. Turns out there were quite a few elements to the crazy cocktail that is *Pretty in Pink* that I never knew about until years later.

For one thing, I learned that Howard Deutch is not Machiavellian. Not that I thought he was a master manipulator. I mean, Howie's a great guy. We've stayed friends all these years. But when it came to one source of filming frustration on *Pretty in Pink*, I'd always blamed Howie for it, until he gave me the true story last year over lunch as I was getting my memory jogged for this book.

It was the nightclub scene in which Duckie, Iona, and Andie are hanging out, Blane shows up, and I'm a dick to him. It's four people around a table, and those scenes take a long time to shoot, because you have to get everybody in single shots as well as the group take. As the day goes on, you've performed the scene many, many times, because when a fellow actor is getting his or her single shot, it helps if the scene partners are off-camera delivering their lines for the sake of flow and realism.

There's a hierarchy, though, as to who gets to do their singles first, and my new-kid status meant my singles would be filmed last. I didn't mind being last, because coming from the theater, I'm used to running scenes over and over and over. I considered it a badge of honor, in fact, that when it came to my singles, I'd be as fresh for the final takes as I'd been at the beginning of the day.

But when it came time to have the camera on me, Molly and Andrew started fucking around with the lines from behind the camera. It was already a tense scene of arguing, but they were making lines up that were even more outwardly hateful, compounded by giggling and laughing between each other. My dander wasn't just up; it was airborne. I thought, *I just did rock-steady off-camera line readings for all you dicktards, and now is when you fuck around, after three-quarters of the day is gone? Where's the professionalism?*

I was really angry about it, and after we finally got the take of me that Howie liked, I went over to Molly and vented.

"What the fuck!" I said. "What was that all about?"

"Oh, well, they told us to try to make you mad so that the scene would be fresher," she said.

That only made me more furious. There was an assumption that I wouldn't be fresh enough to make the scene work, when I'd given no indication that I wasn't rarin' to go. I took it as an insult, and from then on was floored that Howie would feel the need to manipulate me into getting what he wanted, something he'd never done before.

Well, what I learned was that it was John Hughes's doing. Howie said that when John was around, it was not uncommon to hear, "That scene needs a little more something," and then he'd push for more takes, or a different approach to a take. We'll never know if the buttons-unpushed version of my singles would have been better, but out of respect for the late writer of *Pretty in Pink*, let's just say the scene works as it stands.

At least I got confirmation that Howie is a hundred percent mensch, as opposed to 99.9 percent!

I also learned in recent years that Robert Downey Jr. and I are not the same person.

Yes, that sounds like something pretty obvious to know about oneself. Taking that statement at face value, I also know that at no time have I been Dick Cheney, a golden retriever, the guy from the Joe Isuzu commercial, or Sir Francis Bacon. But when I say we aren't the same person, what I mean is: When it came to the part of Duckie, Molly Ringwald wanted Robert Downey Jr., didn't get Robert Downey Jr., and therefore could look at me only as Not Robert Downey Jr.

Now, I knew back then that Robert Downey Jr. (are you sick of seeing that name now?) was somebody talked about for Duckie. I also knew Anthony Michael Hall was offered the part. But what I didn't know until I sat my forty-something self down a few years ago to watch the other interviews on the twentieth-anniversary "Everything's Duckie" DVD edition of the movie was that Molly's view of the original ending would have been mighty different if that delectable (my word) Mr. Downey Jr. had been cast. She would have completely understood Andie and Duckie being together at the end if the sexually attractive (my phrase) Mr. Downey Jr. had been opposite her. But once the romantically unappealing (my inference) Jon Cryer was cast, she simply never bought the ending. To which my forty-something, just-thought-I-was-kicking-back-to-reminisce self responded to the TV, "*Whaaaa?*"

Needless to say, I went over the whole ending rigmarole in my head and started to view it in terms slightly more complicated. Molly was certainly physically ill the day we shot the original finale—something I'm not so negative as to assume had to do with my actual presence—but was there an unknowing thread of actorly sabotage going on? Did she never intend for the ending to work? Had she heard about Robert's masterful work in the subway improv at Stagedoor Manor and convinced herself only an actor capable of that kind of brilliance deserved her character's love? Was the plan to make that Andie/Duckie pairing so unpalatable that the studio would pull Robert Downey Jr. out of whatever he was doing and erase me/

insert him digitally, even though such technology didn't even exist then? Was I really being this paranoid about someone who was only seventeen at the time?

Once I came out of that irritable place, I felt I'd at least earned a few lingering irritations. I may not have given off the most palpably erotic vibe playing Duckie—something I now wish I'd been pushed into working on then—but at least I played the part where this flashy dork was plainly in love with Andie. Mightn't Molly have tried a wee smidgen to pretend that first ending could have been realistic?

Had there been, in some tangible way foiled by a lack of imagination, at least a chance for Andie and Duckie with audiences?

Then again, there were boos at those early screenings, another late-arriving fact to my mental history of this movie.

Only last year, over that aforementioned lunch, did Howard Deutch inform me that those initial test screenings of *Pretty in Pink* weren't just a case—as I was initially led to believe—of audiences politely indicating that they didn't "go for" the ending. As if it were a case of Coke versus Pepsi.

More like Coke versus horse urine.

As Howie explained, "Through the whole screening, Dawn Steel"— then the production chief at Paramount—"is holding my hand, because the audience is just loving the movie so much. They were totally with it, until that moment at the end when she starts dancing with Duckie, and the freeze frame happened. People actually booed."

I had gotten my freeze-frame moment à la Judd Nelson at the end of *The Breakfast Club*, and instead of roars of approval, there were boos. Yikes.

Howie added, "I've never had that happen where just everything came to a screeching halt."

Learning of actual boos altered everything again for me. Was that first ending just beyond the comprehension of everyone? Maybe it was like the famous story screenwriter William Goldman tells in his memoir *Adven-*

tures in the Screen Trade about the reaction to *The Great Waldo Pepper*. They'd made a big period adventure about the early days of aviation, with Robert Redford—then the biggest star in movies—playing a brave pilot whose stunt partner was a young, vibrant Susan Sarandon. Everything was hunky-dory with audiences until they killed off Sarandon in a tension-filled aerial sequence. As much as the filmmakers thought they'd braced audiences for the possibility of a dramatic left turn, they apparently underestimated what people wanted to see—namely, their marquee hero saving someone—and after that, moviegoers simply checked out.

Pretty in Pink was perhaps, without anyone realizing it initially, about a poor girl snagging a rich boy. Maybe even the instant eroticization speculatively attributed to Robert Downey Jr. wouldn't have made that ending work. My costar's secret preference is now to me exactly what it should be: something to roll my eyes over, shrug off, and make jokes about.

I am now, however, in the process of tracking down every single person who booed at that screening and figuring out a way to sign them all up for unwanted magazine subscriptions.

I guess the takeaway is, endings are mysteries.

As it turns out, Duckie's legacy has decidedly benefited from his also-ran status, his right guy/wrong guy alchemy. I got a real taste of that in 2008, when Oscar-winning screenwriter Diablo Cody asked me to make an appearance at the New Beverly Cinema in Hollywood for a screening of *Pretty in Pink* she was hosting as part of a Cody-curated film festival.

She asked me to do a preshowing interview, and in talking about the ending to the crowd, I diplomatically acknowledged that I could see how the original ending might have felt odd, since, I said, "You do invest in the cross-class relationship."

"I did not invest in it," Diablo interrupted with a mild vehemence, her fangirl defenses up. "I was, like, so against it in every way."

This is something I've continued to hear over the years: that if you're in the Duckie camp, a nerd-forever type with sympathies augmented by an inherent distaste and distrust for Blane and all he represents, you think of *Pretty in Pink* as ending bittersweetly, unhappily even, and in fact more realistic than John Hughes imagined it originally when he shunted Blane to the side as Andie and Duckie twirled their way into outsider Eden. I find it especially funny that even fans of the ending as it stands now don't seem to think Andie and Blane make it past the first year of college as a couple. They do all seem to believe she and Duckie are friends for life, though.

I'm always touched by fans like Diablo, whose affection for Duckie lead them to believe an injustice was done upon this sidelined geek. It's heartening to see this outspoken guy I played become a hero to young people who feel ostracized and put-upon, but who might find in themselves the capacity to boast anyway—however misplaced—and move forward. You don't get in this business to avoid having some effect on people. "He's your Duckie"—shorthand for "there's the effeminate heterosexual dork who's always been in love with you"—is even a pop-culture phrase now, known to arise in movies and TV shows. (Its first-known usage, as far as I know, was from John Hughes himself, who during filming pointed out a friend of Molly's and whispered to me, "He's her Duckie.")

Molly added a rainbow-hued wrinkle to the Duckie legacy during a videotaped interview for *Entertainment Weekly*, which was reuniting various movie/TV-show casts for an issue. She, Annie Potts, and I were chattin' away, and when I brought up the notion that Andie and Duckie stayed friends, Molly added, "And I'm sure that Duckie came out by now."

"Ha, ha, ha," I went along, making a joke about how Duckie would be the one at the Gay Pride parade in suspenders with no shirt.

But then I thought about it some more. Did I somehow not pick up on a pretty big thing about this guy I played? I already knew that among the character's champions are gay men and women who saw in Duckie a society-branded pariah who didn't give a shit about what people thought, was comfortable in his own skin, and lived out loud. And for the closeted gay men who in their teens professed open "crushes" on close female friends as a defense mechanism against real feelings, there was probably a certain kinship attached to Duckie's fruitless quest to win over Andie.

I'm honored by that legacy, too, but I have to say that I didn't play Duckie as gay, and I never thought of him as gay. Because, just to set the record straight (ahem), Duckie was in love with Andie. As an into-girls, not-into-dudes nerd. You know how I know? Because I was that same vaguely effeminate, heterosexual dork who, growing up in a more societally rigid time, occasionally sent gaydar meters spinning out of control when he just wanted to win the heart of a girl who wouldn't look twice at him. Saying Duckie was gay, frankly, is a kind of copout, too easy a sexuality tag in this label-busting era for gender roles, too easy an explanation for an outsider losing the girl, and suggests that nobody that flamboyant could possibly be straight. I respectfully differ on that one, Molly.

Duckie is straight, folks. So straight, in fact, that he *did* go to that Gay Pride parade in no shirt and suspenders, because he has gay friends he marches in solidarity with, and if we know Duckie, he doesn't do anything by half measures. That's something you see in all types of people. That's why we love the guy. That's why I'm proud of him.

As for Alan Harper marrying a man . . .

Chapter 13
Fuck 1987

1987. Remember that year?

Aretha Franklin became the first woman inducted into the Rock and Roll Hall of Fame. About time! The Simpsons made their debut appearance, as little cartoon shorts nestled into *The Tracey Ullman Show*. Legendary! Reagan told Gorbachev to tear down that Berlin Wall. Historic! The Canadians introduced their one-dollar coin, nicknamed the loonie. Weird!

Oh, and Jon Cryer's movie career imploded. Wait. What?

To those of you in the acting profession, one of the truest things I can tell you is that planning a career is foolhardy. Maybe Brad Pitt can say, "Bring me a half-animated, half–live action musical about the life of professional French farting performer Le Petomane for me to star in alongside my cat, to be directed by my accountant!" and be relatively certain it will get made and put in theaters, knowing that if it fails, he can make a superhero movie and be on top again.

For the rest of us, it's a little trickier. There's what we want to do, what we can do, what comes to us, what we get to try for, what we actually get, and what eventually gets made. Then that last, kind of important thing called what people think of it.

I was in an envious position after *Pretty in Pink* in that scripts were coming to me, people saw I was talented, and I had goodwill with decision makers. My name was able to get a movie made. It's a form of being hot in Hollywood that can take you in one of two directions: Do more of what got you there in the first place, or do your own thing, because you've now got that power. In its crudest form, it's the choice between pleasing audiences or pleasing yourself. The problem is when you choose pleasing yourself and assume that it runs in tandem with pleasing audiences. That's called pleasuring yourself, and nobody wants to see that. Again, unless you're Brad Pitt.

I never got the repeat John Hughes experience, as Molly Ringwald and Anthony Michael Hall did. I thought I was going to, though, when John's script for *Some Kind of Wonderful* came my way, and Howie was slated to direct it. Howie and I got along like a house on fire—even though I've never understood that term—and the script was great.

As John envisioned originally, the story was more antic, more in the vein of *Ferris Bueller* than *Pretty in Pink*. A high school outcast takes a big leap and asks the most popular girl in school to the prom. To his surprise— and the rest of the school's—she says yes, which leads everyone to tell him it could only possibly be a pity date. The nerd then finds out that she said yes to get back at a jerky boyfriend, whom she's still seeing. His response is to take her on the Date to End All Dates, an epic romantic adventure that at one point included the Blue Angels aerobatic flying squadron. The whole thing was silly, sweet, and big, and I thought, *Wait. What role could I possibly play?* I joke.

Actually, the central nerd role was a different animal from Duckie. This guy had no outsize swagger or offbeat cool. He was a hundred percent geekazoid. That was fine. Paramount's motion picture bigwig Ned Tanen was high on me. John Hughes was on board. Howie was directing.

Let's do this thing! They asked me to come in and read with Mary Stuart Masterson, and although I was sensing that Howie didn't think I was completely right for the part, I kept my fingers crossed.

Then suddenly Howie was fired, and I was out of the picture. Now, I was aware that this kind of thing happened, but it seemed odd.

Well, it was. Here's what happened, according to Howie, who filled me in years later. At the time, Howie was also itching to direct a hotly discussed script of John's called *Oil and Vinegar*, which was a stripped-down, guy-and-a-girl (guess who the girl was going to be) movie that took place entirely in a hotel room. It was an all-night talkathon à la *The Breakfast Club*, and to this day Howie says it was the best script of John's he ever read. Though he was prepping *Some Kind of Wonderful*, he nevertheless got up the courage to tell John he wanted to direct *Oil and Vinegar*.

"Hmmm, okay, I'll think about it," John said.

The next day, Howie went to the studio to work on *Some Kind of Wonderful* and discovered a lock on his office door, and shortly after, he received word that he'd been taken off the movie. In a flash, John had simply turned against Howie. It seems John had wanted to direct *Oil and Vinegar* himself, and interpreted Howie's vocalized interest as a huge betrayal. Now Howie was off *Some Kind of Wonderful*, and Martha Coolidge—who'd made the college comedy *Real Genius*—was hired. Martha didn't like the script, though. Yes, you'd be surprised how often this happens: people campaigning hard for a job they don't really want, getting it, then starting to fuck around with the project.

Martha oversaw a massive rewrite, transforming it from a comedy about a nerd's grand gesture to a kind of somber *Pretty in Pink* love-triangle redo. She then brought in Eric Stoltz—not really anyone's idea of a nerd—and Lea Thompson, both opposite Masterson in the role of the pining best friend called Drummer Girl. Well, the tone change was now too much, so they fired Martha and brought back Howie, only now he was stuck with Eric and Lea, because they'd signed for the movie. ("Stuck" being a relative term regarding Lea, since she and Howie fell in love on the set and got married.) With Howie too grateful to be back in John's good graces to rock the boat anymore, he kept *Some Kind of Wonderful* in its now-serious state, and that's the movie that wound up on-screen.

We could play "what might have been" and say, Okay, if Howie hadn't piped up about *Oil and Vinegar*, unleashing a paranoid malfeasance in John Hughes, I could very well have starred in a broader, funnier *Some Kind of Wonderful*.

But I took it in stride, and at any rate, hearing about the firing and hiring and firing and hiring (even if I didn't know then what it was about) had me skittish about being part of that clusterfuck. Also, I was getting plenty of offers after *Pretty in Pink*, and the scripts were pouring in. The idea was, Strike while the iron's hot, and show the world what Jon Cryer can do when not slobbering all over Molly Ringwald.

Another impetus to line up projects quickly was the fact that I knew I had one surefire dud opening: the aforementioned *Home Front*—now renamed *Morgan Stewart's Coming Home*, in a desperately lame attempt to echo *Ferris Bueller's Day Off*, and with the replacement director (because the first one was canned) taking his name off the finished movie, soon to boast that hallmark of disowned cinema, the pseudonymous, I-don't-want-anyone-to-know-I-made-this-piece-of-shit credit "Directed by Alan Smithee." Alan Smithee was the Directors Guild–sanctioned name that could go on a movie if a director successfully argued that his creative control wasn't represented on-screen. Yes, directors get to change their identities in the name of art and integrity.

The movie still says, "Starring Jon Cryer," though, so tough shit, actors!

I made three movies in a row after *Pretty in Pink* that I really thought would constitute that well-rounded meal of cinematic entertainment guaranteed to satisfy both my artistic needs and an imagined moviegoer merrily exiting a movie of mine, saying, "Is there anything Jon Cryer *can't* do?" One of those movies was going to be a dark indie that would show my edgy side and please critics, the second movie was going to be a big, effects-laden summer blockbuster hit that would please the masses, and the third was going to return me to the high school comedy setting that would please the fans who loved me as Duckie. Because, you know, I give back, too.

Instead, I made one movie that no one saw, then a second movie that no one saw, and then a third movie that no one saw. I wish I'd made *Saw*. People saw *Saw*. They didn't see what I made. Which wasn't *Made*, incidentally. That was a Jon Favreau movie. One that I'm pretty sure no one saw, either.

I calculated my career right out of Hollywood, almost. You can, too! Just follow these three easy steps.

In the 1980s, the movies had a flickering love affair with the punk scene, thanks to talked-about releases like *Sid and Nancy* and *Suburbia*, and documentaries like *The Decline of Western Civilization*. Ballsy, dark little films were getting made right and left, it seemed, and I wanted to be a part of one, because I admired their scrappy attitude. What drew me to this script called *Dudes* was that it not only had a strange, unpredictable story combining punks and cowboys, but it was going to be directed by critical darling Penelope Spheeris, who'd made both *Suburbia* and *Decline*. I loved how she just got shit done outside the Hollywood system. Her movies got made, and she directed what she wanted. You don't get many opportunities to work with people like that, who don't take no for an answer.

Plus, I'd get to hold a gun. My character, a New York punk named Grant, is on a road trip with two friends—played by Dan Roebuck and Flea (yes, that Flea. There are not two Fleas)—when Flea's character is killed by a motorcycle gang in the desert. The other two become cowboys to avenge the death of their friend. So in essence, I got to be an armed punk in Western duds on a mission of vengeance in canyon country. How many times would I get to do that?

Maybe what I should have asked myself is, Am I the *right* person to do that? In all honesty, I knew I was wrong for *Dudes*, but the part of me that loves a challenge said, *You can make this work.*

What happened, though, was that who I was didn't turn into Grant. Grant began changing to reflect who I was. As we started shooting, little bits of the anxious nerd that I am would seep out of my pores during the scenes. It would be in my every reaction, line reading, and movement, even though he wasn't written that way. Penelope ostensibly had a choice to make: Steer me to how Grant was on the page, or accept what she was getting. She decided to go with what I was involuntarily bringing, so she made the part more comedic. But it changed the movie from a cool, dark thriller to something goofier.

We filmed in Cottonwood, Arizona, which was a bleak town surrounded by gorgeous scenery. A local radio station falsely announced that Tom Cruise was in town shooting a movie, so we'd get crowds wherever we filmed, and with only me being of roughly the same size and complexion as the *Top Gun* star, I'd get plenty of strange looks, of the "Wow, he looks very, very different off-screen" variety.

The magical power that movies held over people became readily apparent during this shoot, when I got a knock on my hotel room door one night and opened it to find a woman with a child of about one or two.

"Are y'all with the movie?" she asked.

"Yes," I said. "We're working on the movie. I'm not Tom Cruise, though."

This didn't seem to matter to her. "Well, things are really hard in town," she said. "Would you take me with you?"

"What do you mean?"

"Give me a job, and I'll stay with the movie and leave town."

Not quite sure what to say or do, I think I mumbled something about how we weren't a circus, and that we were already crewed up and I couldn't help her. The desperation in her certainly threw me off. It was as though the otherworldly allure of the film industry that had offered me mere artistic fulfillment was to her the last, best, and only hope for a life for both her and her child. It was a sobering thought.

We also filmed in Los Angeles. One location shoot in particular drove home to me just how much of an impostor I was in the role of a punk. We were at a downtown LA club to film a concert scene with the Vandals, a band whose music I knew somewhat, but whose fan base I didn't exactly consort with. This was a mosh-pit scene, however, with costar Dan Roebuck and me in the middle, and Penelope decided to forgo the risk of clueless poseur extras by populating the crowd with all her punk friends, hard-core types with piercings and Mohawks who were huge, sweaty, and drunk.

The Vandals fire up "Urban Struggle," with its "born to be a cowboy" lyrics and Ennio Morricone–inspired guitar intro, and I know we're all supposed to get our mosh on, but I don't know how this starts, of course. So I just begin pushing this guy, and he looks at me like a fly alighted on his shoulder. Then the meat of the music kicks in, and suddenly fists are flying, and Dan and I are getting hit repeatedly, which I try to laugh off, but which in reality sends me into sheer terror.

"Cut! Cut! Cut!" we hear from Penelope, and everybody stops.

Thank *God*. Everybody's fixing their Mohawks, and Dan and I are ready to nurse our wounds when Penelope yells out, "It doesn't look real! You guys have to really do this!"

Excuse me?! What could "really do this" possibly mean? Are they going to hand out weaponry?

Everyone started up again, and this time people were being hoisted on top of one another. Furious feet had been added to flying fists, and Dan and I were just getting hammered. I was trying to look like I enjoyed this, because my character would, but I have to say, Penelope's fear about poseur extras was unfounded. What she had was a poseur star!

That mosh pit was like a tumble dryer of human beings. None of these guys and girls were jerks, by the way. They were nice people, kids from the San Fernando Valley or wherever, for whom fun was . . . this. And that

Jon Cryer

day, boy, did they get into it. Our cinematographer was the great Robert Richardson, Oliver Stone's guy, who had just come off filming *Platoon* for Stone. For the mosh-pit scene, Penelope had set him up with a shoulder-mounted camera and one focus puller behind him, and when Penelope yelled, "Action!" Bob and the focus puller were essentially shoved into the crowd. Over and over. At one point, Bob was out of breath after she yelled, "Cut!" and he said, "Okay, I just did *Platoon*, but that? That was worse."

Flea's bandmate from the Red Hot Chili Peppers, Anthony Kiedis, would visit occasionally, too, and I remember a nice chat with Kiedis at lunch, after which he walked away and a crew guy said, "Yeah, that guy's got a real bad heroin problem." I thought, *But he's so friendly!*

Flea was at the center of one of the more notorious inside jokes of the shoot, pertaining to a beloved dessert that the craft services people served: bananas and sour cream. As a starter actor of sorts, Flea didn't get his own trailer; he got one of the many dressing rooms on a trailer called a honey wagon. One day he disappeared into his dressing room with a young lady, and after he reemerged he noticed an unfortunate stain on his costume. Conclusions were drawn. He asked for help in cleaning the stain, and a costume assistant put him on the spot by asking what it was.

"Bananas and sour cream," he blurted out nervously.

For the rest of the shoot, this refreshing, delicious snack was marred by a truly unfortunate association. Anytime we'd get our dollop of bananas and sour cream, there was an exchange of particularly distasteful expressions on our faces. Gee, thanks, Flea.

As for Penelope, she was everything I'd hoped she'd be: tough, honest, and helpful. She taught me one of the most valuable lessons I've ever learned as an actor. It had to do with a scene toward the end in which my character, now having fully adopted this cowboy persona, has the drop on the worst of the gang members who killed his friend. We're in a movie theater, my target is watching a Western—ironically—and I pull a gun and point it at the back of his head. The conflict is, *Can Grant do this? Is he that guy?* That's what I needed to feel, and I was using everything I

134

learned at theater camp, every trick I learned at the Royal Academy, and every bit I stole from every great performance I've ever seen. Every tool I ever had. It was all being brought to bear at that moment. The gun is shaking, my face is contorted, I'm calling up the rage, and Penelope yells, "Cut! Cut! Cut!"

"What's the matter?" I said.

She walked up to me and said, "It looks like the gun is broken."

"What?"

"You're holding the gun and it's shaking," she said. "It looks like the trigger won't pull."

"Hold on," I said. "That makes no sense. I'm feeling this! The gun's an extension of what I'm feeling. How is that possible?"

"Well, don't do any of that," she said. "Just hold it."

I'm not usually defiant, but I just wouldn't do what she asked. I couldn't imagine not doing anything with my face. This was a huge moment. You have to see what's going on, right? Well, I just kept working at it and working at it and she kept yelling, "Cut," and telling me it wasn't working. Finally she showed me the dailies, and she was absolutely right. It looked like the gun had jammed, and that I'd be firing if it weren't the case. None of the Sturm und Drang I knew I was projecting came through, and I realized how vast the difference can be between the real emotion inside you and what appears on-screen. It's like the famous editing experiment this Russian filmmaker did in the silent era. He took the same shot of a man's expressionless face and cut it together with a variety of different shots—food, a body in a coffin, a pretty woman—and when he showed the different edits to people, they believed his emotion was different each time. In retrospect, if I'd just held the gun, looked at it, then put it down, the audience would have projected onto me what the emotion was, rather than my thinking I needed to do all the work.

In the end, I had a good time making *Dudes*, and held out hope it might work, but it never got any traction as either a comedy or an edgy indie. That it wasn't the movie I read, because it became something more ridiculous and comedic, is something I feel bad about. I genuinely can't tell anymore if the movie is good or not, although I know it's got its followers—any movie not available on DVD by its very nature develops a cult behind it. Hey, my hardware store guy is a big fan.

After shooting *Dudes*, I was off to London for a movie I knew in my bones had to work. When manager Marty pitched me on a planned reboot of the Superman franchise, the comic book–loving kid in me was instantly seduced. The script was sent over and I loved it. Christopher Reeve had taken the reins on reinvigorating this classic superhero's world-saving status by developing a story in which Superman—motivated by a young boy terrified of nuclear annihilation—decides to rid the world of nuclear weapons. That's some ballsy heroism for ya, and after what everybody seemed to agree was a deflatingly über-campy *Superman III*, this one looked to be doing things right. With producers Alexander and Ilya Salkind no longer involved, Menahem Golan and Yoram Globus—the men behind Cannon Films—were stepping in, and though their reputation was for tacky action films (*Delta Force* and countless *Death Wish* sequels), this was being hyped as their bid for respectability. Besides, Margot Kidder and Jackie Cooper were back! Even the great Gene Hackman was returning as Lex Luthor, in a subplot about the creation of something called Nuclear Man, an irradiated clone of Superman with all the same powers but used for evil. Evil! It all promised something epic and fun. I was going to play his dim-witted nephew, Lenny—the Ned Beatty-as-Otis part, essentially—and damned if I wasn't going to make him the dumbest motherfucker I could. I could not have been more filled with joy and hope and excitement that I was going to be a part of a blockbuster in the making.

That first *Superman* in the 1970s had always been one of my formative moviegoing experiences, one that helped spark in my mind the notion that I needed to one day be a part of creating that kind of magic. If you're of my generation, you remember how tempting those teaser posters were for *Superman*, with that double-down bet of a tagline, "You'll believe a man can fly." I think it's safe to say every kid in the run-up to the 1978 release of the movie was thinking, "Challenge accepted, Hollywood. Alter my perception of physics!" And there we all were in theaters, patiently awaiting takeoff as the movie gave us the origin story, then Smallville, then Jor-El's voice booming across the Fortress of Solitude . . . come on, come on! . . . and suddenly, there he is! The John Williams fanfare begins, Superman appears in full costume, he leans forward gracefully as his feet leave the ground and he glides toward the camera, sweeping out of frame, and *goddammit* if I did not fucking believe a man can fly! Hoot and clap, people. That was serious hoot-and-clap stuff.

My first day did nothing to dispel my initial feeling of promise. We were actually shooting part of the very end first: Lex Luthor and Lenny, their plans having come apart at the seams, try to escape in an open-top 1930s-style car. We're on our way out of town when suddenly the car takes flight. We look down in panic, only to realize we're being transported to prison by the Man of Steel himself.

Although nowadays such an effect would probably be handled entirely by computer wizards and actors in front of a green screen, this was 1986, which means we were on location, using a real roadster, which was hoisted with a crane fifty feet in the air, and Christopher Reeve was in costume on a wire underneath it. Shit, yeah, baby. They were pulling out all the stops on this one. I was in this crazy costume, sitting with Gene Hackman, also in crazy threads, looking down at Superman and making small talk:

"How ya doin' down there, Chris?" I asked.

"I'm okay, Jon," he said with a smile. Probably a forced one, since—as Chris explained to me later—he hated flying sequences because of the painful, bikini-size harness he had to wear.

But that day I had no distracting thoughts of my costar's squeezed nether regions. I was on cloud nine. *I'm fuckin' flying with Superman!* I remember thinking. *This might just be the best day of my life.* I also remember thinking, *It's going to be like this every day!*

It wasn't. With all the vaguely uncertain awareness of impending doom that Mia Farrow experiences in *Rosemary's Baby*, I began to see that *Superman IV: The Quest for Peace* was getting cheesier and cheesier, from the sets to the props to the tone. Even the craft service table and its array of fattening, sugary items was reducing in size. Days started getting cut from the schedule. Then one day I was talking to director Sidney J. Furie and I casually mentioned how he wouldn't need me for a few weeks because of a big, important action sequence he had to shoot.

"No, that sequence was cut," he said.

That seemed odd to me, because it was a pretty massive sequence, one where Nuclear Man was destroying things. I thought, *How do you cut that and have the movie make sense?* I chalked it up to the wisdom of the filmmakers and went my merry way.

All around me, though, it began to feel more and more like people saw this as a job, not something special. Most of my scenes were with Gene, and the Oscar-winning master was genial, happy to chitchat. (His favorite role, incidentally? You'd think Popeye Doyle, but no, he told me it was the blind man in *Young Frankenstein*. The most fun, he said. His favorite movie of his? *The Conversation*.) Gene was also workmanlike. He'd show up, do what was asked of him, maybe have a little fun with it, and then totally put it out of his mind. It was all about the golf he was going to play after he was through for the day, and he couldn't care a whit about the movie. That was something of a disappointment to me, because I assumed we'd all look at this as iconic, honoring this great franchise. In retrospect, Gene probably noticed the corner-cutting, and saw it as the writing on the wall.

Gene did lend me my first cell phone. This was the early days of mobile phone technology, when you held what looked like a large brick to your head. I needed it because I was having problems getting a phone line in my London flat. British Telecom at the time was still essentially a communist organization, incapable of doing the one thing it was built for, which was installing telephone lines. Getting one installed in my flat was an ordeal, and when it finally was installed, I entered another institutional nightmare when I realized they never left me a number for it.

What follows is the Kafkaesque exchange I had with the BT operator.

Faceless BT bureaucrat lady: How may I help you?

Me: Hi. Could you tell me the number I'm calling from?

FBTBL: [Pause] Why do you want to know?

Me: Well, because the BT guys just installed the phone, and they didn't tell me the number.

FBTBL: Why didn't they do that?

Me: How would I know? You sent them.

FBTBL: I didn't send them.

Me: Okay, okay, you personally didn't send them. Someone at BT did. Anyway, it doesn't matter who sent them. The bottom line is, they installed a phone and didn't leave a number. Is there any way for you to tell me the phone number I'm calling from?

FBTBL: No.

Me: Maybe I'm not making myself clear. Is it that you don't know the number I'm calling from, or you can't tell me? Or won't tell me?

FBTBL: Oh, I know what it is.

Me: Oka-a-a-y . . . great. It's sitting there on your computer screen. You could tell me right now but for some reason you don't want to, even though I'm in the house, and calling from the number.

FBTBL: Well, you could have broken in.

Me: I . . . What? I'm breaking into somebody's house to find out a phone number?

FBTBL: Yes.

Me: That doesn't make any sense! Just tell me the damn phone number!

FBTBL: No.

She never told me the number. As long as I lived in that flat, which was approximately two months, the only calls were outgoing ones. The only way to call me was with Gene's phone, after which I'd hang up and call them back on the BT phone. As for the production, they had to send the car a half hour early and someone knocked on my door.

In the midst of the shooting, I got a little taste of home in the form of a visit from David and Artie, who had spent the previous two weeks on a spur-of-the-moment cultural tour of Italy, but had run through their funds after four days. So when I saw them emerge from customs at Heathrow Airport, they looked like hollow-eyed, emaciated immigrants from sub-Saharan Africa. I'd been working pretty much nonstop for almost a year now and was missing them acutely. So I rushed them back to my flat post-haste. When we arrived those hollow eyes set upon something that must have mystified and shocked them: a suitcase full of British pounds sterling. Why did I have something that you would typically only find in a Guy Ritchie movie? The production was giving me a cash per diem that I was never using, because I'm basically a hermit when I'm on location. No restaurants, no nightlife, no gambling addiction, no drug dependency. The money was, literally, piling up.

David's and Artie's faces were truly dumbfounded. They'd been without money for a week and a half, and had hardly eaten because of it. So we went to a local Chinese restaurant to fatten these boys up. David agonized over what to order, because he was still in a scrimping mind-set. He'd say "I want this, but *what if it's not enough?*"

"Then we'll order more," I said.

His eyes welled up, but he held back. I felt like a benevolent aid worker in the Sudan.

The rest of their stay, we spent our nights playing poker using the pile of real British money instead of chips. Of course, each night "the house" had to collect everybody's winnings, which was usually met by disappointed *aww*s from David and Artie. But we had a great time when they were there. These were the friends, after all, who knew me better than anybody, who had seen me through every tough time I'd had, and celebrated my good times without a hint of weirdness. When they left, I had the sense that this was my new life: having experiences beyond my wildest imagination, and getting to share it with them.

By the end of shooting, I was pretty curious about how it would turn out. I came back to the States and began working on my next movie, *Hiding Out*—we'll get to that one—so I was too preoccupied to worry about *Superman IV: The Quest for Peace.* In fact, I felt a surge of excitement all over again when I heard that the Smithsonian was going to open a comprehensive exhibit on Superman, tied to the film's release, and they asked me to attend a big press event there. In Washington I reconnected with Chris, which was nice. He and I didn't get many scenes together in the movie, but anytime we got to talk in London, we'd end up talking about New York theater, which is where he came from. He was always concerned about how I was doing. Chris was about as approachable and friendly as they come.

We met for lunch in advance of the Smithsonian event, and I was literally rubbing my hands together in anticipation as I said, "How's the movie?"

"It's a mess," he said. "An absolute mess."

My hands went from well rubbed to clammy.

"Cannon ran out of money toward the end of principal photography, and a huge amount of stuff we were supposed to shoot just never got shot," he said. "I was scheduled for six months of flying work. We did maybe a month. We had to cut all these scenes that pertained to the stuff we were missing, so now the movie barely makes sense."

I was mortified, absolutely crestfallen. Chris had begun distancing himself from the fact that the movie stemmed from an idea of his, but he was a good soldier, even showing up for a publicity event like the Smithsonian's. I left that lunch in a state of semishock, but I held out a glimmer of hope that it would come together in some way.

I was visiting my grandparents in Indiana when the movie opened, so we all went to check it out. One of my favorite things about the first *Superman* was the opening credits, which practically screamed, "Prepare for *epic*." There was that spectacular John Williams overture, and a space backdrop against which these names whooshed at you or away from you like flashes of celestial blue. It was awe-inspiring and, frankly, over-the-top, but boy did it psych you up for awesomeness.

Superman IV, on the other hand, opted not to pay for fancy credits, and tacked on a ripoff opening with video-produced effects that looked like the beginning of *Reading Rainbow*. Names appeared with a cheap ghosty trail and then fled behind the horizon of Earth as if they had something to hide. This was not the movie I had hoped it was going to be. Nobody was going to hoot and clap at this crap.

How was I in the movie? As with that scene I had a problem with in *Dudes*, I finally grasped that I was trying too hard, especially when my getup—pleather and leopard prints and ridiculous hair, a marriage of metal, glam, and new wave—did all the work for me. You never forget your first pair of skintight faux-leather pants, by the way. Mostly because the smell you produce at the end of the day, after sweating in them for hours, is an exceptional thing.

The movie had created its own scent, too, one even my sweet grandmother picked up on, because after twenty-five minutes, she turned to me and said, "Oh, honey, this is terrible."

So much for the big blockbuster in my master plan. . . .

One of my post–*Pretty in Pink* perks—there's some alliteration for you—was a holding deal at Paramount, which included an office on the lot and the chance to develop scripts and make movies. For the actor who gets it, it's a monetized ego boost—I'm going to be a Hollywood producer!—that promises richer involvement in your destiny. For the studio, it's a way to keep an actor from working somewhere else, as they methodically block you from ever actually making anything of your own. Marty Tudor and I figured that out pretty quickly, as our repeated cries just to get a printer for our hovel of an office repeatedly went ignored.

After that deal ended, we split and opened up an office on Sunset Boulevard, which was where *Hiding Out* came together. After the disappointments of *Morgan Stewart's Coming Home* and *Dudes*, neither of which had planned release dates, and the sketchy feeling I had upon returning from filming *Superman IV: The Quest for Peace*, I really felt the need to take control of the reins, and produce and develop something, the quality of which I could oversee. That project was *Adult Education*, a comedy about a grown man returning to high school. It was a fun, broad concept, and addressed my particular niche, since I was a twenty-two-year-old who still looked very young. I'd be in a high school comedy again, and the last one I made seemed to go "pretty" well, if you catch my drift.

So of course we changed it into a thriller. My character was now on the run from the mob. I was a producer now, and I fancied myself knowledgeable enough to know that if we could just turn *Adult Education* into *Beverly Hills Cop*—laughs and excitement! comedy and violence!—then we'd have a hit. Suddenly making audiences laugh wasn't important enough for me. We could go deeper. The protagonist needed the threat of death to keep his impersonation ruse going, because the jeopardy would then really juice the comedy.

We hired writer after writer to do the rewrites for what was now *Hiding Out*. The problem was that with every subtle change, other parts of the script were affected. There's a logic in your head as to how it should all be, and we kept ignoring the stuff that really needed to work on paper, which were the funny bits. By the time we started filming, we had successfully ironed out a really dark opening, and it simply didn't set the right tone for the stuff we wanted people to find humorous, which was essentially the rest of the movie.

You know who picked up on this dilemma early? Dino De Laurentiis and his daughter Raffaella, who were bankrolling us. At one point we had sent them rewrites, and we went in to meet with Dino and Raffaella at the De Laurentiis Entertainment Group offices on Wilshire Boulevard. This father/daughter pair were a fascinating combination of genuine characters—the thick Italian accents, the enormous eyebrows—yet real Hollywood veterans. We'd heard they didn't like the rewrites, that they felt there were two movies there, but I chalked it up to the fact that the scripts had to be translated into Italian so they could read them, that something was lost in the translation.

At the meeting, where Dino sat behind an enormous desk, he gave his notes, and then there was a long pause.

"But you gonna be-a the funny guy, right?" he said, then began gesticulating wildly with his arms, in what I can only imagine was the universal sign for going broad.

Now I paused. Dino had agreed to make the movie because he wanted the *Pretty in Pink* guy. The "funny guy." I knew the nature of the movie had changed, that I was not going to be the funny guy, but I also knew the answer to this question was very, very important.

"Yes, Dino. I'm gonna be the funny guy."

"Okay," he said. "We'll make-a the movie."

To direct we brought on Bob Giraldi, a highly regarded commercial director who made the legendary "Beat It" video for Michael Jackson. Bob had a great veteran's strut. He'd seen everything, and even though this would be his first feature film at the age of forty-something, he was skilled at being up-front about his opinions without being obnoxious about them. At one point he looked at me, pointed generally at my entire frame, and said, "You're gonna do something about this, right?"

I said, "What do you mean?"

"Well, you're gonna work out a little, get in shape."

"Bob," I said, "I'm playing a stockbroker. I don't recall any nudity in the script."

He said, "Yeah, but . . . you know . . ." and then pointed at me again, as if there was overtly something lacking in my appearance. I agreed to get more in shape, and he suggested a gym on New York's East Side that was the neon-lit, teased-hair, pastel-colored exercise emporium of Sonny Crockett's dreams. This was where Bob worked out, and the first time I went there, he noticed me in the locker room, said, "Hey, Jon!" and walked over completely naked. Although I was uncomfortable—never imagining I'd get a gray-pubic-hair visual to accompany my mental image of the director of the movie—it did reinforce the idea that this is the kind of confidence you need to be a director. You just can't care what anyone else thinks.

As for the casting process, I remember a very young Winona Ryder coming in to read for the part of Ryan, the high schooler who befriends my character. We all sat around uncomfortably, because even though she was a sweet girl not trying to be coquettish at all, she was strikingly gorgeous and exuded an effortless sexiness that we grown males in the room knew would be completely inappropriate to comment on. We also saw a future Academy Award winner who was incredibly wooden and bad. (Sorry. You're not getting that name.) We eventually cast Annabeth Gish, who had a charming soulfulness to her without being sexy. (Not that she isn't a sexy woman now, but back then it wasn't her vibe.) The problem was, though, that in deliberately avoiding that tricky chemistry—because it would have suggested an inappropriateness when one character isn't of age—it also deprived audiences of their need to see a spark between two people. We were so scared of it, we looked at it logically instead of emotionally.

By opening weekend in November of 1987, I had invested much of the year to *Hiding Out*. I was in it from the beginning, overseeing rewrites, helping get the director attached, pitching in on casting choices, even being all over the marketing and ad campaign. The movie was what I wanted it to be. It tested well with audiences, too. But opening weekend it was just not a movie people wanted to see. That's when I learned a central fact about testing: Pleasing random moviegoers you've asked to see your movie, who don't know what to expect, and who come out and say, "Yeah, that basically worked," is different from people wanting to see your movie. And people just did not want to see *Hiding Out* when it hit theaters.

Performers are prone to the illusion that if they could just run the ship, it would all work much better. Well, this was the project that made clear to me the limits of my expertise. Making movies is hard. It's a process so convoluted, and so charged with the unsteady anticipation of what audiences want, that you understand why the few who've been successful at it multiple times are considered so valuable in the industry, and why they make tons of money. I walked away from *Hiding Out* with serious questions about my judgment. I had thought I was setting myself up for a varied career of different types of movies and different types of roles, but it didn't exactly work out that way. It was a tough lesson to get after almost two years since *Pretty in Pink* had come out, but it was a lesson with a punishment attached: With four flops in a row, it seemed I had effectively squandered all the showbiz heat I'd acquired from playing Duckie.

Fuck 1987!

Chapter 14
So We Did Something Strenuous

Before 1987 became the 1987 of "Fuck 1987," it was more of a regular 1987, except for the fact that I learned I had a very minor, rare, weird form of cancer, a lump that attaches to the underside of one's skin. It's called dermatofibrosarcoma protuberans, and if you are considering getting cancer, this is the one to get. First, it's very rare, which sort of makes it valuable, right? And best of all, it metastasizes in only five percent of patients, so I highly recommend it.

But in every other way, 1987 was a good time: I was enjoying my bachelor pad in New York and making movies, living what I determined to be the ideal existence for a working actor. Learning about the lump was a left turn, but the doctors said it was easily taken care of by way of an operation. They'd simply cut it out of my chest.

The operation went smoothly, and I was told to go home and rest. I can do rest. I like rest.

"Don't do anything strenuous!" they said. Thumbs-up to that, medical professionals!

I was chilling out in my apartment later—probably watching reruns of *Mr. Belvedere*—when I got a phone call. Who should it be on the other end of the line but a certain someone I hadn't heard from in four years. This certain someone was a she, and a very attractive she at that. Actually, this Very Attractive Certain She (VACS) was an easy memory to call up, you see, because VACS was the one who, during my senior year of high school, took my virginity.

"I'm back from college," she said. "I'm not with that guy anymore."

Oh, I thought.

"Oh?" I said.

"Yes." she answered. "Are you around? I want to see you."

You really never forget your first, whatever the circumstances surrounding it. In the case of my sexual education growing up, I definitely didn't put much faith in the idea that my first time would happen easily. I was simply too perplexed by what it took just to get a girl to look at you, then look at you twice, much less talk to you, then perhaps convince her to see you alone, then see you *alone* alone, followed by the part where clothes come off, and then the hoping and praying the girl doesn't hurriedly put the clothes back on before she lets you do highly personal things to her.

Again, though, it starts with the social stuff. My buddy David Dennis was the type of freewheeling social animal I dreamed of being at that time, a smooth talker who could charm adults and peers alike. Girls especially. Listening to David talk with Artie about the opposite sex was like being a student in the best seminar ever, even if a lot of it went over my head. It was pretty plain that they were intimately involved with girls at the ages of fourteen and fifteen, whereas my concurrent experience amounted to unfulfilled crushes marked by moon-faced silence, while a virtual loop played in my brain of fantasies that involved instant reciprocal love because I'd saved the object of my affection from drowning or, more realistically, a moving train. Listening to David and Artie, however, I found it painfully clear that I had a way to go, since they were getting into the kind of anatomical detail and procedure that didn't make sense to me. Basically it was a lot of me going, "Really, how would she . . . ? Doesn't that hurt . . . ? But she's someone's daughter! . . . Do you have to brush your teeth?"

It would be a few more years before I had the wherewithal to make a move and get serious with a girl. It happened just after I turned eighteen. At the time, my summers were at Stagedoor, but during the school year, I'd keep sharp by doing Jack Romano's winter workshop productions at the Carter Theater in the Times Square hotel of the same name. Fun fact: The Hotel Carter would end up being voted "the Dirtiest Hotel in America" for an impressive three years running during the mid-2000s, but back then, it could only aspire to such accolades. It was during rehearsals for one of Jack's musicals that I met her.

I was learning the choreography for a dance scene, trying to stay focused on the task at hand, when I was paired with a beautiful redhead. Immediately my laserlike attention shifted to her. Smiles were exchanged and chatting took place, and we discovered we had been in another production together before but had never noticed each other. We realized how odd that was, and in a strange way, it forged a bond. We began hanging out, my jokes making her laugh, her dry sense of humor winning me over, and suddenly in rehearsal one day, we were holding hands. It seemed natural. Something was happening here! I picked up her hand to look at it more closely, and I noticed a ring on her finger.

"What's this?" I asked.

"Oh, I'm engaged."

Not expecting that. "Sorry? Engaged?"

"Yeah, he's away at college right now," she said. "I've known him for a long time."

I dropped her hand like it was the wrong end of a torch.

Then she took mine again.

Uh-oh.

The two of us began dating, and it was the perfect mixture of innocent and forbidden you'd expect from a nervous novice and someone more experienced but exploring her options: four-hour makeout sessions with no sex. We'd meet up and go to movies, and I was falling pretty hard. Mom met her and liked her. All that was missing was dealing with the guy who was missing.

Then he came back from college, and she told him she didn't want to be with him anymore. But he took off, and she was crying all the time, worried about him in a way that was indicative of something deeper, and she broke it off with me. She explained that her ties to him were hard to break and that since she'd planned her whole life around him, she felt as if she couldn't break from that path. It seemed like faulty logic to me, and overall the split was hard to take, but by this point, she'd been accepted to a university in another state—shocker! where he was enrolled, too—and I knew I'd have to get over her and accept that this was just a fling.

That is, until she called me one day that summer following my senior year, said, "I have to see you," rushed over, and gloriously seized my virginity on the floor of my mother's office. (Sorry, Mom.)

It was capital-A Awesome. It was, to combine euphemisms and get at something romantic and carnal, making sex. Then she was off, probably back to that guy, and just like in the movies, the melancholy plunk of the Police's "Every Breath You Take" filled the apartment, and I was like, "Aww, fuck." Nobody explained the part where you want that feeling again, you miss the person immediately, and realize, *What if I never see her again?*

I'll be honest: I really never did expect to see her again, until I got that call years later as I recuperated in my apartment. There was a severe case of déjà vu going on, too, because that magical day in my youth was preceded by an "I have to see you" phone call, and here I was hearing her say to me over the phone, "I want to see you."

Who am I to say no to visitors? I'm practically an invalid! Nothing strenuous about catching up with an old friend. Right, Doctor?

As soon as I saw her in my doorway, looking no less beautiful than the last time I'd laid eyes on her, I thought, *Well, well, well, it has been a lo-o-o-o-ong time.*

So we did something strenuous.

This time there was no running out. She stayed, and we rekindled that flame until it was a nice little glow. After a while we decided to take this intimacy into a public space and go see a movie. We chose *Innerspace*, the sci-fi comedy in which Dennis Quaid plays a pilot miniaturized by science to a microscopic size, and Martin Short plays the hapless guy who gets injected with him.

I wouldn't call the movie's humor ironic, but the experience was, because as I was watching Martin Short's insides get shaken up, the wound I wasn't supposed to strenuate began to grow, and grow, and grow, until it was baseball-size and creating a strange bulge under my shirt. It looked like it was about to pop out of my sternum. At that point, I turned to her and said, "It hurts too much; we have to go."

At Roosevelt Hospital it took seemingly ages for them to admit me for surgery, because I wasn't outwardly bleeding. What *was* leaking, though, was this romantic reunion with my old flame, who with each passing hour in the emergency room was getting in more and more trouble with her family, who apparently had forbidden her from seeing me, since it had become easy to blame me for poisoning her semiarranged marriage. Eventually she had to leave the hospital—probably never to see me again for real this time—and with perfect emotional timing, my wound opened up as if I were a character in *Alien*. Surgery, please!

Not that I needed any more body ache to go with my heartache, but because the wound was now open, they couldn't give me an anesthetic, which meant they operated on me while I screamed bloody murder. But I learned something interesting that day about one's pain threshold: Once you hit the top, that's it. It doesn't go higher than that. A paper cut hurts like a motherfucker, but a big gaping hole in your chest doesn't hurt that much more than a motherfucker. It may be prolonged, but it doesn't go from, say, ten to twenty. It just hurts like it hurts. Get a tattoo while you're at it, I say.

Let me conclude by saying, it all gave new meaning to the phrase "When she left, there was a hole in me."

Chapter 15
Don't Make Me Gary Sandy

Famous true story: When Marlon Brando was a Broadway sensation snapped up by Hollywood at the end of the 1940s to make his first movie, *The Men*, Lew Wasserman—head of the talent agency behemoth MCA—told one of his junior employees to pick up Brando at Union Station in downtown Los Angeles and drive him all over town, since Brando didn't drive. The kid became so adept at catering to the rising star's every need that when Wasserman finally got around to asking Brando who he wanted at the agency to represent him, the actor said, "I want the kid who's been driving me around."

From then on, even Wasserman couldn't get Brando on the phone. He'd tell people they had to call Jay Kanter first. Kanter went on to become one of Hollywood's top agents, representing Marilyn Monroe and Grace Kelly to boot.

That story was the basis for a new television sitcom I was pitched in 1989 as a starring vehicle, called *The Famous Teddy Z*. Its creator, Hugh Wilson, liked the idea of turning Kanter's origins into a Hollywood satire about a mailroom kid who, after a chance meeting with the biggest star in town, is tapped by the actor to be his agent. I liked the idea, too. But the bigger question was, was it really time to do television?

Nowadays, the idea that television is a step down from movies sounds ludicrous, what with the deluge of praise heaped on shows like *The Wire*, *The Sopranos*, and *Breaking Bad*. Matthew McConaughey's winning an Oscar for *Dallas Buyers Club* at the same time you could watch him at home in the HBO series *True Detective* pretty much tore that wall down for good. For actors who want to go where the good roles are, toggling back and forth between movies and television is sound career advice.

But in 1989, that divide between the glamour and prestige of film and the familiar factory feel of television was very much in place, and if a movie actor decided to shoot a TV series, it signaled that one's career at the multiplex was over. And at the end of the eighties, based on the film scripts I was being offered, it seemed pretty clear to me that I was hanging on to a life in film by a slimmer and slimmer thread.

So when my agents and managers told me there was a real market for me to do something in television, I knew I was looking at the proverbial step down. But the prospect of working with writer/director Hugh Wilson was appealing. Though he'd made films (*Police Academy*), his clear métier was TV: He'd created highly entertaining shows with interesting characters, namely the hilarious ensemble sitcom *WKRP in Cincinnati* and the critically acclaimed *Frank's Place*, which at the time of its brief 1980s run was lauded as a TV show with the vibe of a good film. There was already buzz about *The Famous Teddy Z*, too: that it was going to be a fun skewering of insider Hollywood. The lure of being part of something hot was pretty attractive for someone whose last film role was a one-day cameo in the immediately forgotten *Penn & Teller Get Killed*.

"Great," I told Hugh at the pitch meeting. "Just don't make me Gary Sandy."

What did I mean by that? For one thing, it has nothing to do with Gary Sandy's talent. And yet it has everything to do with Gary Sandy's talent. Gary Sandy is actually a really good actor, his leading-man looks belying the fact that he's got comedy skills and character-actor chops. But it was his handsomeness that banished him on *WKRP* to being the nice guy in the middle of all the nutty, funny people. He was much more gifted than being a wacky comedy's straight man.

"Please," I implored Hugh, "don't make me Gary Sandy. I don't want to be the nice guy in the middle of all the crazy. I want to be involved in the crazy."

"Don't worry," he assured me. "I will not do that."

When the script came in, I read it, and I was Gary Sandy.

"Hugh, I'm fucking Gary Sandy!" I said to him at our next meeting. "Should I start feathering my hair now?"

"I know, but that's the way the dynamic is, because he's the fish out of water."

"But I don't get to do any of the fun stuff!"

"Eventually you will, Jon," he said. "I said you will, and you will."

This sounded vaguely like a sales tactic. But it didn't matter. Based on the script, I just didn't respond to the character of Teddy Zakalokis, who was pretty much the innocent surrounded by agency venality and industry nuttiness. Venality is fun. Nuttiness is fun. Innocence is boring. So even with that rush of adrenaline I got from being in trade headlines for doing a deal to star in a hot series, I turned down the script.

Then the yelling and cajoling started. Hugh called to yell at me. CBS chief Kim LeMasters called to fiercely cajole. The pressure to return to the project was intense, so in good faith I offered to step back in and be involved with reading at auditions for the other parts, even though my deal wasn't done. Manager Marty was playing it tough, as he'd learned to do in the features world, telling everyone I was still attached, but that all the deal points hadn't been worked out yet.

But as we got closer and closer to a cast being finalized, it was considered something of a shock that my deal hadn't closed. This was apparently not the television way. In the midst of one of the auditions, with the first read-through scheduled for the next day, Hugh stopped to take a call. When he got off the phone, he said, "Hey, Jon, can we go out and talk in the hall?"

"Sure."

His tone reminded me somewhat of that of a schoolkid being beckoned by the teacher for a chat, and then I remembered the stories of Hugh's famous temper. We walked around a corner, and suddenly his face twisted into one of Hulk-like fury.

"What the hell is going on here?!" he barked.

"I . . . I don't know what you're talking about, Hugh."

"Your agents haven't made a goddamn deal! They're still fucking around!"

"I don't even know what the deal points are," I said, which was true. Marty kept me insulated from all that. But cornered like this, I was sputtering. "I . . . me . . . deal points . . . agent . . . Gary Sandy . . ."

"Are you allowing this?!" he yelled, his volcanic mug closing within inches of mine, while I tried to dodge the spittle flying from his mouth as if it might be lava. It was mortifying. "Because I'm not going to let you ruin this!"

At this moment, a CBS executive walked by and said, "Oh, hey, Hugh!"

In a flash he turned around, cracked a smile, and said, "Hey, how's it goin'?"

"Hugh," the executive says, "is it true you punched out Bill Dial?"

Hugh let out a warm, collegial, "Ha, ha, ha," all hail-fellow-well-met with the guy, but he didn't say no, and once the exec was out of his sight, he turned right back to me with his rage face. "Listen, Jon, stop fucking around, and *make this deal*."

"Yes! Yes! I'm gonna make the deal. I'm gonna make the deal," I shot back, wiping Hugh spit from my face.

That night I called Marty like a petrified shopkeeper who'd just had his business threatened by protection-racket goons. Marty told me not to worry, that the deal would be made when the deal would be made, and that some things were worth fighting for. I acquiesced to the wisdom of my manager and calmed down. The next day I went to the studio, excited for the first read-through. Hugh came to my dressing room and said, "I'm sorry, Jon. This is not going to work out. You're fired."

I'm what?

"In TV, you don't mess around with your deal like this," he said. "This is not how it works."

He'd even gone so far as to have Marty banned from the lot. Now it was my turn to fiercely cajole, so I called Kim LeMasters and said, "What the hell's going on here? I've been actively involved from day one. You know my level of commitment. What's this bullshit about barring my manager?" I also might have cried.

He apologized, which is an odd experience, to have the head of a network telling you he's sorry. (When LeMasters resigned later that year after his fraught reign, I fully expected to read in the trade reports, "Frequently cited as a major reason was his apologizing to Jon Cryer.") Our talk was good, so I called Marty and said, "Make the fucking deal." And that was that. Rehearsals started right away, and we were off and running.

The headiest news for me as we began working on the pilot was who had been tapped to play my outsize, big-personality Greek mother. We were working on the script one day when Richard Dubin, one of Hugh's writers, said "By the way, the woman playing your mother is going to be Lainie Kazan from *My Favorite Year*. She's going to be that character." Everyone couldn't have been more thrilled. Kazan's twinkly boisterousness as the Brooklyn Jewish mom who charms Peter O'Toole's dashing movie star was a scene-stealing tour de force, and I thought, *If she brings that to* Famous Teddy Z, *it's going to be classic.*

The writers just changed the name, made her Greek, and handed it to Lainie, ready for the magic to happen, only to learn she had no intention of doing it that way. She didn't want to do *My Favorite Year* all over again, and yet it was clear this was the only way the character was going to work. They tried to dress her like a woman from the old country, but she hated her costumes, too, and let everybody know. Every time the writers tried to make an adjustment, it was still within the region of overbearing ethnic mama that Lainie just didn't want to live in. In the end, this great actress was fired, and I was floored.

How could this have happened? A part so perfect, tailor-made to a gifted actress's strengths, tweaked by writers willing to make it work in whatever way she wanted, yet doomed to *not* work because a proud performer simply didn't want to repeat what was arguably her most popular role. At the time, I was more shocked than anything else, because the vibe was that we'd locked down the perfect actress for the perfect role. But even though it seemed like she was shooting herself in the foot, I respected her as an artist for saying, "You know what? I've done that already. Why don't we come up with something else?"

It would be a while, though, before I made the connection between Lainie's intransigence and my post–*Pretty in Pink* mind-set. Did I want to make *Duckie 2: Electric Boogaloo*, or an animated Saturday-morning cartoon where Duckie solves crimes with the Harlem Globetrotters, or *Alien vs. Wacky Geek*? (Well, okay, that last one, yes, had it been written.) No, but would it have killed me to take advantage of a popular persona? Maybe not, but who's to say a series of Duckie-clone movies would have been any better or more successful than the career-engineered diversity portfolio of duds I did make? We'll never know, will we? So will you stop reminding me?

The Famous Teddy Z was a quick education in all aspects of getting a show on the air and trying to keep it on the air. Classes involved Being in Every Scene 101, Studies in Learning New Lines Every Week, Introduction to Early Critical Hype, Alex Rocco Appreciation (he crushed it each week as the sharklike veteran agent), Introduction to Varying Degrees of Script Quality, Introduction to Great Ratings, Intermediate Ratings

Decline, Principles of Hiring One's Realtor, Brother-in-Law, and Best Friend for the Writing Staff (which Hugh did), Advanced Script Rewriting and Rewriting, and Advanced Ratings Decline. And after all that, graduation seemed a pipe dream: Just over halfway through the 1989–90 season, CBS expelled us.

That being said, Hugh—who could be charming and genial, but overall kept any possible personal affection for me under wraps—made good on his word: He did try to give my character more fun things to do, but it was too little, too late by that point. As for Lainie's replacement, Erica Yohn, she was tasked with a character who was now a grandmother, and so stereotypically old-country she "tok lahk dees," which, sadly, deed nawt wirk. Besides, the home-and-family stuff was Hugh's sop to the network heads, who thought people would relate to it. But viewers were bored, and the show was always at heart an office comedy anyway.

The cancellation of *The Famous Teddy Z*—a show that never lived up to its early heat—pretty much knocked the wind out of me. The movies that didn't work at least weren't roller coasters the way this had been: I'm in, I'm out; I'm in, I'm fired; I'm in, critics are in, audiences aren't, then the network isn't. There were emotional bruises on me by this point, and I felt as if I had further reason not to trust my instincts when it came to my career choices. I'd made the proverbial step down from movies to do television, and when even that didn't shine a light, it left me clinically depressed. Weight gain, slurred speech, and an intense need to not give anybody a reason to be disappointed in me busted up my relationship with my girlfriend at the time, the beautiful and kind Jane Sibbett, who had played my girlfriend on the show. She wanted marriage and kids, and I was so shot emotionally I didn't even know how to be myself.

It would take doing theater again in my hometown to bring me back to a place of healthy artistic purpose. And a place in which I tried to get somebody fired.

Chapter 16
The Art Garfunkel Role

The lure of movies and television, and my meteoric flameouts at both, left me with only one obvious career choice. No, not porn. Back to theater. In 1990 an offer to do a play that sounded exciting enough to consider came along.

The call came from Martin Charnin, an acclaimed Broadway writer and director, who famously conceived, wrote the lyrics for, and directed the musical *Annie*. His track record is long, going all the way back to the original production of *West Side Story*, in which he played—wait for it— Big Deal, the same character I played in my junior high production. Yet we can assume Martin's audiences were able to hear him, unlike mine, who surely wondered what the Big Deal was with the hamster-voiced zombie kid. But I digress.

Martin sought me out because he'd secured the rights to stage *Carnal Knowledge* as a play, and he wanted me for a role. Jules Feiffer's decades-spanning dissection of male sexual dysfunction via a pair of college pals and their relationships with women was originally conceived as a play, but Mike Nichols thought it should be a film, and in 1971 it was one, with Jack Nicholson, Art Garfunkel, Candice Bergen, and Ann-Margret. What Martin wanted was to stage its New York debut as a play, and I would play Sandy, the Art Garfunkel role, the sensitive guy. Since that was virtually the only part that wasn't played by a legend—no offense, Art, but I mean "acting" legend, and don't get me wrong; you were still great in the role— I would have the smallest shoes to fill of any cast member. Boy, that still doesn't sound nice, does it? I take it back: Art, I quivered at the prospect of failing to do justice to your Sandy. There.

The reality is that the role of Sandy—introverted and maladapted— appealed to that part of me that still wanted to prove that I wasn't Duckie, whom somebody once described as Jerry Lewis with a bit of Jerry Lee Lewis thrown in for good measure. Of course, evidence suggested I should have milked that persona for a while, but if I were the type to take plain facts and actually heed their portent, I'd never have tried this whole acting thing to begin with. And I liked that a respected director I admired had come to me with an interesting part that would allow me to be an actor, not a highly paid circus act.

Plus, Martin said he was going after John Cusack, hot off of *Say Anything*, for the Nicholson part of Jonathan—a callous womanizer—and Brooke Shields, hot off of being hot, for Candice Bergen's role, the shy Smith grad whom Sandy marries. That casting sounded exciting to me, so I committed to it.

The next phone call from Martin: "We're not getting John and Brooke. It's going to be Judd Nelson and Justine Bateman."

O-kaayyy. I readjusted my sense of the project's interestingness in my head. Well, Judd was working the same complicated-guy thing that Jack Nicholson emanated so effortlessly, so I figured that could benefit the project. And Justine had a certain dry, cynical Bateman-family delivery that if not quite reminiscent of the next-door-girl persona Candice or

Brooke give off, suggested a possibly intriguing route to take. Filling in the Ann-Margret part of the emotionally troubled, coquettish girlfriend of Jonathan's was *Northern Exposure* star Janine Turner.

As rehearsals started, what immediately struck me was that I had some pretty quirky costars. New York theater folk aren't terribly enamored of Hollywood types who swan into town to do a play, and judging from the eccentrics around me, I was beginning to understand what they were worried about. Justine was in the middle of her poetry-slam phase, which meant she would, unsolicited, burst into bouts of verse when the moment seized her. Janine's character had to attempt suicide at one point in the play, so she set about an archaeologically obsessive search of the depths of her psyche that matched her character's bleakest, darkest impulses. She appeared to be driving herself insane. This manifested itself in bizarre outbursts and her occasionally sitting against a wall with her legs splayed and banging her head into the floor. (Phenomenal flexibility, that Janine.) Judd, meanwhile, worked his rebel persona, wearing a leather jacket and army boots unlaced—because tying one's shoes is somehow too conformist—and showing up to work on a motorcycle, no matter how snowy the weather. He also papered our entire dressing room with pornography—specifically nude women with the heads snipped off—to get into a misogynist's frame of mind. (Either that, or I never picked up on the signals he was sending me.)

I'm pretty sure he was used to always being the most unorthodox member of whatever cast he joined, so when Judd was faced with Janine's wackadoo tomfoolery he actually seemed flummoxed. How do you top that? He'd often circle the rehearsal space muttering to himself in frustration. Upon my arrival at the theater I'd usually be greeted by the following tableau:

Justine: (Shouting at full volume) "All the tinsel's melting down the tree / The bulbs explode in prickly sparks!"

Janine: (Pounding her forehead on the stage) *Bonk! Bonk! Bonk!*

Judd: (Pacing) "Mutter, mutter, mutter . . . *Un*believable . . . mutter, mutter."

After about a week of this Judd simply started showing up late in order to minimize his work time with her.

Now, I'm not saying I don't have my own odd work habits and mannerisms, but being the experienced New York theater hand in this foursome, I knew how to comport myself as a professional, so I just tried to slog through and be the guy who kept the wheels turning. Janine provoked head scratching, for sure, and I could understand Judd's irritation—after all, he had the most scenes with her—but what increasingly irritated me was Judd's lateness, and acting as if he didn't even want to be there. One time he was tardy enough that I decided to rehearse with his understudy. When Judd finally showed up, he saw me working with his understudy and said, "Oh, *perfect!*" Then he turned around and vanished for the rest of the day.

That was the straw that broke this camel's back. I went to Martin that very night and said my piece. "Listen, Martin," I said, "this thing has just been a bizarre ride, but you've got to fire Judd. What he did was inexcusable. You don't stroll into rehearsal late, then turn around and walk the fuck out."

Martin looked at me wearily. "Okay, okay, Jon, I'll think about it. That's a big step, but I get it. I'm trying to keep this show on track."

"I understand," I said. "It's a horrible thing to ask, but it's simply egregious what's going on."

Was I feeling a little self-righteous about theater protocol, since I had gone through a somewhat ignominious Broadway firing myself as an in-over-his-head youth? That experience was surely running through my mind, but however unready I was on my first Broadway gig, I at least showed up for work. Janine may have revealed herself to be odd, but she was at least there, trying to put something together. Judd's rebel shtick seemed more important to him than getting the play up and running.

The next morning, a downcast and ashen Martin gathered that day's rehearsing cast together for a big announcement. They didn't know what was coming, but I did, and I was starting to feel some relief.

"Listen, I'm sorry to say this to everybody, but I've got some news," he said. "We fired Janine."

Wha-say-huh? Janine? I looked around. No Janine. My eyes seemed to grow exponentially larger in their sockets as my brain kept wanting me to say, *Um, wait, wait! What part of "You've got to fire Judd" did you not understand? Did your ears stop at the J sound?*

As everyone processed the news by creating a low rumbling of shocked voices, Judd showed up, was apprised of the situation, and spoke. "Okay, great," he said. "I think we all knew it wasn't working. I'm sorry it came to this, but we've got a show to do." Judd did not seem sorry. Something was up.

Later I cornered Martin, expressed my deep dissatisfaction with his interpretation of my complaint, and learned that I wasn't the only one who'd shown up that night with a workplace beef. Apparently, right after I left, both Judd and Justine came to Martin and asked that Janine be canned. Evidently behavior that I had determined was bizarre but well within the boundaries of committed character work was, to my fellow actors, simply too wack job to countenance on a daily basis. Showing up late or not at all? That was apparently okay. I couldn't help but imagine what Martin thought: Three of his stars show up, one after another, to request one of the others is fired. Did he just go with the majority vote?

The news, when it got out, was catnip for theater wags, and *The New York Times'* Alex Witchel wrote about it in her column by implying that the campaign to oust Janine was cooked up by the three of us. Which was . . . close? I couldn't exactly call to complain about that one. "Hey, Alex, just a minor error there. I wanted *Judd* fired." That would make a printed correction more gossipy than the original item.

Which leads me to the other aspect of this production that had me dispiritingly shaking my head like a comedy-team straight man with a lap full of soup spilled by his nimrod partner. Witchel referred to Judd, Justine, and me as "the Brat Pack at *Carnal Knowledge.*" *TheaterWeek* featured us on their cover with the headline, "Brat Packers Go Off-Broadway in *Carnal Knowledge.*" Labeling us Brat Packers was essentially the marketing plan for the show in action, and when I heard that it was the promotional idea all along, I thought, *Oh, great. They're going to hate us.*

This was New York theater. This wasn't a Hollywood movie. What should have been promoted as an important piece of theatrical writing from a satirical master being given its New York stage premiere was instead being associated with a sneered-at moniker born out of a negative 1985 *New York* magazine piece about hotshot twenty-something actors in one well thought-of movie (*The Breakfast Club*) and one ridiculed movie (*St. Elmo's Fire*).

And besides, *I wasn't in the Brat Pack!* I never socialized with Emilio Estevez, Rob Lowe, or Judd during the term's heyday. I didn't want to be associated with what was perceived as a gimmicky clique that rubbed people the wrong way. Not when I'd been concentrating on a return to my theater roots. Yet here was this play that I was proud of in spite of its internal strife, being sold in a way that was like dangling red meat in front of snarky critics, or confirming the worst fears of theater devotees suspicious of anything Hollywood corrupting their beloved art form.

The hoopla surrounding the firing of Janine, however, briefly supplanted any concerns I had about how our *Carnal Knowledge* was being positioned. Death threats have a tendency to do that. Yes, that's correct. During previews the theater received a death threat on my life from a crazed Janine fan, and again, I couldn't exactly respond with a composed letter in response that said, "Dear Psycho, I wanted *Judd* fired. My costars are the ones who disapproved of your beloved Janine Turner, who I think is a celestial being of bottomless talent. Yours, Jon." Plus, if Judd was then murdered, I would have felt bad.

It was a strange feeling to go on in a play after knowing that someone has put it in writing that he or she plans to kill you. Almost anybody else in the same situation can hunker down somewhere, or take comfort in knowing that the person didn't know his address, or where he might be. But if you're in a play, there's a specific place everyone knows you're going to be every night, you're standing in front of a roomful of strangers, and it's not as if you act in front of a bulletproof window. Theaters are not that safe. For God's sake, President Lincoln was shot in a theater; they're death traps!

The death threat spooked everybody, and it made Martin, a guy who'd seen everything in his decades in the theater, pretty jumpy. One day my friend Andy, a New York City transit cop, came to the theater to say hi before the matinee. He was standing outside, and as I casually walked out to greet him, I noticed Martin approaching Andy, who's a big guy.

"Hello. Can I help you?" Martin asked.

"Yeah, I'm waiting for Jon Cryer."

"Oh, okay," said Martin, who then noticed that tucked inside this man's jacket was a revolver. Martin started sweating. "Hey, so why do you want to see Jon?"

"Oh, we're old friends. I just wanted to stop by. . . ."

Now, imagine you're Martin, racked with unease about the safety of one of your actors, and you've just been presented with new visual information about a stranger who wants to see him, in the form of a hidden weapon. The words, "Oh, we're old friends; I just wanted to stop by," suddenly sound like something Edward G. Robinson says before he rubs somebody out. And there's his prey, me, walking into the line of fire.

A panicked Martin just started pushing Andy, right as I was approaching, and yelling, "Why do you want to see him? What are you going to do? Do you know this guy, Jon? *Do you know this guy?*"

"It's okay, it's okay!" I shouted. "Martin, I know him! I know him! It's okay!"

Considering that Andy had no idea who Martin Charnin was, but knew I had gotten a death threat, that could have gone a lot worse if you look at it from Andy's point of view. But fortunately everyone lived, we opened, and we got murdered instead by the reviewers.

The knives were indeed out for "the Brat Pack off-Broadway," and they were arguably the worst reviews I've ever received for anything I've been involved in. Judd and Justine got it worse than I did, with the *Village Voice* calling Justine an assortment of wooden items, a totem pole, whatever. It was weird, because Judd and Justine were actually terrific in the play—once Janine was gone, they both loosened up and dug right in—and after a few weeks of tepid crowds, the word must have gotten out that it was better than the reviews, because audiences got fuller and more enthusiastic. Maybe it was morbid curiosity, people expecting it to be bad and discovering they liked it, but when we heard they wanted to extend the run, we all felt vindicated.

I even reconsidered my feelings about the way it was promoted. If the goal with the "Brat Pack" push was to get butts in seats—critics be damned—it did do that. Maybe we made some new theater fans that way. Who knows?

Judd's rebellions, meanwhile, tapered off somewhat. If the stage manager insisted he be there thirty minutes before showtime, he'd show up twenty-five minutes before. Plenty of time to get ready, but also nodding to the power he knew he held. There were pitfalls to that rebel persona, though, usually in the guise of assholes in bars who wanted to prove their manhood by picking a fight with the tough guy from *The Breakfast Club*. I saw it happen.

One night, half an hour before showtime, Judd hadn't arrived. Twenty-five minutes before, our resident rebel was still absent. At the fifteen-minute mark, no Judd Nelson. Then the stage manager got a phone call: Judd got into a bar fight and was in jail. The word went out to the understudy, who had a night job as a waiter, and this guy had to throw off his apron, jump in a cab, and speed to the theater. Meanwhile, I went out to the lobby, where I knew Judd's girlfriend at the time—*Playboy* Playmate Tawnni Cable, one of the headless pinups in our dressing room—was waiting with her plus-one, a guy named Richard Schenkman, who'd been directing her that day in a video for *Playboy*. I broke the news that Judd wouldn't be going on that night, but after the show Judd showed up. He'd made bail, and was ready for more, I guess.

"Let's go out for a drink!" he said.

The best thing that came out of *Carnal Knowledge* was meeting Tawnni's director friend Richard. We became fast friends over shared interests and senses of humor and the strange coincidence that we lived near each other in both Los Angeles and New York. We agreed to hang out more when we were back in Los Angeles, and Richard made good on that with an invitation to a party that promised an entrée into a very exclusive, iconic showbiz world.

Scientology!

I joke. Just turn the page.

Chapter 17
And This Is Tuesday, *Ha, Ha, Ha, Ha, Ha, Ha*

By the end of the eighties I was pretty disappointed that my stardom hadn't introduced me to a behind-the-scenes world of sexual debauchery I assumed was de rigueur in Hollywood. Although I got into show business because I loved acting and performing, there was always a secret part of me that wanted the embossed invitation to the hush-hush orgy, the casual Malibu cookout that suddenly turns into a vigorous game of nude Twister, or the night out at the swanky club during which gyrating lesbians pull you into a back room for a private show in which they pass cigarettes back and forth. (I like girls who smoke, remember.)

And yet I had been unmolested by Hollywood decadence.

Enter my friend Richard, friend to Playmates, director of *Playboy* videos. We'd been pals only a few months when he said the magic words: "Hey, want to come to a party at the Playboy Mansion?"

Um, did Han shoot first?

This was it! I was going to the notorious home of the twentieth century's foremost sexual hedonist and nudie-pictures purveyor, Hugh

Hefner. Score! It was the infamous Pajama Party, too, when all the girls wore lingerie. So it wasn't just attending a soiree at the Playboy Mansion— the three-hundred-and-sixty-degree view would be scantily clad women! And, boy, I'd heard tales—vivid, mythic tales—about the Grotto, the rock-enclosed Jacuzzi heaven that hosted erotic escapades that defied the imagination.

I was going to get to see all of this? And maybe get some other senses involved, too? Don't get ahead of yourself, Cryer.

I had to buy pajamas, of course. I was pretty sure I wasn't supposed to go in boxers and a T-shirt. This wasn't a come-as-you-sleep party. (Technically that's a wet dream, but I hate puns.) I bought a cheap flannel combo at Macy's, figuring the satin look of Hef was not mine to imitate. I was a newcomer. I had to earn the satin. That would come when I was a regular.

Richard and I pulled up to the mansion in Richard's 1974 Corvette Stingray, which boasted a vanity plate that read, BONDAGE, and I was too in-the-moment to think about what it looked like for two guys in pajamas to get out of a car that said, BONDAGE. I was all atwitter, because I was prepping myself for the A-list, all-star bacchanal that awaited us behind the security guys with the guest list. This was my Steadicam moment from *Goodfellas* when Lorraine Bracco gets ushered through the back of the nightclub, introduced to a world of status and power, but that makes me Lorraine Bracco and Richard Ray Liotta, so let's scotch that comparison. I was excited; let's just leave it at that.

The doors open, we walk through into a tented backyard, and my eyes are like a heat-seeking paparazzi Terminator, ready to zero in on all the big names, your Nicholsons, your Beattys. . . .

The first face I recognize is Ed Begley Jr.'s.

Okay, not the biggest star, but a talented character actor! He was friendly, too. I introduced myself. Ed was talking to a couple of gorgeous women, and I'm thinking, *This is the place where Ed Begley Jr. talks to the hottest babes. Well, then I'm a natural. I can't lose!*

Next up: again, not exactly James Caan level. It's Chuck McCann, star of the Sid and Marty Krofft show *Far Out Space Nuts*. Well, he's a star to ten-year-olds! He's cheery, too, having a good time in his bedwear.

Then we got to some A-listers. Tony Curtis was there, and I almost lost it. I love so many movies he made: *Sweet Smell of Success*, *Some Like It Hot*, *Spartacus*. Now we're starting to ramp up at this shindig. On one of Tony Curtis's arms is a beautiful blonde, and on the other, her identical twin. Twin hotties! The evening is heating up. I walk over and say, "Hi, Mr. Curtis, I just had to introduce myself. My name is Jon Cryer, and it's so nice to meet you."

"Hey, I'm Tony," he said, then indicated to the girl on his left—"This is Monday"—then the girl on his right—"and this is Tuesday. *Ha, ha, ha, ha, ha, ha . . .*"

The girls laughed, too, a sort of "this is a joke he's made several times already" snicker. And I couldn't help but think about the trajectory of a pair of lives in which attractive sisters come to Los Angeles, stars in their eyes perhaps, and wind up sexualized punch-line accessories for an aging actor for whom their twinness is the draw. That must be a strange existence.

The marquee factor—new or old—pretty much ended at Tony Curtis. There weren't very many other celebrities there that night. What there was, though, in the department of has-been design, was a multicolored disco floor with a spinning ball. Now, disco floors were cool. *Ten years prior.* This was 1990, however. You wouldn't willingly have rented one for a wingding then. They weren't even ironic yet. What undoubtedly happened in the 1970s was that Hef thought he could save money on the rental of a disco floor by just buying the damn thing, and now he was simply trying to amortize the enormous purchase price of a trendy item bought at the height of the trend by whipping it out for his yearly Pajama Party.

As you might gather, I don't look at a dance floor and necessarily think, "Time to dance." Neither did anybody else, it seemed. There were only two people on the floor, but at least they were both beautiful women. One was a stunner with incredible Crystal Gayle–style long hair down to her calves, halfheartedly swaying, but it was enough to generate something tantalizingly magical. This girl with the glowing mane was moving in a way that looked like slow motion. It felt like a classic Playboy Mansion image to me. Not so iconically classic but no less mesmerizing was the other beautiful woman, who was in a wheelchair. Of late, it turned out, the magazine had made an effort to broaden the types of women they showcased, so in the interests of unclad diversity they'd introduced the Paraplegic Playmate, and here she was—another striking blonde in regulation lingerie—zipping around that dance floor, occasionally showing off a well-timed spin-and-wheelie in sync with the music.

She was enjoying herself. But she was also clearly drunk, which made for an unusually tense situation in my mind. She'd scoot that wheelchair right up to the edge of the disco floor, then wheel herself back in, and for the love of God, I thought she was going to fall off each time. It was like watching those gym boogie-ers in *It's a Wonderful Life* when the floor opens to reveal the swimming pool, and they're blissfully unaware that they're now literally dancing on the edge. But she'd also get so close to the Crystal Gayle girl that I just knew that long hair would get caught in the wheels and Crystal Gayle Girl would be pulled down Isadora Duncan style toward humiliating injury. I just kept thinking I was looking at the before scene in a terrible slapstick comedy. Again, I don't look at dance floors the way most people do.

I walked away from that scene and picked out of the crowd *Screw* magazine founder, Al Goldstein, which seemed odd, since I thought *Screw* and *Playboy* were competitors. I guess the Pajama Party is some kind of men's-mag détente. But next to Goldstein was Hugh Hefner himself, and next to Hef was Kimberly Conrad, the woman he was going to marry, or, as the magazine hyped, Hef's "Playmate for a Lifetime." (Words that didn't exactly prove to be true.) Richard introduced me to the two of them, and as they walked away I turned to Richard and said, "Well, she seems nice."

"Yeah, she's okay," he said. "But the parties used to be so much better before she came along." According to Richard, the word was, no more Fellini-esque carnivals of sin, and instead, nice get-togethers that ended at reasonable hours.

My heart sank. "Wait, wait," I said. "You mean this is never going to devolve into something wanton and libertine?"

"Nah, probably not."

"No devolving? No moment where everybody pops Quaaludes and G-strings are tossed to the wind?"

"Wouldn't bet on it."

"Why didn't you tell me!" I said. "I expected a den of iniquity!"

The sadness was brief, though, as Richard began introducing me to Playmates he knew. Boobs have a tendency to distract, and two particularly glorious ones arrived, belonging to the stunning Petra Verkaik, who was one of my favorites of the magazine's recent centerfolds. Petra wasn't in a nightie. She was more dressed for a slumber party, in a T-shirt that stopped midthigh, but it was still enough that in chitchatting with her I had to stop every other word I said from being, "Wow." Petra and Richard were apparently getting set to fly down to Puerto Rico for a shoot, and she said to him, "We're going to have a great time!" and walked away.

Richard seemed unfazed by this. "You know, she's such a game gal," he said nonchalantly. "If you ask her to go bowling or grab dinner in Koreatown, she's always up for it."

"Richard!" I said. "Why aren't you married to her?" It seemed shocking that someone that gorgeous, nice, and fun wasn't *his* "Playmate for a Lifetime."

He seemed surprised at the suggestion. I knew his type was tall and thin, not petite and curvy like Petra, but he just seemed faintly amused more than stirred. I guessed Richard to be the type for whom work was work, and when you have a type, you're blind to other possibilities. I, on the other hand, was instantly sad when Petra wandered off. But again, only for a moment, because then my eyes drifted across the room and caught sight of an exquisite golden-haired gal in silk pajamas, standing next to another equally va-va-voom blonde. Talking to them was another blonde, but it was Ed Begley Jr., who doesn't count. He's more sandy-haired anyway, I'd say.

No more of this two-girls-with-one-guy business. It was time to actually strike up a deep conversation with one of these dazzling female partygoers, so I walked up with my mapped-out reason to talk to Ed, and luckily Ed's an easy guy to start talking to. He introduced me to one of the blondes, then referred to the other as "her daughter." Whoa! Beauty across generations here! It seemed the daughter's father was an unspeakably groovy, handsome B-movie actor famous in the sixties, and as she and I talked it became clear that her father and Hef were such good chums, she practically grew up at the mansion.

"You want a tour?" she asked with a sweet smile. "You want to see the Grotto?"

My mouth went numb. I think I said yes, but it might have just been a lot of vigorous nodding. *Now we're talkin'! A gorgeous blonde is offering to take you to one of the world's most famous nooky spots!*

We made our way to the Grotto, which was populated at that moment by an eighties television star whose name I've forgotten and a bikini-clad woman he was chatting up with bald-faced intentions. But even without a gaggle of swinging guests, the image I'd had of this magical land of wet-and-wild wantonness was being quickly supplanted by the reality in front of me: that the Grotto is essentially a dingy pool with prefab rocks. It looked surprisingly ersatz. Then there was the powerful stench of chlorine, and while I wouldn't call chlorine the most aphrodisiac of perfumes, one is probably grateful that something is killing a communal recreation "lagoon" that I'm pretty sure by this point was thirty percent water, thirty percent body oil, and forty percent Jimmy Caan's sperm. Taking in the scene, I thought, *If this were the pool facilities at a hotel I were staying at, I'd be calling the front desk to request a cleaning.*

Something about the scene seemed to irritate my adorable tour guide, though, because she turned and said, "Want to see the game room?"

The game room! As in "Yes, I'm game!" Now, that sounded like a provocatively private bit of naughtiness, a place where only those familiar with handcuffs, stirrups, and safe words need enter? A lair of intimate recreation where maybe losing was as much fun as winning? I was ready for a wall collection of whips and straps, but . . . no, it's an arcade you'd find in any mall, and the only person in there was Jonathan Silverman playing pinball.

I was still in the company of a pretty young thing, though, and I decided that if the party and the mansion were considerably different from my expectations of them, talking to a nice girl was worth my mental energies.

"So, you grew up here?" I asked.

"Yeah, yeah," she said. "It's kind of a wild place, but it's pretty cool. My dad and Hef are friends, and though my mom and dad aren't together anymore, he still lets me come."

"That's nice," I said. "Well, it's certainly a pleasure meeting you."

"I know. It's so freaky that I'm meeting you," she said. "I'm superexcited about tomorrow, because I'm taking my driver's test."

"Oh? How old are you?"

"I'm fourteen."

For the second time that night, my mouth went numb. Look, I'm no operator, but you make an assumption about the age of a female allowed to stroll the grounds of the Playboy Mansion accompanied by a man she's never met before, and you allow yourself to imagine where that encounter might lead. And now that mental projection was being replaced by visions of me knocking on doors in my neighborhood, alerting people that I'm a registered sex offender. With that final break in my evening of shattered expectations, I said, like the twenty-four-year-old father figure I immediately felt like, "Okay, well, we're going back to your mom now."

The party was also winding down, and security was making the rounds informing people of such, shooing people out. Once back with the mom, I politely said, "Well, it was very nice meeting you and your daughter."

I turned and left, looking for my friend Richard. Suddenly I felt a tug on my arm, and it was the mother. With what I can only describe as a conspiratorially suggestive tone, she said, "It seems like you guys were getting along great. If you ever want to say hello, here's my daughter's number."

She handed me a piece of paper with a phone number on it, but all I could see were the words *statutory rape.*

Out of her sight I tossed the number, and then allowed myself to feel dejected, realizing that if I'd just stuck with Richard, I would have talked to Playmates. They were his work colleagues, for Pete's sake. His beautiful, stunning, supersexy *adult* work colleagues. I, meanwhile, picked the fourteen-year-old. I had struck out at the Playboy Mansion. I found a small ledge to sit on, where I decided to wait for Richard, and took the moment to stare off into space.

Suddenly, my zoned-out pity party was interrupted by a sultry yet remarkably inebriated voice.

"Heyhowzitgoin?"

It was my last best hope for the evening, the sexy Paraplegic Playmate, who was ready to continue this merrymaking somewhere else, was definitely of age, and for some reason had picked me as the guy to make something happen. Now, don't get me wrong. This was a beautiful woman seated before me. But if my judgment was sound enough to kick Jailbait back to her pimping mom, it was also sturdy enough to avoid a scenario in which one party was so unbelievably hammered she makes four words sound like one. And who, might I add, was already operating semiheavy machinery. It was time to bring this anything-but-decadent excursion to a polite close.

"I'm sorry," I said. "I'm pretty tired, and I think I'm just going to go h—"

Thump-thump.

She wheeled over my foot.

"Why, yes, I'd LOVE to discuss the latest episode of *The Banana Splits*!"

Thumb in mouth, check.
Diaper on outside of pj's? Check.

Me and my sister, Robin, during a momentary lull in hostilities.

All photos courtesy of the author unless otherwise noted.

My lovely mother, Gretchen, with her shy, retiring son.

By the age of three, I was almost 74 percent cheeks.

Me, my sister, Robin, and my dad circa 1968.

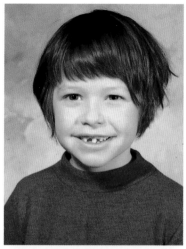

Well, I got one side brushed.

Almost there . . .

BAM! Stylin'!

The "Boys of Room 116" at Stagedoor Manor (*left to right*): David Quinn, me, Adam Warshofsky, and David Bache.

I played "Perchik, the fiery revolutionary with the outrageously billowy white shirt," in Stagedoor Manor's production of *Fiddler on the Roof.*

The Cryer household for many years (*from right to left*): Shelly, me, mom, and Robin.

I'd like to say surrealist Luis Buñuel took our Fire Island Polaroids the summer I was seventeen, but I'd be lying. That's my friend Anthony's head in the sand. The park ranger? We never saw him again.

To this day, when Sarah Jessica Parker sees me, she asks me to remember to buy milk on the way home.

David Dennis, me, and David's brother Eric flanked by a chicken and a king. Don't ask. Also refrain from inquiring about my shoulder pads.

Me and the cast of *Brighton Beach Memoirs*. That's my dressing roommate, Anita Gillette, in the red coat in front, and yes, that is a sullen Elizabeth Perkins bottom right.

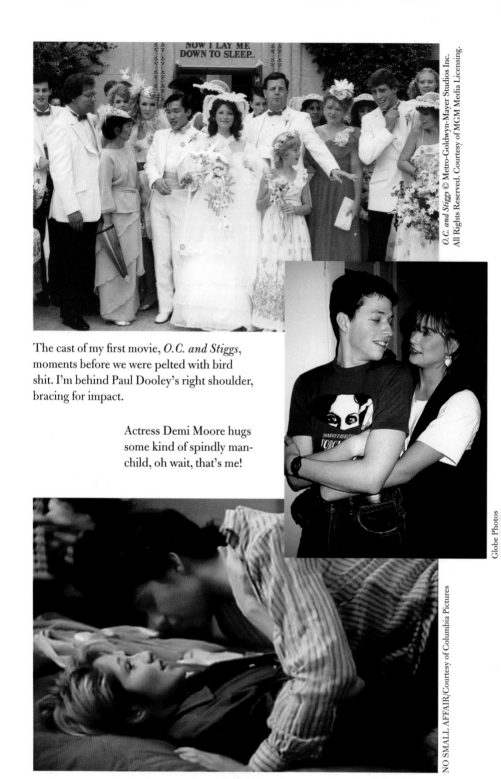

The cast of my first movie, *O.C. and Stiggs*, moments before we were pelted with bird shit. I'm behind Paul Dooley's right shoulder, bracing for impact.

Actress Demi Moore hugs some kind of spindly man-child, oh wait, that's me!

Here's a shot from my first screen test for *No Small Affair*. That's Ellen Barkin I'm manhandling there. Or maybe she was manhandling me.

I'm really hoping you can tell which is me and which is Molly Ringwald from *The Facts of Life*. What could possibly have been the cause of our lack of sexual chemistry?

Playing Duckie for John Hughes changed my life. He's a freakin' word in romcom terminology, for Christ's sakes. RESPECT!

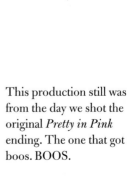

This production still was from the day we shot the original *Pretty in Pink* ending. The one that got boos. BOOS.

			2 Rich crou...
	PROPS: Album		
	END 3RD DAY - TOTAL PAGES: 3-1/8 pg		
4TH DAY	INT. RECORD STORE - DAY	1 - ANDIE	227 Broadway
		2 - DUCKIE	Santa Monica, CA
THURSDAY	Sc. 122 (D-6) 2 pgs	4 - IONA	
JUNE 6			ATMOS
	Duckie's hot to trot.		3 Stand Ins
			1 Wel Wrk.
	PROPS: Knee pads?		
	MUSIC: Playback		
	CAMERA: 2 Cameras		
	INT. RECORD STORE - B		

The production thought Duckie's lip sync would only take a third of a shooting day. Ha! As you can see, at least they were considerate enough to ask about knee pads.

Yes, even Superman has a stand-in. While Christopher Reeve had long lost his enthusiasm for flying work, I looked for every excuse to hang out. Here's a rehearsal for the shot where he drops me off at prison.

In this shot from the set of *Superman IV*, I asked Gene Hackman to pose like he'd never met me before. Mission accomplished, Mr. Hackman.

Here's the phone that British Telecom installed as well as the cell phone that Gene Hackman lent me. Yes, I was frustrated enough with my phone to take a picture of it.

This actually happened: Gene Hackman and I were riding in an open-top roadster, and suddenly we got picked up by Superman and flown to prison.

David Dennis, me, and Artie Martinez on the set of *Superman IV*.

Here's David Dennis with a pile of British pounds while I was in London shooting *Superman IV*. This is the happiest he's ever looked.

Jon Cryer, Catherine Mary Stuart, and a big blurry gun in this production still from *Dudes*.

I took this Polaroid with my goth friend Tiffany after the producers of *Dudes* had my hair dyed black to see if I could pass for a hard-core punk. They hired me anyway.

Shooting *Dudes* in the desert with Flea from the Red Hot Chili Peppers and Dan Roebuck.

MAROWITZ ON *THE SECRET RAPTURE* AND MICHAEL FEINSTEIN

TheaterWeek

November 26, 1990
$2.50 / $3.00 Outside NYC

Karen Byers

Judd Nelson

Justine Bateman

Jon Cryer

Brat Packers
Go Off-Broadway
in *Carnal Knowledge*

Carnal Knowledge made the cover of *Theater Week*. Who wouldn't want to see a play starring this group of glowering hipsters?

Here actor Ben Daniels welcomes me to London theater in the Old Vic production of *900 Oneonta*.

© Henrietta Butler/ArenaPAL

Here are me, David Beaird, author of *900 Oneonta*, and his assistant/girlfriend, Shevonne, moments after David had read reviews comparing him to several of the twentieth century's great playwrights. You'd have that look on your face too.

Who's that guy in the background of this production still from *HOT SHOTS!*?

Revelation 2:27 "And be ye warned: The fourth sign of the apocalypse shall be Jon Cryer on the cover of *Jet Magazine*."

While at the Cannes Film Festival with *The Pompatus of Love*, I managed to convince the French Air Force to strafe the beach to promote the film.

Photo by Chris Lee

Conductor Paul Gemigniani, Martha Plimpton, Neil Patrick Harris, and I screw up entertainingly during rehearsals for *Company* at Lincoln Center.

The cast of *Company* performs "Side by Side by Side" (*left to right*): Jim Walton, Patti LuPone, me, Jennifer Laura Thompson, Aaron Lazar, Katie Finneran, Craig Bierko, Jill Paice, Stephen Colbert, Martha Plimpton, and Neil Patrick Harris.

Joseph Marzullo/WENN.com

We rehearsed *Company* at Pearl Studios in midtown, a place brimming with theatrical energy and invention but not air-conditioning.

Photo by Jill Paice

DRESSING ROOM E

COMPANY STEPHEN COLBERT

COMPANY JON CRYER

America's favorite fake right-wing blowhard and I shared a tiny dressing room and many scantily clad, intimate moments because of it.

Two and a Half Men first aired in the fall of 2003 and was an instant hit, something I'd never experienced before.

Perhaps the show owed its phenomenal success to the low-key, understated marketing campaign.

Lisa, me, Charlie Sheen, and Brooke Mueller—just a pair of young newlywed couples.

Here's Chuck Lorre handing me the slate after I directed an episode of *Two and a Half Men* for the first time. They don't give me flowers anymore.

For seven years *Two and a Half Men* was more fun than any of us had any right to expect. Then it got interesting....

The cast of *Two and a Half Men 2.0* backstage at Carnegie Hall moments before we were introduced for the first time.

Photo by Ashton Kutcher

My wife, Lisa, and I were married in June 2007, after which we commenced filling our days by running places while holding hands and smiling. That's what being married is, right?

My wife, Lisa, my son, Charlie, and my daughter, Daisy.

Chapter 18
Oh, Yeah, Charlie Sheen

The first emotion I felt when I read the script for *Hot Shots!* was a mixture of elation and relief, because it was not only goddamn hilarious, but the first really good script I'd gotten in a long stretch of diminishing offers. Jim Abrahams, of the ZAZ team (David Zucker, Abrahams, and Jerry Zucker), who changed forever the movie parody genre with *Airplane!*, had branched off on his own to craft with coscreenwriter Pat Proft a wicked sendup of the jingoistic pageants of machismo and war action that we'd all been bombarded with since the release of *Top Gun*.

And can I just say, I thought *Top Gun* was slick, manufactured crap, as artificial as whatever goes into a Twinkie, dumber than cardboard, and written so that every line felt like a slogan. Its recklessness bothered me, too: that this was about air force pilots who negotiate international incidents with . . . missiles? And who the hell were they fighting at the end? If you're looking for modern warfare devoid of context or clarity, *Top Gun* is your movie. And frankly, can anybody ferret out what's going on in those fight sequences? They were universally lauded at the time, but to my mind they represent the dawn of Cuisinart editing techniques, in which there's just enough fast motion and rapid firing and loud music to distract you from the fact that it's impossible to follow the fighter choreography. And *ugh*, that ridiculous shot of the cockpit canopies inverted over each other: "Ha, ha! Get it?! He's taking a Polaroid of the other pilot! This guy really *is* a maverick!"

And one other thing. I like Kenny Loggins as much as the next guy, perhaps more. I've often found myself giddily singing along with "I'm Alright" from *Caddyshack* even though I clearly don't know the lyrics. But one can only imagine when Tony Scott called him to ask that he pen a song for this film, Kenny bought a "fighter pilot lingo" set of refrigerator magnets, slapped them on his Frigidaire, copied down what was there, randomly picked three power chords, and started collecting his royalties.

Where do I sign up for the movie takedown of this shit?

It was a smaller part, the sight-challenged Jim "Wash Out" Pfaffenbach, but I was really pumped. *Hot Shots!* felt like a chance to get back into the fraternity of feature films after being left out in the cold due to my calamitous movie choices in the 1980s. This was 1990, though, so the new decade was looking up. I had to audition for Jim Abrahams, but he really laughed at how I combined deadpan line readings with ridiculously crossed eyes (a skill of mine), and a couple of days later I learned that I got the part.

In two important ways, the production of *Hot Shots!* was completely unlike *Top Gun*. For one, we didn't have the support of the military, because we weren't a two-hour recruitment film for enlistment, as *Top Gun* shrewdly was. So instead of getting an aircraft carrier at sea for those sequences, our production guys had to actually be *clever*: They built the prow of an aircraft carrier on a cliff in Palos Verdes, so when we shot on the deck toward the horizon, it looked as if we were on the ocean. That's movie magic, people.

The other way was initially worrisome, then pragmatic. During the shoot, the first Gulf War broke out, in January of 1991. I remember, the night U.S. forces started air strikes on Baghdad, switching on my TV and being mesmerized by the green glow of the invasion footage on CNN, and when a huge potted tree blew over at my next-door neighbor's house, I was so startled by the sound I screamed. But the reality was, when we were out filming in the Mojave Desert, surrounded by actors in uniform and trainer jets leased to the production, I thought, *Wow, none of this is going to be funny when people start dying.* But the Persian Gulf War turned out to be astonishingly brief (at least, that's what we thought at the time), and what we now had was a villain we could name in Saddam Hussein, so they added a scene of him catching a bomb while listening to Neil Diamond. So unlike *Top Gun* and its cowardly inability to actually identify the enemy its characters are combating, we named names and, ironically, added actual hard-edged realism to the fighter-pilot genre!

Let's see, what else? Oh, yeah, Charlie Sheen. (How long were you waiting for me to talk about him—be honest?)

We'd met before *Hot Shots!* actually. We both auditioned for a movie years prior that never got made, and I remember thinking he was friendly, talkative, and strikingly handsome. That hadn't changed when we remet on *Hot Shots!* but what had changed was his level of stardom, and that he was prone to tabloid-worthy incidents—he'd accidentally shot Kelly Preston in the arm that year (Oh, Charlie, you scamp!) and famously enjoyed recreational mind-altering substances.

It did surprise me that Sheen was making *Hot Shots!* frankly, because he wasn't some Leslie Nielsen type trading on years of journeyman work and getting comic juice out of a has-been status. Sheen still had marquee power. It had been only five years since *Platoon* and *Wall Street*. But he had made one of the umpteen *Top Gun* knockoffs the year prior—*Navy SEALS*, which fizzled—so he was uniquely qualified to do a full-on parody. It was also immediately obvious that Charlie was born to do the kind of precise, straight-faced, never-overplayed line delivery that movies like

Airplane! and *Hot Shots!* need to sell their brand of silly. Charlie just turned on that great charisma and swagger, and we were off. He needed almost no direction adjustments from Abrahams.

It was also clear that our star was deeply invested in partying, and made no apologies about it. Charlie was hitting clubs and strip joints almost nightly—not with me, because we weren't socializing—but his extracurricular fun never seemed to affect his work. As the production got going, he might roll in an hour late in the morning in his convertible, with then-squeeze Ginger Lynn in the passenger seat, but once makeup and hair were finished with him, Charlie hit his marks and got everything on the first take. One could not help but respect it.

Meeting Ginger Lynn, who had been a figure of some eminence in fantastical imaginings of mine inspired by filmic works typically found on store shelves shielded by a flimsy curtain, was interesting. Sort of like meeting your office buddy's girlfriend. She wore jeans and gingham shirts, nothing leathery or heeled or tied around her in suggestive ways, as one might expect—hope?—to discover about the casual wear of adult-film stars. You could sense the eyes darting toward her from the male crew folk, but she was polite and sweet and kind of regular-gal boring, to be honest. I do remember being struck by how petite she was. I thought, *So that's why guys look so big in those videos. It's a trick of perspective.* That's my theory and I'm sticking to it.

Speaking of perspective—like that segue?—I had absolutely none when I had to sport Wash Out's ridiculous eyewear, the glasses that looked thick enough for fishbowls. When I'd get direction like, "Okay, we need you to come over here, then run down these stairs," I'd say, "You do understand that I'm blind with these things on? I'd be *falling* down those stairs, if I could even find them." I'd literally have to memorize spaces like a legitimately blind person.

Being in a movie like *Hot Shots!* you really appreciate the time, thought, and effort that goes into getting a well-crafted joke to play. It is often a mysterious art, but with a scientific side: When you get a laugh, you know it works. One day we were shooting the bit in which Wash Out is dragged by an ambulance and slammed into the back of it when it stops, after which he stands up, responds to a concerned query by saying, "Why, thank you, Andre. I'll have the veal piccata," and falls out of frame. But every time we reached the beat with the veal piccata line and falling down, it wasn't funny. We all huddled over the video-playback monitor like lab technicians at a microscope, trying to suss out why the gag wasn't landing. Was it the fall? Was it the wrong kind of pratfall? Was it the way I said the line? The line itself? You'd have thought we were trying to solve a murder.

Eventually we hit upon a look I gave between saying the line and falling. I would glance at the other characters before falling, or just look anywhere, and that killed the joke. I had to say the line, not look anywhere, and fall. Then, almost as if by magic, it was funny. In much the way my gun scene in *Dudes* was radically altered by the smallest of gestures, I realized the same thing applied to jokes predicated on exactness.

The success of *Hot Shots!* in the summer of 1991 was immensely gratifying. I was finally in another hit, and one that gave me renewed confidence in my ability to make people laugh. Eventually the mechanics of comedy would prove to be the place for me, but before that could happen, I made another stage detour, to do a play that would lead to some of the best highs of my life as an actor and, in one fateful night, one of the lowest lows.

I really like this foreshadowing thing. Don't you? Don't you just want to go right to the next page and find out what I'm referring to? I mean, do you really need to go to the bathroom? Tell you what. Just hold the book in your hand while you do your business. I don't care if you get pee on it. Ladies, that's unlikely to happen anyway, but, guys, that's a distinct possibility. And yet, hey, it's your book. Unless you got it from the library. In which case, now you know what those discolored splotches are in other books you borrow. And you thought they were coffee stains.

Sorry. This got weird. Just turn the page.

Chapter 19
That Time the Very Worst Thing Happened

"Here 'tis," he drawled, dropping into my hands what felt like a phone book, its weight heavy in my palms. The dropper's name was (and is) David Beaird, and he was (and is) a playwright known for being, shall we say, eccentric. Which is to say batshit. Yes, I was about to have yet another outlandish guy named David in my life.

"It's my new play; it's a little long," he deadpanned.

It was indeed "a little long," as it was conspicuously in excess of three hundred pages. It was also bound into separate volumes, I assume so that the brads tenuously holding it together would not be overtaxed. It was titled *900 Oneonta*, which sounded mysterious, to say the least. It seemed I was holding a terrifying magnum opus wrought from the pain of a playwright's tortured soul, the kind of self-indulgent (and did I mention lengthy?) exercise in introspection that actors, or pretty much any friend of the playwright, must slog through every now and then out of loyalty. I regarded it queasily.

"Can't wait."

Little did I know that this play would lead to that time the very worst thing happened.

First, some context. Back in 1989, David had directed me in the Los Angeles premiere of Howard Korder's play *Boys' Life* at the Los Angeles Theatre Center, and we'd bonded over that piece's particular and twisted journey to the stage. What happened was, Korder had submitted an early draft of his play to the Theatre Center dramaturge quite a while before it became an off-Broadway hit. So when said dramaturge decided to mount the play in LA for the first time, he just assumed it hadn't changed.

Ah, but it had, as we were informed by the playwright's lawyer, who by chance had come to a preview performance. We were performing *the wrong ending.* So we found ourselves on the afternoon of opening night staging a completely new denouement that utterly altered the arcs we'd spent weeks toiling over to bring all of our characters to satisfying conclusions. It was as panicked as you'd imagine. Lots of knees-bent running about. But in the middle of it, David, who'd up to this point in rehearsals been by turns mercurial, brilliant, bizarre, manipulative, depressed, and exultant, was now suddenly, eerily calm.

I've found that when shit goes down, crazy people often handle it very well, because the world is finally conforming to their worldview. Instead of freaking out, David simply, methodically blocked the new ending and hoped for the best, a completely rational approach, considering the circumstance. Actually, come to think of it, that is probably the best attitude for a director to have at all times.

At any rate, I admired him greatly for this, and to his credit, the cast of *Boys' Life* rallied and put on quite an opening night. It would turn out to be one of the oldest stories in show business: An amiable and oddball bunch of actors is cast in a troubled play; they're thrown a curveball at the last minute; the plucky director and cast band together to assemble an inspired and magical fix; they stage a triumphant opening night; and it all leads to the big finish: crushing reviews and the show closes quickly.

But that was not the very worst thing that I was talking about.

The so-called "actor's nightmare" actually varies from actor to actor. Some are stricken with the "I'm suddenly in a different play" type, in which he or she is ready to do one play when abruptly, everyone around them is performing another. There's also the "why am I naked?" variation, where you're doing a familiar play, but inexplicably nude. There's also the "I mysteriously can't remember lines that I've known backward and forward for months" dream, which is pretty self-explanatory. And not far down the list of dreadful scenarios that keep actors dramatically waking up in a cold sweat (perhaps the reason why they are so good at that in the movies) is the "something happens that absolutely, irretrievably stops the whole fucking show" nightmare.

Now, up to this point, the one that haunted me specifically was sort of a combination of the "different play" and the "naked" situation. I'd dream I was playing Eugene in *Brighton Beach Memoirs* and everyone else was doing *Sweeney Todd*. Plus, I was also nude and holding some sort of cricket bat. And Orville Redenbacher was playing Mrs. Lovett. But as terrifying as this was, it was also perversely comforting, because I was pretty sure that particular scenario was very unlikely to play out in real life. Not the different-play part, or even the naked part, pretty much just the Redenbacher portion, 'cause he's totally dead.

Well, I'd like you to know that now I've got a new nightmare, one that I actually got the chance to live through.

But first, I got to live something of an actor's dream scenario. Allow me to explain. To my surprise, the ream of paper that David Beaird handed me was no boring exercise in artistic indulgence but rather a full-throttle, holy-shit, grab-you-by-the-throat, magnificent piece of writing (although, yes, a little long). I finished it in one sitting and immediately let David know I wanted to do it.

And thus began a several-year process of workshopping it, submitting it to theaters, and begging producers to mount a production. Turns out, nobody in their right mind—in the United States, at least—wanted to touch it with a ten-foot pole. But in 1993, an enterprising young British producer named Kate Danielson finally saw its potential and got the Lyric Hammersmith Theatre in London to take a shot. What's more, British Equity was willing to allow two American actors to be in the production. I was both gob-smacked and chuffed (which are Britishisms for "speechless" and "thrilled"). This would be my British theatrical debut, with a great part, in a play that I loved, at the legendary Lyric Hammersmith Theatre. That's right, *theatre* with an "re"! This was no small potatoes. The Lyric had a terrific reputation for groundbreaking plays and musicals, and the theater itself had survived two world wars and was known far and wide for its beautiful performance space. Designed and built in 1895 by legendary theatrical architect Frank Matcham, it had been lovingly restored piece by piece in 1966. We could not ask for a more perfect environment for our production.

As David and I packed our bags and jetted off, we were joined by Leland Crooke, an actor of such enormous and remarkable skill that he's the living embodiment of the injustice of fame in the entertainment industry. If the business were fair at all he'd be as well-known as Daniel Day Lewis. He's that good.

We arrived in London exhausted but elated and made a beeline for the home of our play. When Kate greeted us at the door and led us into the lobby of the theater, I took the opportunity to sneak a peek at the stately performance space. Kate noticed my prying and said, "Beautiful, isn't it?" then added, "That's where they put on their marquee productions. We'll actually be doing our play in the studio."

Wait. What?! We were not going to be thrilling audiences on the Lyric Hammersmith's main stage? The one designed in 1895 by legendary theatrical architect Frank Matcham? That survived two world wars? And had been lovingly restored piece by piece in 1966?

As I managed to blurt out a bewildered, "Oh," she gestured toward the stairs, and as we descended she continued. "The studio is where they put on their edgier productions; it's really a better place for our play." And with that she flung open a dilapidated set of double doors to reveal the "studio," so-called because it's much more inviting to tell performers they will be playing in the Lyric Hammersmith studio than the Lyric Hammersmith basement. It was what they call a "black box" theater, basically a room painted black, crammed with seats, above which lights are hung from rafters. I was disheartened but not discouraged. This would just have to do.

The first week of performances made it clear to me how difficult it is to launch a new play by a foreign playwright whom nobody has ever heard of. We played to tiny audiences, their tininess only enhanced by the fact that the theater itself was tiny to begin with. But people seemed to enjoy it. I worried about what critics would think, given that they'd be attending the show along with only about a half dozen other patrons. "I don't give a shit about the critics," David would bluster, then add with a grimace, "I mean, have you ever actually met those people?"

Now, because we weren't on the main stage at the Lyric, we were officially considered a "fringe" production. Fringe productions don't get the same treatment that the big-budget West End shows get. Even if critics had attended the first week, their reviews wouldn't actually hit the papers until their respective editors felt that there was enough room to print them. So for the first three weeks of our four-week run, not one single paper ran a review.

Consequently our audiences remained minuscule. We soldiered on bravely. Performing for British theatergoers is still a thrill, even if you can count them on one hand. The British actors who'd gamely come on board had turned out to be a notable group of thespians in that to a person, they were dedicated, good-natured, inspired, and professional. Not a nut job or asshole among them! And while our UK colleagues enjoyed themselves immensely, they were baffled as to why a play that they been so excited about hadn't gotten a press reaction.

But when the deluge came it was sudden and monstrous. We got word one night that a few papers would run notices the next morning, so we stayed out extra late drinking that night in order to grab the editions as they first hit the newsstands in the wee hours of the morning. When they arrived, David, his girlfriend/assistant, Shevonne, and I each grabbed whichever issue was closest. Drunkenly pulling issues of the *Daily Mail*, the *Evening Standard*, the *Daily Telegraph* and *The Times* off the stands while simultaneously trying to appear as though you really couldn't care less about what the reviews say is harder than you think. We frantically spread them out on the ground and scoured them for any sign of a reference to our play.

Now, when one happens upon a review of someone's work in a publication and one is in the presence of that particular someone, one's first impulse is to read the review aloud, to include everyone in the exposition. However, if you've gone through the excruciating experience of a read-out-loud review that veers into highly insulting territory, you'll understand when I say that virtually every actor I know squelches that impulse and reads reviews silently.

That is, until you come across a line like the one I read in the *Telegraph*:

"The play is a glorious and sometimes disgracefully enjoyable triumph!"

When you hit a line like that, you shout it to the rooftops.

I stammered, "Hey, guys . . . this one says, 'The play is a glorious—'"

"'Nails you breathless to your seat!'" screamed Shevonne from behind her open *Evening Standard*. "'A spectacular feat!'"

Just then I spied the headline of the *Daily Mail* review in gigantic letters: "A Triumph of Genius and Faith!"

"Holy crap!" I shouted as Shevonne held up a copy of *What's On*, shouting, "'One hell of an evening out!'" Now we both screamed. And just as shit was getting crazy, I noticed that David was, once again, suddenly, eerily calm.

But this moment was different. This was the moment that I got to watch as my friend David read *The Times* review that opined that his play was "as if Eugene O'Neill, Tennessee Williams, and an American Joe

Orton had collaborated on a play." That's right: One of the most influential papers in London had just compared him to, arguably, the three greatest English-language playwrights of the twentieth century. Too bad he didn't give a shit about critics.

The lines around the block started the next morning. With only a week left in the run, seats were at a premium. We were excitedly informed that fistfights had broken out. This was probably not true, but we actors are easily duped when people tell us that audiences simply must see our work, lest they resort to physical assault. The Lyric extended the run for a couple of weeks but then ran up against visa limits on the American actors. So we played our last weeks to packed houses, hoping there might be some other life for the play.

A month later, after Leland and I had come back to the States, the word came. We were asked to move the production to the Old Vic Theatre (again, with the "re"!), the esteemed playhouse where Lord Laurence Olivier had founded the National Theatre. The illustriousness of our new location was mind-blowing enough, but what really pleased us was that we were finally going to be able to stage *900 Oneonta* in a space big enough to capture the grandness of our production.

The play itself is a rip-roaring piece of Southern Gothic. I used to refer to it as the play Tennessee Williams would have written if he ever tried crack. But then I found out that it was completely possible that Williams had, in fact, tried crack, and the result was not this play. That being said, *900 Oneonta* follows Dandy (played by Leland Crooke), the ancient, dying patriarch of a wealthy, rotten-to-the-core Louisiana family, and his efforts to find a suitable heir to his vast fortune. The only trouble is, his heirs are fuckups and he's in the midst of a massive coronary, which, as you would imagine, imparts a certain urgency to the proceedings.

Dandy spends the first act making out his will while confronting his brood with every awful unspoken truth he's kept hidden over the years, cackling with glee as they scramble to get a piece of his legacy. I played Gitlo, the spineless, craven, frenetic grandson whose attempts are particularly desperate. Complicating Gitlo's efforts is the fact that the only one in the family Dandy has any actual affection for is my character's wild-eyed, redneck, heroin-addicted brother, Tiger (you can get away with these kinds of names in a play that takes place in the American South, but place it pretty much anywhere else and people will just laugh you out of the theater). Our alcoholic, incestuous, bipolar mother, Persia (see?), and broken, nymphomaniac sister, Burning Jewel (oh, for Pete's sake), round out the squabblers, with the dad, a maid, a priest, and a lawyer on hand to witness whichever way this fiasco turns out.

The play rockets along manically, but then, the first jolt: At the end of the first act the main character, Dandy, the motor for all this action, dies. The guy the whole play is about is gone. Where the hell do you go from there? Well, the second act starts with the disclosure that due to a curious proviso in Dandy's will, Gitlo's brother, Tiger, inherits the entire fortune if he merely signs on the dotted line. If he fails to do so within an hour, though, the estate will be donated to the local church. Tiger is also de-mented enough to throw it all away just to spite the rest of his kin. Without any break in avarice, the second act explodes into an even more frenzied struggle, this time to convince Tiger to keep the money and "save" the family.

Just when all looks lost, into the middle of all this bursts Tiger's half-caste prostitute girlfriend, Palace (sure, why not), a character we've heard about through the entire play, but not seen until now. Palace rips through the family with the purity and power of a tornado, blasting their hypocrisy and greed and setting Tiger straight. Her character knocks the play on its ear and catapults the action to its shocking conclusion.

Palace was an electrifying, star-making role, and when the production moved to the Old Vic, Sophie Okonedo joined the cast to play her. Sophie would go on to be nominated for an Oscar for *Hotel Rwanda* and win a Tony for *A Raisin in the Sun*, but at this point she was still an unknown—albeit a gorgeous, shatteringly talented one. Her friend Ben Daniels also joined the cast to play Tiger, which was ironic in that while he was playing the doomed, surly, lunatic junkie, he was actually a very sweet, jovial man.

During rehearsals, I'll admit that at first I wondered if this soft-spoken, apprehensive, British Nigerian Jewish girl and this lovely gay guy could pull off these hot-blooded, fucked-up, backwoods, hooker-and-dopehead Louisiana lovers. But my concerns could not have been more misplaced. Once performances began, I used to look forward to Sophie's big entrance in the second act every night. I had the honor of her cue line. After a marathon of high-decibel infighting, Tiger has just given away all the family's money to the church. Everyone's devastated. Burning Jewel is weeping, Persia is passed out on the couch, and Gitlo (me) turns on Tiger furiously, spitting (in my Southern accent), "You didn't have to do that! You didn't have to ruin all our lives!" (I pronounced it "lahvs," because, you see, I am a master of dialects.) There'd be a dramatic pause; then Sophie would charge on from stage left, bellowing, "Tiger! Did you took that money or not!" and proceed to wipe up the stage with all of us. It was fun to be there for Sophie's instant command of the stage, and exhilarating to watch her stun the audience before steering the play to its end.

In retrospect, I suppose I should have seen it coming. The show had been running for a couple of months to enraptured crowds, the theater was a joy to play in, the new set was spectacular and haunting, and I was performing in a critically adored, honest-to-God West End hit. Something had to go wrong.

Sophie's main mode of transport around London was her bicycle, but one day she'd had an accident. We suspected it was a bit more serious than she let on, but she was nothing if not a trooper. She showed up to work, took a couple of painkillers, and vowed to carry on despite her injury that day. The show must go on! We cherished her dedication.

As performances go, that night's was turning out to be a fairly unremarkable one. The audience was a little less responsive than usual, but that was it. We still had time to bring it around. The second act proceeded in a very businesslike manner, but I hoped for a little spark to ignite our rapport with them. An actor never knows what will suddenly engage a crowd in a new and special way. It could be a tiny moment of intimacy, slightly different timing on a joke, an instance of true spontaneity, or (ominous chord) something else entirely.

The descendants fought as they did every performance. Tiger, as he did every night, gave away the money. The family lay scattered about the stage in shell-shocked dismay. Burning Jewel was crying, Mom was passed out, I turned to Tiger, as always, and howled in rage, "You didn't have to do that!" And then I added a hint of self-pity to my reading of the last bit: "You didn't have to ruin all our *lah-ves!*"

And then there is that dramatic pause.

That very long dramatic pause.

That dramatic pause that is now milking the moment a little bit too much.

That dramatic pause that is now a big, long, unnerving, and gaping dramatic *silence* as all of us on the stage realize:

There's no Sophie.

Eyes grow wide. Panicked glances dart among the cast. Tiger is dumbstruck. Burning Jewel has stopped all pretense of sobbing, and our mom, supposedly in a stupor, has secretly opened the peeper facing upstage to surmise what the hell is going on.

In an only somewhat pathetic attempt to deny the obvious, I trot out probably the oldest tactic in the actor-trying-to-hold-the-show-together arsenal: the repeat-the-line-again-and-hope-the-right-thing-happens-this-time gambit.

I work myself into an indignant growl: "You didn't have to do that." I add a "No!" for good measure and then yelp with increased volume, "You didn't have to ruin all our *l-a-a-a-a-ahves!*"

More silence.

I strive mightily to resist the urge to turn around and look stage left to see if maybe, just maybe, she's just hanging around there, waiting to come onstage. I hammer my gaze at Tiger. However, he no longer seems like Tiger. He seems a lot more like Ben Daniels, a nice, concerned guy whose eyes plead with me to figure out what to do next. That's it; I can resist no longer. I turn stage left, only to realize to my horror that my character has no reason to look that way, unless he is, say, expecting a character we've never seen before to burst onstage and bring the play to its conclusion. I whip back around and lamely continue my angry tirade with the only epithet that comes to my mind at that moment: "You . . . *jerk!*"

Ben can't seem to muster a reply. More agonizing silence.

My mind races. *Shit! If Sophie doesn't come on, there is no way to end this fucking show! We're screwed! Is there anything I can say here? Jesus Christ, anything?! Fuck! There has to be someth . . .*

Just then I remember a monologue that my character used to have at this point in the play but that had been cut for time. Amazingly, it jumps to mind. *Maybe if I vamp long enough she'll show!* I launch in: "Y'own fuckin' lah-f so shot to hell, no 'mount of good fortune fallin' on ya like this here today . . . fell right on yo' head!"

Ben's eyes, already saucers, distend further.

I continue. "No. You had to pull everybody else down." It occurs to me that Ben has never heard this monologue before, because it was cut in previews of the first production, when someone else played Tiger. He thinks I'm just making this shit up off the top of my head. I blunder on. "You ain't gonna live long, brother. I can see into the future here, all a sudden, an' I see you dead." Ben looks more and more alarmed with every word. "Real fuckin' cold." He must be thinking, *Jon has lost his bloody mind.*

It's now when I take another gigantic pause in the hope that somehow, some way, Sophie has gotten to stage left and has just been waiting for a gigantic pause (such as this one) to shoot into the action.

Nope.

I take a deep breath and menacingly finish off the monologue: "Ain't a threat; it's a promise. You're dead, Tiger. So live fast. You a walkin' ghost."

A-a-a-a-a-and that's it. There wasn't any more of it. I try to figure out how to extend the monologue, but it's a little hard to top threatening your brother with murder. I've got nothing.

Ben sees that I'm finished and finally manages a reply:

"Gitlo . . . shut up."

Oh, that fixes everything. Thanks, Ben. I look at Burning Jewel. Nothing. I look at the priest. Nothing. Dad. Nothing. I look stage left. Still nothing.

Then, from stage right, Guy Manning, who plays the lawyer, pops in and shouts, "I got Balford Sartor on the phone!"

Guy actually has this line later in the play. When he says it, I am supposed to run offstage to answer the phone. At this moment, Guy Manning is my favorite motherfucking guy on planet Earth because he's given me a reason to *get the hell offstage.*

"God grant me a golden tongue!" I say, and head right. I stop when I hear the booming sound of footsteps behind me, and I turn to realize that inexplicably, almost everyone in the cast is now following me offstage. Gitlo's sister, Tiger, the maid, my dad, even the priest all seem to suddenly have a compelling interest in answering this phone call with me. I turn to look at them and they all mumble variations of, "Balford," "Yes," "Very important," "To talk . . . yes." I can't blame them, so we all head off.

Once in the wings I whirl on my castmates with a fierce whisper: "What happened to Sophie!?" Many freaked-out replies. Nobody knows. Rumors fly. Furious speculation. Then a stricken Guy nearly shouts, *"Susan's still out there!"* We all turn to realize we've left poor Susan Tracy, the actress playing Mother—the one who was supposed to be out cold—lying outstretched on the chaise in the middle of the stage with no one else there. She's just lying out there while the audience sits in stunned, bewildered noiselessness. It was like in *Full Metal Jacket* when the platoon left that GI bleeding out in the middle of sniper alley.

I bark/whisper, "Never leave a man behind!" and exhort Ben and the priest back out onstage to retrieve her. I often quote *Raising Arizona* in times of stress, and then send other people to fix things. Turns out the guy playing the priest, Kieron Jecchinis, was actually in *Full Metal Jacket*! He was exactly the man for the job. He and Ben venture out cautiously. Then Ben's brilliant improvisational mind kicks in as he haltingly says, "Preacher, let's . . . take Mama . . . upstairs."

Thanks again, Ben. He and Kieron manfully attempt to hoist Susan on their shoulders, which is harder than it looks, and carry her up the stairs. Ever so slowly.

Out of nowhere a thunderous metallic *thump*!

I turn to see that the massive riveted-steel fire curtain has dropped to the stage. I know that's what it is because it says across it in huge letters, FIRE CURTAIN. Apparently James, the stage manager, has decided to put this performance out of its misery.

At this point, the audience must be thinking the play has just ended, or there is a fire. And what an ending: My brother gave up the money, I vaguely threatened his life and got a phone call that everybody in the family as well as our household help and a local clergyman needed to take, and then Tiger helped Mama upstairs. Great stuff. At this point, they were probably hoping for the fire.

The word *smattering* was coined several hundred years ago just to describe the amount of applause we experienced at that moment. Other words to describe it are *hesitant* and *confused*.

The stage manager's voice comes over the PA with the incredibly smooth, reassuring calm of a BBC newscaster during the Blitz. "Ladies and gentlemen, due to unforeseen circumstances, we must suspend the play momentarily. We will resume shortly. Thank you for your patience."

Backstage, I'm admiring James's placid delivery when he spins around and full-on shouts, "Where *the fuck* is Sophie!"

Now that the shit is, once again, truly going down, I'm disappointed to note that due to the lack of assholes and crazies in our company, there's no one to become suddenly, eerily calm!

Costumers, dressers, even the wig maker are hastily dispatched to scour the dressing rooms, basement, and wings. I can hear doors being flung open and slammed shut, the thudding footfalls of people bounding up and down stairs in a frenetic search. More rumors fly. Did she quit? Is she out at the pub? Abducted?

"Here she is!" Claire, the wardrobe assistant, appears at the bottom of the stairs with her arm around a sobbing Sophie Okonedo. "I'm so sorry," Sophie says through intermittent heaves. Turns out the painkillers she took for her injuries knocked her out. She hadn't even changed into her costume when she went out like a light. "I'm so sorry," she repeated to anyone who'd listen. "I'm so s—"

"Fuck it!" James barks. "Get out there!"

The cast hastily reassemble onstage. "We'll start from the line before her entrance," I urgently say, like I know what I'm doing.

There is an electric moment just before the curtain rises. If we didn't have the audience's full attention before, we certainly have it now.

Up goes the fire curtain; I compose myself, work up an angry head of steam, and start in: "You didn't have to do that, Tiger. You didn't have to ruin all our lah-ves!"

Dramatic pause.

Nothing.

Seriously, nothing at all.

Are you fucking kidding me?

I do the slow-burn take of all time as I pivot stage left.

From the blackness of the wings I hear a choked sob. Then a sniff. Then the imploring voice of Claire plaintively begging Sophie, "Just say 'Tiger. . . .'"

My shoulders collapse in despair. I give up.

Then from stage left I hear a tiny, timid, tremulous, "Tiger . . . ?"

Thank Christ! I turn around. Sophie is standing onstage, but something is off. I realize she is still completely in her civilian clothes. Somehow this trailer-trash Louisiana prostitute buys her clothes from H&M. She cautiously ventures, "Did you . . . took that money, or . . . not?" as though she's never said any of those words before in her life. The maid chimes in with her line, "What she doin' here?" Burning Jewel screams, "Git yo ass outta here!?" Sophie gains volume and confidence on her next line; she starts prowling the stage, a bayou hellcat in a sporty, reasonably priced ensemble.

At one point she gesticulates wildly, something she'd always done at this moment, but this time it's special because all of her civilian bracelets (that she doesn't usually wear in the show) fly off her wrists, arc across the stage, and clatter to the floor.

But God help me, the audience is rapt. They explode with laughter at the slightest provocation. They gasp at the dramatic revelations, and openly weep at the tragic ending. The actual end of the play is greeted with a standing ovation and hoots of enjoyment.

Oh, well, if that's all it takes to get you guys interested.

As you may have guessed, because of that night, my new actor's nightmare is the "something happens that stops the whole fucking show" one. Even though this one turned out okay in the end, it is something I never wish to live through again.

In Sophie's defense, it's hard to play a character that shows up only an hour and a half after the show starts. You are required to be there a half hour before curtain up, but must sit around on pins and needles, waiting for your entrance. It's an odd sort of purgatory. You're neither in the show nor out of it.

900 Oneonta was eventually nominated for an Olivier Award (the British equivalent of the Tony Awards) for best play. David Beaird lost the category to a play by Arthur Miller, pretty much the only great playwright of the twentieth century who had not been mentioned by that *Times* reviewer. The play ran long enough to end up at yet another theater, one where, as legend tells it, Sophie missed her entrance again. By that time Eddie Izzard had taken over the role of Gitlo from me.

I suppose I'll have to read his book to find out how that one turned out.

Chapter 20
Corn? When Did I Have Corn?

Who doesn't love a good, juicy rumor?

Specifically, who doesn't love a good, juicy rumor about Carol Channing?

Not I, as I sat among friends one night many years ago. I'd been performing in London on and off for the past nine months and had returned to an America that hadn't even noticed I was gone. So I decided to do a bit of career resuscitation with a small burst of publicity. The next day I was scheduled to appear on *Late Night with Conan O'Brien*—this was in the midnineties, early in the show's run—and I knew that I would be appearing alongside the great singing and acting Broadway legend Carol Channing. Actually, the conversation about the offer went like this:

My publicist: They want you to go on *Conan.*

Me: Okay. Who else is on?

My publicist: They got a monkey. And Carol Channing.

Me: Great. Count me in.

Mentioning my coguests to my friends around me that night, someone chimed in with the promise of scurrilous Carol Channing dirt. She knew somebody who had been on tour with Channing in a production of the show she's most famous for, *Hello, Dolly!* Notice how this particular rumor—I'll get to it—is already two persons removed before you even read it. Keep that in mind.

What I heard that night was that Ms. Channing, while being an incredibly nice lady to work with, might have had uncontrollable digestive-tract issues. I'll spare you the gory details of what my friend regaled us with—maybe just teasing you with Channing at one point saying in her unmistakable Kewpie doll rasp, "Corn? When did I have corn?"—but let's just say it was not the type of unconfirmed gossip about a famous person you want swimming around in your head the night before you're about to meet said famous person.

The next day I arrived at 30 Rockefeller Center and was greeted by a perky NBC page. Mere moments later, Carol Channing walks up, friendly, gracious, lively, sporting those big glasses that memorably sit on her lollipop head, and wearing . . . a beautiful white pantsuit. White. Like a pesky little virus, the rumor I'd heard the previous night wormed its way into my brain, as I thought, *Boy, I sure hope that's just not true.*

In fact, I tried to spin this worry and what I was seeing into something positive: *Actually, with that outfit, she's incredibly confident if she is,* I thought. *That might just blow the incontinence rumor out of the water!*

Pleasantries exchanged, the page said, "Ms. Channing, Mr. Cryer, come this way." We're led to the elevator, we step in, and the door closes, after which I am suddenly struck by the unmistakable smell of what I can only call, without mincing any words, poop. We're talking a stench, something pervasive, unignorable, and not artificial. This wasn't a cut-rate cleaning chemical, or the lingering after-odor of a lunch left out too long. It was something biologically processed, released organically, and making its home in the atmosphere.

My brain was now working overtime. *Oh, no*, I'm thinking. *Carol Channing—Broadway legend—has lost control of her bowels right before she's about to go on a TV show wearing a white pantsuit! This woman's a stage icon! This can't be happening!* It had to be maybe the most awkward and discomfiting moment of my life.

I looked over nervously, and she was smiling. Not a care in the world. But when I glanced over at the page, I was met with a decidedly sheepish look. She knew, too. She knew, too! And still that odor was all over, daring you to transform every muscle in your face into an expression of disgust.

When the doors finally opened, I walked out quickly, while the page motioned in one direction and said, "Ms. Channing, your dressing room's down this way." I barely let the page get out of her mouth where my dressing room was before I urgently motioned her aside.

"This is terrible!" I feverishly whispered. "Somebody's got to do something! You smelled that, right?"

"Yes," she replied.

"Carol Channing just lost control of her bowels in the elevator!" I hissed.

A confused look settled over the page's face. "Oh, wait, no, no," she said. "We just brought up the monkey in that elevator."

When I told Conan that story much later (not on the air, of course), he couldn't contain himself. He thought it was the funniest thing he'd ever heard. I'm just grateful there was no real crisis and that the only thing helplessly leaking was my overactive imagination. Carol is indeed a Broadway legend, and now that I think about it, a woman of such incredible grace and poise that she never once said out loud or let on with her face what *she* had to have been thinking: *Boy, that Matthew Broderick smells like* shit.

Chapter 21
P-Choo . . . P-Choo! P-Choo!

When actors are in high demand they get offers left and right. We may end up having meetings with directors and such, but we won't have to actually audition. We won't be asked to prove we can do the part. But those periods are few and far between. The rest of the time actors spend a large portion of our lives auditioning.

Hot Shots! had been a hit, but hadn't revived the demand for me as a performer, so I auditioned quite a bit.

When people hear I tried out for and didn't get the role of Chandler on *Friends*, the prevailing response is that it was the biggest of missed opportunities. That I was "this close" to landing an incredibly popular role. That I could have starred on one of the most beloved and defining sitcoms of the 1990s.

"Oh, what might have been," they say, when the right response is, "Boy, that show would have been a lot different."

Actors get roles for all manner of reasons, and they don't get roles for a similarly wide variety of reasons, too. The subtleties in tonality that land one actor a part while making every other actor not right for that part can be incredibly hard to distinguish, and often come down to a strange mixture of prejudice, talent, luck, and circumstance.

In the case of Chandler, I was doing *900 Oneonta* in London and got a call at three a.m. from Marta Kauffman, one of the creators/producers of what was then titled *Six of One*, an incredibly funny and intelligent woman, yet evidently someone who didn't understand that the Earth actually rotates, causing night to fall in places that aren't Los Angeles. But never mind. When Marta calls, I wake up, and she quickly said, "I'm writing this script and I want you to put yourself on tape for it. We have a casting director in London who can do this, but it has to be a rush, because we're casting now."

I was groggy when the phone rang, but now I wasn't. I said, "Okay, great! Can you send me the lines?"

"Well, do you have a fax machine?" she asked.

"No, but I can hook up my computer to the phone line here, and receive a fax on my computer!" Were you to be reading that response of mine in 1993, you might just think I was from the future, so snazzy was my technological capability at that time. What I didn't grasp, though, was that the British phone jacks didn't work with my Yank modem jack, and I didn't have the proper converter. (So much for that snazziness.) But I managed to rig a connection, which took an hour to get working. (Why wasn't I in *War Games*, again? Never mind.) The fax came in—it's now four a.m.—and I got down to the business of prepping for the audition.

The Chandler monologue she sent over was a riot, and I could tell it was a great character. The next day, on very little sleep, I met up with a British casting director, who recorded it, then sent off the tape to Warner Bros., where . . . apparently no one got it. I learned this later from Mark Saks, a friend (and Stagedoor alum) in the casting department there who said that the tape was stuck in customs, and that they'd cast Matthew Perry without ever seeing it. *Oh, what might have been*, you've already started thinking, I can tell.

Well, the reality is, I was terrible on that tape. This is not just me trying to make myself feel better about a lost part, excusing how tired I was,
or misinterpreting the British casting director, who didn't seem to get any
of the jokes. This is an assessment with independent verification from my
casting director pal Mark, who eventually saw the tape once it cleared
customs, and will vouch to anybody who asks that had that tape made it
through and been seen by everyone, I would never have gotten the part in
a million years.

Besides, here's the only sane, realistic way to look at that never-was
opportunity: Matthew Perry is fucking great on that show! *Friends*
wouldn't be the same sitcom with me playing Chandler. Matthew's distinctive line delivery and physicality were a gold mine for those writers, and that was something only he had. (I heard it was based on the
mannerisms of a close friend of his.) Matthew deserved every bit of
the massive success he got from it, and frankly, it personally feels great to
lose a part to somebody who knocks it out of the park. What feels terrible
is when the great role goes to someone who fails at it. That's when you
start wondering if the people in charge didn't know what they wanted,
and that if you'd just had the chance to read for someone else, if, if, if, if . . .
That's a spiral you want to avoid.

Around that time I had another, similar situation regarding an audition. I was on a late-night flight from Los Angeles to New York, reading a
script for an independent movie. Ah, independent movies: a chance to
work incredibly hard in terrible conditions for very low pay on a movie
that no one will ever see. Plus, they wanted me to come in the very next
morning. That's woefully little time to prepare, and the situation wasn't
helped by how confused I was by the story, which shifted back and forth
in time, and the brazen talkiness of the lines involved—long foulmouthed
monologues, one of which I was supposed to read at the audition. Getting
in at midnight, drowsy and bewildered, I thought, *This is really brutal. I
don't know how I'm supposed to do this.* I was dreading going in to audition
the following day.

Then, in the morning, a call came from my sister. Her mother-in-law had taken ill, requiring her and her husband to go out to Long Island on very short notice. Would I take care of my niece while they made this sudden trip? Yes! I now had a reason not to audition: family emergency!

I called the producer, who was not thrilled about the news. "We were really excited about seeing you. Are you sure you can't come in? Bring your niece!"

I said, "My niece is four. You want me to do this filthy monologue in front of my niece?" (Reason number two: I'm a protective uncle!)

"Please, we're begging you to come," he pleaded.

"No, I can't. I'm sorry."

Well, that part was Mr. Pink and the movie was *Reservoir Dogs*, Quentin Tarantino's iconic calling card as a talent to watch. That movie put him on the map, and yes, what helped put him there were the outlandish time shifts in the plot, and the legendary cursing, the stuff that for some reason dissuaded me from auditioning. That was a hard-won lesson in being open to new things. The truly funny part of my refusal to try out, however, is what I realized after the movie came out and caused a sensation: Had I gone in and done that vividly profane monologue with my cute little niece sitting on my lap, how could I have *not* gotten that part? Quentin would have loved that shit!

But again, the saving grace of my misreading of the situation was that Steve Buscemi was great as Mr. Pink. As it stands, the movie works, and they got the right guy.

Sometimes your own prejudices sink you before you can even allow yourself to do well. When I was a teenager, I scored a meeting with an Oscar-winning filmmaker at his Upper East Side apartment. While I was excited about auditioning for a man whose work I admired, the script for the movie was, I thought, complete crap. I was eighteen years old, you see, and had seen several movies, thus acquiring critical thinking skills vastly greater than those of an Academy Award–winning director. As I was doing the scene for him at his dining room table, I'm almost positive he could detect in my eyes the diminishing interest in having to read dialogue I thought was so dumb and clichéd.

Well, the director was John Avildsen of *Rocky* fame, and the movie was *The Karate Kid*, and after my intellectually disdainful interpretation of young, bullied Daniel, Avildsen asked me to sit in his kitchen while he brought in the next kid: Ralph Macchio. I perched myself in such a way that I could surreptitiously peek in on Ralph, who delivered the same scene I had just read moments before. But where I had bought out emotionally, he was simply, directly sincere. Ralph read the lines with apparently no greater goal than meaning what he was saying, and sounding as if they were occurring to him for the first time.

I wasn't surprised to hear he got the role, but when I saw the movie eventually in its smash box-office run, the triteness I was quick to brand it with had been replaced by something honest, charming, and rousing. It drove home the lesson that sometimes the things we consider clichés can be transformed if they're done with a complete lack of cynicism. Every story's been told. It's how you tell it that makes the difference.

Sometimes you know the movie's going to be interesting, the part's going to be great, and yet you're utterly stymied by something about the actual audition. I auditioned for *Platoon* to play Bunny, the cocky young soldier eventually played by Kevin Dillon. It was an intense scene, involving killing a one-legged Vietnamese man, and on top of that, writer/director Oliver Stone had created a special audition script that combined the dialogue of several characters into one. That often stems from there not being enough dialogue for the character to make for a whole audition. The other characters' dialogue allows a director to then see a lot of different facets in one reading.

What made the audition uncomfortable was that I couldn't answer a key question: How do you act out shooting at a one-legged Vietnamese person without a prop gun, a well-timed sound effect, or, for that matter, a one-legged Vietnamese person? Do you do it with your finger and thumb extended, the way a kindergartener might when playing cops and robbers?

Do you pantomime holding a nonexistent gun? Do you bring in a real gun at the risk of scaring the producers and/or getting the cops called but also being forever remembered as a *badass*? And in the act of killing, do you make a sound, or say, "Boom! I'm shooting now!" In the end, I went with a variation on the kindergartener that was lame yet somehow audacious in its stupidity.

And just let me add this: You haven't lived until you've seen the face of the director of *Natural Born Killers* as he watches you scream, "Dance! You one-legged motherfucker, dance!" and then finish off with a finger-pointing, "P-choo . . . P-choo, p-choo!"

Please refer to the "eventually played by Kevin Dillon" sentence above to be reminded of that audition's perhaps inevitable result.

Then there are the auditions that just go south due to circumstances beyond anyone's control. I was the first actor to audition for the lead role in the Coen brothers' *The Hudsucker Proxy*, due to the fact that I lived two blocks from their New York apartment at the time, which was on the Upper West Side right next to Riverside Park, where I grew up playing with my friends. It was as simple as Joel and Ethan were gearing up to try people out, they knew I was in town and so close, and did I want to swing by and read it? Well, sure!

As I got ready to try out in their home, I remember saying to them, "Wow, this will be the first time you've heard your screenplay read aloud by somebody else." They took a moment and cautiously said, "Yeah." I seized the chance to joke, with a little seriousness, "Then if anything's wrong with this, you've got to fix it. It won't be my fault, right?" They seemed to find it funny.

It was a pretty relaxed audition, and we were having a convivial time when there was suddenly a frenzied knock. It was a woman who lived next door, and she was freaking out. "My husband fell!" she cried. "He was getting out of the bathtub and he just collapsed! Can you help?!"

So we all rushed over to their apartment, and there on the floor was this elderly man, dazed, completely naked, and wet. We gathered around him, asking if he was all right, assisting him to his feet, and securing a towel around him. It was painfully obvious that we were trying to avoid looking at the parts of this man that are usually hidden in normal social interactions, but really, on somebody that old and naked, there's no good place to look.

After we parked him in a chair, the extent of our actual ability to "help" when none of us were doctors (at that point I couldn't even say, "I play one on TV" yet) became abundantly clear. In fact, I'm not sure it "helped" this elderly gentleman at all to know that not only Duckie, but also the guys who directed *Barton Fink* and *Raising Arizona* got to see him without his clothes on. We made small talk as we waited for the EMTs. After the medical team arrived, we said our good-byes to this big, old naked guy, who appeared to be in good hands. It seemed the time to bid adieu to the Coens, too, and we exchanged awkward "well, that was memorable" farewells. I didn't get the part, but for a brief time there it certainly felt as if I'd been in a Coen brothers movie.

By the time I cowrote, produced, and starred in my own movie, *Went to Coney Island . . .* (hard work? check; terrible conditions? check; low pay? check; no audience? *check!*), I'd had enough experience auditioning to know a lot about the process. But then I got to see it from the other perspective, as the one doing the hiring, watching hopeful after hopeful come through the door and show what he or she had to offer. I considered my years in the business an invaluable resource in picking the right cast, but I also naively assumed each actor we were going to see had the chance to win the part. If you get the opportunity to try out for a role, why show up if you don't have that belief, right?

That's why it was shocking to then see actors I revered from Broadway, films, television, wherever, come in to read for this tiny indie and just blow it. I was even stunned a few times. (Sorry again. Names are being withheld to protect my pretty face.) The first couple of instances I felt sort of a sinking in the pit of my stomach, but the more it happened, the greater was my realization that auditioning is not just something very hard that an actor endures, but also a process that by its very nature fells many very quickly, for—as I mentioned earlier—a wide variety of reasons.

If you're not right for a part, no amount of preparation, confidence, or invention is going to get you there. I watched actors step up and nail it, yet they weren't right for the part. How did I know? I just knew. Think of auditioning as going full throttle toward what can only be a halfway mark: Once you've done your job going up for a role, the rest is absolutely beyond your control. It's an epiphany that has given me tremendous peace going into auditions now, because I think of them like this: If I'm the one, I'm going to get it, and if I'm not, no sweat.

My advice, then, to aspiring actors is to enjoy the ride. Do the hard work, make your choices, but then have a good time: Say hi to the casting director you haven't seen in a while, catch up on current events, wave with a smile to the colleague in the waiting area you think is your competition, then get the fuck out and go have a nice meal with a friend.

You'll have a healthy life as an actor if you realize auditions aren't missed opportunities. They're parts you weren't supposed to get.

A final note about the *Coney Island* auditions. Actors are pretty used to reading for a part opposite a director or casting person delivering the other lines with barely any emotion or affect. It's not as weird as it sounds, because you want to be able to focus on the man or woman vying for the part. But because this was my movie and I was going to be sharing the screen with whomever we picked, I read with the auditioners. This one young man came in, and between us we delivered a mighty fine scene. At the end, you could sense the exhilaration from him, and he turned to me and said, "Wow, thank you. That was great!"

I said, "Hey, no, thank *you*! Thank you!"

We offered him the part the next day, and a couple of days after that, I ran into him on Sixth Avenue. "Dude," I said, "you're going to do the part, right?"

"Yeah! Yeah!" he said excitedly, before adding, "And by the way, you're the best reader I've ever worked with. *You* should act!"

Chapter 22
Not Really an Answer to the Winter Part

When the cheaply made comedy *The Brothers McMullen* became an indie sensation at the Sundance Film Festival in 1995, it seemed to spark a wave of similarly talky, shoestring-budgeted relationship movies set in as few locations as possible. The vibe among moviemakers and budding creative types suddenly seemed to be, *No excuses. Quit sitting around in a bar complaining about your lack of work opportunities. Sit around in a bar and make a movie!*

Actually, my friends and I had come to that conclusion years before.

By the early nineties my film career was in the doldrums, which had done wonders for my free time, so I did a lot of hanging out with my New York friends Richard Schenkman, the director, and Adam Oliensis, an actor and playwright. One day we looked at our combined skills—directing, writing, acting—and realized, *We've got most of what we need right here!* We came up with a story about guys like us in New York, single and struggling to understand who they are and how women fit into their lives, and decided each of us would go off and write scenes alone, then come back and hash them out with the other two. About a week later we had a movie script about four guys and their romantic misadventures, which we called *The Pompatus of Love.*

A natural theme emerged from our individual writing sessions: that we were a generation of guys raised to believe that communication fixed everything, but we were discovering that it also had incredible limitations. In spite of the barrage of words you could exchange with a prospective mate, you weren't immune to further cloudiness just from talking more. (The title refers to the line from that Steve Miller song "The Joker," which has spurred a million "What the hell does 'pompatus' mean?" conversations. More on that later.)

One of the scenes Adam wrote really nailed the idea that honesty is a tool used as much to control and/or hurt others as any willful deception. "Just say what you mean!" this girl says, and the guy responds, "You can't say what you mean, because the saying is tiny, but the meaning is huge!"

We kept the script deliberately loose and rough, a free-form jazz improvisation of sorts, and though we originally envisioned it as a DIY project, we suddenly got a surprising amount of interest from actual producers, including *Moonlighting* creator Glenn Gordon Caron. When the usual Hollywood stalling tactics of interest and disinterest started to irk us, though, we set a date for ourselves: If we didn't get it set up by such-and-such day, we were just going to shoot it with whatever we could scrape together ourselves.

Then the appointed day arrived, and we did our gut check. I'd been able to save some of my money from TV gigs, and Richard and Adam had a little bit of money as well. Plus, they knew people who had money. Then Richard worked an in with a financier who knew Kristin Scott Thomas. She wanted to be in the movie, which led to French money, because Kristin was especially revered as an actress in France. *Et voilà*, it was a real movie.

We were amazed. We had wrought something from nothing, a real film from the three of us sitting around bellyaching. And we were going to be shooting in New York, our hometown! I hadn't shot anything in New York since that Zestabs commercial when I was four. We had a cast that included Adrian Pasdar as a womanizer, Tim Guinee as a verbose playwright, and Adam as a lovable lug of a plumber. I played an overanalytical therapist. The women in our characters' lives were played by Kristin, Mia Sara, Dana Wheeler-Nicholson, Kristen Wilson, and Paige Turco.

One of my favorite memories from putting the movie together was Richard telling me about a singer/songwriter he knew who had been a backup singer for Michael Jackson, but wanted a solo career. He asked her early on if she'd record a new version of "The Joker" for the movie, and she said yes. Then he asked me to go see her at a club on the Sunset Strip, and she was terrific. I remember thinking, *Why isn't she huge?* Well, she soon was. It was Sheryl Crow.

We were a tiny indie movie, but in New York, as long as you're willing to pay for a cop, you could get the same treatment *Law & Order* gets. When Richard was directing a scene in the Times Square triangle between Seventh and Broadway—one of the city's busiest, most iconic locations—he simply asked our cop, "Can we shut down the traffic?"

"Okay," the cop said, and promptly halted Times Square traffic so we could shoot. Cars were honking, bystanders were pissed, but it felt like we had this magical cinematic immunity. Normal human rules did not apply. I remember at that moment I looked up at a Jumbotron and saw a pop music top-ten countdown, and there she was: Sheryl Crow. She now had a hit single. It felt as if the world were bending to meet us. This was surely a good omen that we were onto something.

Again, my delusion about these things caught up to me. Going to the Cannes Film Festival market to sell the film proved to be a learning experience as a producer. There was a real disconnect for me between the opulence and glamour of the Croisette—the famous promenade lined with huge ads for blockbuster movies on one side, and a beach full of topless women on the other—and the dingy hotel suite we were set up in by the company that was representing us, where we had to sell the movie to buyers from around the world. The level of bullshit showmanship involved to hawk a movie was something my heart was just not in, and I had money in this labor of love. That part of the business—the razzmatazz P. T. Barnum aspect, schmoozing a guy with five theaters in Lichtenstein who might be interested in your film—has never been a talent of mine, although Richard did try to bed one of the potential German buyers, and I thought that was awfully sweet.

Also, our financier turned out to be a complete douche. One of our production assistants was a great guy named Phil who was dating my sister, Robin. As a favor, he took the job making no money, but figured he'd be getting a wealth of on-set experience. One night he was slated to drive actors back to the production office, and we were so tired that a bunch of us leaned on him to do so as quickly as he could, whereupon he got a speeding ticket. I told our moneyman that the production had to pay the fine, since we'd told him to go fast, but this asshole refused. It wasn't even a lot of money, but for Phil it was more than he had, and he eventually lost his license for a while over not being able to pay the fine.

Another dickish thing the guy did was, well, lose the film rights. When he never paid the Screen Actors Guild for residuals—a minuscule amount—the union had the movie seized, and they eventually sold it for less than ten thousand dollars without our knowledge. A movie that cost a million dollars to make was sold for a pittance because of this prick. I'm proud of *The Pompatus of Love*, even though it didn't exactly set the indie world on fire. And we did get an unqualified rave in *The New York Times*, which is never not fun.

But did you know that we also solved one of rock music's great mysteries? That's right, people: In the course of making this movie, I found out what the hell *the pompatus of love* means.

Richard, Adam, and I had been as puzzled as everyone else about the meaning of this enigmatic lyric. That its definition was essentially unknowable was a part of the metaphor we were constructing about love. But it had to have come from somewhere.

See, Steve Miller was a huge fan of fifties R & B; he quoted several famous lyrics in both "The Joker" and another song he wrote called "Enter Maurice." If you recall, "The Joker" went like this: "Some people call me Maurice, / 'Cause I speak of the pompatus of love." Well, "Enter Maurice" featured this doozy: "My dearest darling, come closer to Maurice so I can whisper / sweet words of epismetology in your ear and speak to you of / the pompatus of love."

Richard and I were content to let it remain unknown, but while we were in postproduction, a friend of his alerted us to the fact that there existed a doo-wop song called "The Letter" by a group called the Medallions, which had a spoken verse that appeared to contain the line, "Oh, my darling, let me whisper sweet words of epismetology and discuss the pompatus of love." Jackpot! Clearly there was a link.

But Steve never talked about it in interviews. Ever. Neither confirmed nor denied. For me, the resemblance was just too close. The Medallions song was written by its lead singer, a guy named Vernon Green, but we couldn't find any sheet music to check on the lyric.

So here's where it gets weird. Flash-forward to the release of the film, and I'm on *CBS This Morning* promoting it at the ungodly hour of four a.m. They ask me what the title means and I mention the Medallions and how the lyric is just too close to be a coincidence. Later that day my publicist gets a call from none other than the only other dude in California who was up at four a.m.: Vernon Green himself. He left a number.

We had a great conversation; he talked about growing up in LA with polio in the 1940s and what inspired him to write the song.

"You have to remember, I was a very lonely guy at the time," Green said. "I was only fourteen years old, I had just run away from home, and I walked with crutches."

The song was supposed to be a letter to the woman of his dreams. I asked him what the words meant. Turns out what Steve Miller heard as "epismetology" was actually "pizmotality." Pizmotality! Of course! I thought. That means . . . um . . . uh . . . What does that mean?

"Pizmotality was a way to describe words that were so secret they could only be spoken to the one you loved," he explained.

"Oh. Okay. And what about 'pompatus'?" I inquired, barely containing my anticipation.

He paused, cleared his throat, and said, "That was 'puppetutes.'"

Now it was my turn to pause. "Beg pardon?"

"Puppetutes," he clarified (sort of). "It was a word I made up to mean a secret paper-doll fantasy figure [like a puppet], who would be my everything and bear my children."

"Uh-huh . . . Sure. That . . . makes . . . sense," I ventured. "So one of the great rock mystery lyrics is actually kind of a misquote?"

"I don't know. I've never heard the song."

"You're kidding," I scoffed.

"Nope."

I played "The Joker" over the phone to him and he erupted with laughter.

"That's it!" he said through cackles. "That's it!" He seemed pretty sure the song was referring to his lyric. I was too, quite frankly.

We ended the call on a high. I was glad that my movie gave me the chance to be the guy who made him aware that his legacy would include having influenced one of the defining hit rock songs of the seventies, as well as clearing up one of its most enduring perplexities.

If anything, *The Pompatus of Love* gave me a taste of what's possible when inventing a movie from scratch. We told ourselves we could make a movie, and we did. For someone who aspires to be an artist, that is intoxicatingly empowering.

When Richard and I tried to tackle an independent film again, we seized on an idea that was less commercial, came from a deeper place, and held more meaning for me personally. It arose out of two incidents from my past that I fused into one story.

Remember my life-changing evening at the theater, seeing *Star Wars* with my mother's boyfriend and his son? The son, Anthony, was younger than me by a few years, but he was a great kid. He got along with David Dennis and me, so we looked at him like a little brother of sorts. David and I lost touch with him over the years, until one day around 1989 I was hanging at Sal's, the pizza shop where David worked, when we heard a rumor that Anthony was homeless and living in Central Park. Never one to miss skipping out on a responsibility in order to fuel a distracting curiosity, David exaggerated his concern for our friend and insisted his boss let him off from work and that I join him in looking for Anthony. I felt like I was in school all over again, enabling my hooky-playing buddy. We certainly never thought for a moment that what we heard about Anthony was true.

One of the first places we "looked" was Sheep Meadow, because it housed a big encampment of hippie kids. We walked up to a girl and said, "We're searching for a guy named Anthony; have you seen him?"

"Yeah, I've seen him," she said, and smacked this pile of clothing, which then stood up and revealed itself to be Anthony—a disheveled, out-of-sorts Anthony, who remembered us, but was definitely going through a personal low in his life.

Whoa. It *was* true. We were taken aback, partly because this was the first place we'd stopped, but mostly because our larkish excursion had turned a corner into something we weren't really prepared to face. Anthony seemed to be on something, and wouldn't talk to us when we inquired as to his well-being. He asked for ten bucks, and I gave it to him, and told him if he needed anything else—a shower, change of clothes, whatever—to just ask. David and I walked home shell-shocked. For me, it was as if this charmed experience of mine—fame, money, living my dream—had been replaced by an alternate universe in which shit can go bad.

The other incident that inspired the movie happened around the same time. David called me up one particularly cold New York day and said, "We've got to go to Coney Island."

David's enthusiasm was often just enough to get me to say yes, but occasionally I had to prod. This was one of those times. "David, why do you want to go to Coney Island during the winter?"

"We're gonna ride the rides! The Cyclone, the Parachute Jump! The Wonder Wheel! All that stuff!"

Not really an answer to the "winter" part, so I said, "I'm not sure it's open."

"Sure it is," he said. "It's New York."

I wasn't doing anything else, and logic wasn't going to dissuade him, so I left a note for my girlfriend at the time saying simply, *Went to Coney Island on a mission from God. Be back by five.*

We hopped on the D train and rode it all the way out to Coney Island, and, of course, it was closed.

But we walked around anyway, and it struck me how this historic destination for amusement-seeking New Yorkers could seem so haunted and vaguely terrifying when devoid of humanity. It was an absolutely surreal experience, like being stuck between a glittering past and a devastated future.

This feeling deepened for me when I realized later that David was going through some personal crises of which I wasn't aware. I'd always known that David drank and used drugs from a very early age. Although I always like to say about our friendship—and believe I did, earlier in this very book—that I was his conscience and he was my reason to be naughty, I never indulged in the parts of David's life that involved anything worse than raiding Mom's liquor cabinet. David's life had been hard: The operation he had at twelve to lengthen his shorter leg had worked in terms of preventing scoliosis, but it also left him in a state of fairly constant pain, so that by the time he was fourteen he was smoking cigarettes and weed and drinking heavily, and by sixteen he was using cocaine.

It was never David's wont to push anything on me. In fact, he and Artie—an enthusiastic coke user who could swill stunning amounts of beer—often claimed they weren't high when they clearly were, going so far as to feign ignorance one day when a packet of coke fell out of David's pocket. It was the full-on "how did that get there?" routine. They were oddly protective of my innocence. They wanted me to just be who I was, and I was fine with that. In many ways, David had a presence of mind stoned, drunk, or coked up that I didn't possess cold sober.

But over the years, as our lives diverged, the effect of all that self-medicating and the psychological problems underlying it were starting to show. I'm pretty sure David was high that day at Coney Island, for one thing, and as I would learn, the real reason he wanted to go to this usually cheerful place at so chilly a time of year was less about the weather outside than staving off whatever the gathering storms were inside him.

While Richard and I were holed up in our crappy hotel room selling *Pompatus* at the Cannes Film Festival, my mind kept coming back to these incidents. In looking for a way to process them, Richard and I wrote a movie called (unsurprisingly) *Went to Coney Island on a Mission from God: Be Back by Five*, about two guys—local neighborhood dudes—who hear that an old friend is homeless and head for the eerily abandoned New York tourist destination to find him. I wasn't thinking about making something with box-office juju. I just wanted to use art to process these equally strange experiences of mine, in the hopes that maybe others might feel some kinship toward it. Richard wanted to direct it, and it was low-budget enough that I could put up half the money.

And where was that money going to come from? Doing something I didn't want to do.

If you suddenly got an image of me in front of a dry cleaner's on a very friendly West Hollywood street (see pages 76–77), let me stop you right there. I don't mean that. Get your mind out of the gutter. My eyes are up here. I'm referring to an acting job I didn't want to do, but that paid me a lot.

Ten years before, I had an idealistic view of the compensatory aspects of acting professionally. The last big movie offer I got after the career firebombing that was 1987 was a hotly hyped project called *Young Men with Unlimited Capital*, a fact-based movie about the two twenty-something business types who created Woodstock and got swept up in the world of rock and roll. The deal was for me, Ralph Macchio, and Robert Downey Jr., and the pay was going to be really good. So my manager made the deal. Then Macchio pulled out, followed by Downey, and the movie fell apart.

My deal was pay-or-play, however. During a phone call, I asked manager Marty, "What does that mean?"

He said, "It means, even though they're not going to make the movie, they still have to pay you your salary."

"That can't be right," I said. (I know, I know. Stop gasping.)

"Well, it's how it's done."

I wasn't finished. "Is there anything to be gained by not taking the money?" If Marty's eyes were popping out of his head at the possible loss of a substantial sum of money, considering his cut, his voice didn't betray it. "Because I don't do these things for the money. I want to make the movie. I don't want to screw over these people who are offering me money to be in their movie. They're already hurting anyway since it fell apart."

Marty's voice was calm and only mildly schooling. "No, Jon, they're paying for your time commitment, because you're a valuable part of this. This is the way business is done. They're used to it. They knew it was pay-or-play, they agreed to it, and now they've got to pay you off. There will be no hard feelings, I promise."

And he was right. Honestly, these studio suits don't even respect you unless you're willing to bend them over and give them a good financial rogering, because it helps them accept you as a valuable commodity if you treat them like you're a valuable commodity. "Fuck you; give me my money," is no different to them from, "Nice doing business with you."

But I felt guilt about it. Still do. I always come to whatever I'm doing from the mind-set of an artist. And yet around the time Richard and I were trying to get *Coney Island* made in 1997, I decided to put those ideals away to make art happen, and it felt weird. I had been offered a pilot for a sitcom created by Chuck Lorre, who would later make *Two and a Half Men* but at that time was known as the guy behind *Grace Under Fire* and *Cybill*. I would play an IRS auditor asked by his brother, played by Jim Belushi, to run a nightclub left to us by our dead father. I liked Chuck, I liked Belushi, but I didn't think the character—an uncomplicated nebbish—would be fun, so I turned it down.

That's when I learned that the sexiest word you can say in Hollywood is *no*.

First they offered me more money. Second, they offered me even more money. Third, they offered me even *more* more money. I've had only a few calls from Marty where he's giggling. This was one. The amounts increased until it was so much money I realized, *I can finance* Coney Island *with this*. It was a thirteen-episode commitment, and I'd get paid even if it didn't go past the pilot stage. But I kept saying no. It reached the point where the read-through for the pilot was on a Monday at noon, and when noon passed, they offered me more money.

At twelve thirty p.m. that Monday, I finally said yes, at which point they said, "Great! Get over to the 20th Century Fox lot now, because you've got a read-through to do."

By the time I got there, everybody had been waiting an hour and a half. But Belushi strolled over, said, "Hee-e-e-e-y!" then picked me up, flung me over his shoulder, and carried me to the table, where he promptly dropped me into my chair. Rounds of, "All right!" and, "*Yeaaah!*" and, "This is gonna be *great!*" filled the air as we settled in, but it had gotten so hot in the studio that the AC had to be turned on, huge AC vents that happened to be directly above the table where we were doing the read-through.

The noise of frosty air coursing out of this machine to blanket us was, to put it mildly, deafening. It was so loud that the actors had to shout their lines above the air conditioner just to be heard, the barking sameness of everyone's delivery effectively killing every joke. Meanwhile, panicked

PAs frantically tried to figure out how to shut off the AC. What ensued was the single most disastrous read-through I've ever been a part of, with nary a laugh to be had.

Rehearsals started, and everybody's game face was on. Plus, a sterling cast was assembled, including Polly Draper, and the legendary Abe Vigoda and Tom Poston. That was all great. But all the while I kept feeling weird, because I'd taken the gig for the money. I just could not engage. I never felt good about it. When audience night arrived for the pilot, all the executives were there, agents, friends, family. Pilot-filming night can feel like an opening night on Broadway, and this one was thick with excitement.

When a glitch in editing meant that an outdoor scene we'd prefilmed on a big downtown street wasn't ready, Belushi got all amped and said, "Let's fuckin' do this!" We just performed it again for the audience, and they went nuts. They loved the rest of the show, too, and were on their feet at the end.

I looked around and thought, *This is going to be a success.*

Then I thought, *Oh,* shit.

None of it felt real or organic or good to me. I dreaded its getting picked up. Here I was, still looking for a hit show after a few tries, but what I came to understand was, what I wanted was a job my heart was in. This wasn't it.

Then, like a balloon being pricked, suddenly the network decided Polly Draper wasn't right, and when further casting searches proved fruitless, they threw up their hands and didn't go ahead with the pilot.

To which I said, "Thank *Christ*," took my chunk of money, called Richard and said, "We're golden," and hotfooted it back to New York.

Coney Island came together after a few hiccups that may or may not be familiar to people who toil in independent film. First, a funding source's promised money didn't arrive, which meant I had to front the entire cost of completing principal photography, and once that was finished, we'd run the risk of being stuck with a bunch of great stuff on film, but no money to put it together into a movie.

Second was a nail-biter that we didn't see coming. We had cast Ione Skye of *Say Anything* fame as our female lead just a few days after she had moved to New York City. It was a coup to land her on such a microbudgeted film, especially since I considered that Cameron Crowe film without a doubt the best teen romance of the eighties. We'd notified her agent what days that we'd need her for shooting, but the night before her first day, he called me around ten p.m. to inform me, basically, "We don't know where she is."

Turns out, she was still in the middle of her move, and her agent couldn't reach her to give her the call time. He had phoned her old place, and even her mother—but no one knew where she was. She'd had a phone installed at her new place, but stunningly, nobody actually knew the number. He assured me that he had left her messages and that she'd get back to him.

So we were on location the next morning, in the middle of Rockaway Beach, with a hundred extras who were working for free, and no leading lady.

I'm on my cell phone, pacing back and forth, calling everyone I can possibly think of, and her agent is saying to me, "Look, if you have to hire another actress, I understand."

He understands!? Where were we going to get somebody? She's already an hour late and we're supposed to be shooting! I'm not very good at yelling at people, but I'm getting pretty heated with this guy. So I call another agent and line up the availability of the actress who was our second choice. We're moments away from hiring her. At this point I've got two calls going at once: I'm begging one agent to make a deal on one, and screaming at Ione's agent on the other—when a guy walks by with no ear. I'm shouting in the middle of Rockaway Beach and there's a man on the promenade with absolutely nothing but a hole in the side of his head.

Richard spotted him, then turned to me solemnly and said, "I wept that I had no cell phone, and then I met a man who had no ear."

I burst out laughing, and as I doubled over there came a shout: "We've got her!"

Turns out that a resourceful production coordinator had taken it upon herself to check at Ione's brother's apartment, and sure enough, there she was, sleeping on the sofa. She had no idea we were looking for her. The coordinator drove Ione to the location, she slipped into her wardrobe, and the production continued as though this mishegoss never happened. I shudder to think that had no-ear guy not stopped me cold, I'd've booked that other actress and never gotten to make a movie with Ione Skye.

Once principal photography was finished, I had to wait till I got a few more jobs, just to make enough to get the film out of postproduction. Our final snafu was when a sound-editing house in Hollywood that we hired on the cheap went into bankruptcy, trapping our film behind closed office doors. Our reconnaissance of the sound house had revealed only a mildly vigilant receptionist between us and our film elements. Once again, Richard sweetly volunteered to sleep with her to regain our stuff. It turned out to be unnecessary, though; in the end Richard only had to distract her while I pretended to use the bathroom but in fact made off with our finished edits.

Though our film never made it into any of the big festivals, it had a nice life at smaller festivals around the world, from Rhode Island and Canada to Ghent, Belgium, and even Oldenburg, Germany. Though reviews were mostly positive, a particularly negative one came to be a major milestone for Richard and me. The critic referred to us as "the worst high-profile filmmakers currently working." To which Richard and I rejoiced in unison, "We're high-profile!"

Festival audiences, however, really took to it, and though it's not necessarily a movie I would entertain making today, it holds a special place for me, as the title says, as a mission of sorts. Like David and his all-encompassing enthusiasm, *Coney Island* took hold of me for a while, and seeing it through felt like a major accomplishment.

Perhaps the most interesting side benefit of making it was that it documented most of old Coney Island, a lot of which is gone now. I've read comments on the Internet that say it captures the park at its most haunting and otherworldly, and I find those very satisfying sentiments.

My time in the trenches of independent film was an education in many respects. I learned Richard Schenkman is a great guy to have in your foxhole, and that all those people who tell you not to put your own money into movies are only half right: You won't make a dime, but it will be worth it anyway.

Chapter 23
The Mechanics of Jokedom Department

What is it that I do best?

When I think about that question in terms of my career, it can be boiled down to two "aha" moments that I had while starring on a couple of sitcoms in the nineties.

The first was on *Partners*, a buddy comedy that debuted in the fall of 1994, and was created by two writer/producers from *Friends* named Jeff Greenstein and Jeff Strauss (known collectively as "the Jeffs") and directed by Jim Burrows, perhaps the most highly regarded director of situation comedies, well, pretty much ever (*Taxi, Cheers, Friends*).

As we were rolling film on the very first shot of the pilot, the second assistant was having difficulty with the digital counter on the slate. She tried a couple of abortive claps and then started fiddling with it. In the meantime the camera was still rolling on a single shot of me that was being shown to our studio audience over the monitors.

As I patiently waited for the issue to be resolved I looked into the camera momentarily and the audience started to laugh—a nervous, low roller that subsided quickly. But as the time stretched on, my eyes drifted back and forth from my castmates to the camera again, and each time the laughs got bigger and bigger. I was not mugging or reacting or making any facial expression whatsoever. Just sitting there. And the audience apparently found this hilarious. When the slate was fixed, we proceeded with the scene and the audience was already on board, hooked into these characters and laughing from the first line.

After the scene I joined Jim and the Jeffs at the writer's monitor. They were intrigued by the crowd's reaction and, of course, as people in the business of comedy, trying to dissect it.

We batted it around for a while, and went at it from every angle, until finally I realized it was this: They were laughing at the very idea of me. That I exist in physical space the way I do is just kind of somehow inherently ridiculous. Now, most people, when they come upon this kind of information, would probably have been insulted, but not me. I was thrilled. From the moment I realized it, I accepted it as the gift I truly think it is.

It dawned on me that comedy turns everything I've ever been ashamed of about myself into an asset. My weaknesses, my fears, my anxieties, even my posture, all of them give the audience permission to laugh at me, and laugh they do. And something about the live-audience format for sitcoms came into play as well. Perhaps the close-up attention of the camera combined with the broad-stroke rapport with actual human beings who are watching the show and reacting in real time sparked a discovery in me.

I'd always thought movies were where I wanted to shine, but this was giving me a whole new direction.

The other "aha" moment came on another series I did with the Jeffs called *Getting Personal*, an office comedy that was on the air briefly in 1998.

One day Jeff Strauss gingerly approached me and said, "We have a scene where we might set you on fire." He paused, perhaps waiting for a reaction. I had one.

"Might?" I said.

"We're *going* to set you on fire," he clarified.

The setup was that my character was going out on a blind date with a girl who was very clumsy. She was gorgeous, but she kept hurting me in various ways. It started slowly with a spilled drink, moved up to slamming a car door into my crotch, and ended in a restaurant scene in which we have an intimate moment, I reach across the table to hold her hand, and a candle sets my sweater on fire.

As written, I was supposed to react in a manner something along the lines of, *"Ohmygodohmygodohmygod, I'm on fire! I'm on fire! Fire! Fire! Fire!"* In other words, how anybody would probably react. The real joke was supposed to be what followed: My date grabs a champagne bucket and pours a bunch of ice cubes on me, which does nothing to put out the fire.

But I saw a chance to do something here. My character had been through so much already in the episode that it seemed funnier if his reaction might be as if he fully expected the evening would come to this. We rehearsed the scene, and the way I did it was I looked at my flaming arm, paused, and then said with the blankest expression on my face: "Oh, my God. I'm on fire."

The producers enjoyed it, but I could see the worry in their eyes.

"You sure that's how you're going to do it?" one of them said.

"Let's see what the audience says," I replied.

It killed in front of the audience. I felt it was a gutsy move on my part, for three reasons. One, it was a choice my producer was unsure of. Two, it isn't exactly a realistic response to suddenly being on fire. And last, if it didn't work, I would have blown the gag *and* be sitting there ablaze. Not that I thought the crew wouldn't douse my arm because I spoiled a joke, but you know, weirder things have happened in show business.

Ultimately, it was a moment in which I wanted to assert myself in the Mechanics of Jokedom department, and when it worked, it gave me the belief that I know a thing or two about laugh lines, that you can sometimes take an offbeat approach and it adds that extra bit of surprise. Knowing how much reality and how much ridiculousness with which to imbue a joke can take a lot of mental energy, and it's actorly work I take much pride in.

Oh, wait. Is that what you thought was the big reveal about what I did best? Sitcom lines?

No, no, it's fire gags. I am the *king* of fire gags.

This goes way back to when David Dennis and I used to play Careless Gas Station Attendant. (Again, not really a game, per se, but . . .) David smoked, so he had cans of Ronsonol lighter fluid just lying around. We'd create a puddle of Ronsonol in the street, then run a line of it along the ground, ending in a trickle along either his or my leg. I'm not even sure we went so far as to playact the gas-station-attendant part. We just lit the puddle, and the flame traveled our little pathway until one of us was slapping at our leg going, "Ah! Ah! Ah!" while the other would scream with delight. I promise you I didn't strangle animals in my spare time.

Anyway, when sitcoms offered a chance to learn the exquisite craft of fire gags, I accepted with the unflinching resolve of Kurt Russell in *Backdraft*. This specialty was going to be *mine*. The comedy gods would know my name by the look on my face when my character realizes his arm/leg/hand/whatever is ready to char marshmallows.

I've been on fire a handful of times on *Two and a Half Men*. Nobody approaches me gingerly anymore. Now it's, "This week we're setting you on fire in a new place." Each time I look that producer back in the eye and say, "Bring it on. With accelerant." The time I did a bit where they'd genuinely lit my crotch on fire for the close-up, but then decided to use computer-generated flames for the wide shot, I shook my head and grumbled, "Pussies." Then they thought they'd really gotten me when years later the producers said, "This time, Cryer, it's Alan's bathrobe. Get ready for an inferno, bucko."

"Oh, when I burn," I shot back, "I *sizzle*." (I might be remembering this exchange wrong, but let's just say I was ready.)

One does not take fire gags lightly. The things that can go wrong are legion, even though you're slathered in flame-retardant gel. A burn that goes on too long leaves a scar. An improperly controlled burn could travel someplace else very quickly. If there's a prop nearby nobody realized was flammable, you could burn down the set. The burning bathrobe was the hottest I'd ever gotten, because the heat travels up your arm if you've got it at your side, so it was important to keep my arm perpendicular to my body until the absolute right moment.

Take a fire gag for granted and it will bite you in the ass. You've got to have a healthy respect for the flame. She's a cruel mistress, pretty and warm one minute, a storm of devastation the next. But I've got her number.

What do I do best? you ask.

Light up a room, motherfucker.

Chapter 24
We Who Labor in the Shadow of Giants

It's not hard to fall into a narrative about yourself created in your own mind or by others. It's one reason reality TV is so appealing: Think your life is interesting? Fear that it's not? Let show-business professionals mold it into something TV viewers want to watch week after week! With actors, though, who can become public figures based on their abilities yet still carry plenty of doubt about their worth to anyone, the tendency to interpret your life as a story of destiny is ever-present. Frankly, the world is a lot less concerned about us than we think.

Here's an example. In 1998, after *Getting Personal* was canceled, I got a call one day from Danny Jacobson, the creator of *Mad About You*, who wanted me to fill in on very short notice for a guest role on his latest endeavor, the ABC sitcom *Two Guys, a Girl and a Pizza Place*.

Danny said, "There's a character we've been talking about all season, we cast a guy, he came in, we did the read-through, rehearsals, run-throughs, and it's just not working. It's an important part."

"Sure," I said. "When do you need me?"

"Monday. We shoot on Tuesday."

Today was Sunday. Yikes. "Absolutely, I'm there," I said. I like Danny, and it felt good to help out a friend. I showed up Monday, started rehearsing, and quickly decided to base the delivery style of the character—a dickish college professor—on an old acting teacher of mine who was so soft-spoken that everything he said sounded incredibly condescending. The writers loved it, the actors howled, everybody enjoyed it, so I did it on Tuesday night when we filmed, and as if completing a circle, the audience was hooting with pleasure and having a great time.

Three scenes into the show, however, everything stopped. The producers came over to me and said, "Jon, the network wants you to stop doing that, the way you're doing this guy."

I was dumbfounded. "But we've already shot three scenes of me being this guy."

"Yeah, well, we're going to go back and reshoot them," one of the producers said. "It's coming off too arch."

That may have been the case, but when I started up again, dialing down the character so that he just came off as a regular guy, you could tell the audience was confused. We finished the show, then stayed late to reshoot the first three scenes, and I was mortified. I felt like such a failure. What was supposed to be a lark, a save-the-day scenario that had been encouraged by the warm, laugh-filled reception of everyone around me, was somehow a fiasco. The network had to have been furious: stopping the show, ordering reshoots, getting an actor to change his whole concept. Now I was just as furious. *Fuck these people! ABC is an asshole network! Fuck the whole history of ABC! This is why they struggle in the ratings! Hiring actors who do their best, then cutting them off at the knees!*

I was really commandeering a freight train of self-loathing and outward disgust in my brain, and putting myself in the middle of this cockamamie narrative in which I had made the Wrong Decision, and

ABC was blackballing me out of sheer hatred for how I'd screwed up their show. I went home in the darkest of snits, pretty certain that if Charles Schulz were to draw me at that moment as a Peanuts character, he'd give me one of those angry black squiggle clouds over my head to signal deep, abiding perturbedness.

Cut to a year later, and I received a script for a pilot called *People Who Fear People*. It was really funny, but on the day of the audition, I had a few minor crises that almost made me late. I arrived in time, though, with my adrenaline pumping, and subsequently crushed it. I killed in that audition room—laughter, applause—everyone was having a great time. Right after I left, though, I realized something. I had just read for ABC! The people who hated me!

Well, no, Jon, they didn't hate you, I was forced to tell myself. *You made that up. Last year you did a solid for a friend in need; the network thought you were going a little broad, so they asked you to tone it down. Everything was fine, and you turned it into a personal tragedy on a par with Waterloo.* Grateful over having woken up from this self-destructive fantasy, I heaved another sigh of relief that I'd been distracted enough that morning by daily-routine hiccups to not remember the network I was auditioning for. I could only imagine the futile undercurrent of paranoid ire that might have infected my tryout otherwise. Instead I walked in oblivious to personal drama and, as I found out later, got the part.

Narratives are a big part of our enjoyment of life, but it's good to remember occasionally that they're not always reality. They're something imposed on reality so that we can make sense of it. I was privy to another instance of this after I filmed that ABC pilot and learned that the network would be putting it on its fall 2000 schedule.

People Who Fear People—later to be renamed *The Trouble with Normal*—would be my fourth gig as a series regular in a decade, after *The Famous Teddy Z*, *Partners*, and *Getting Personal*. None of those shows lasted more than a season, although *Getting Personal* counts as two because it debuted in the spring with a short batch of episodes, got re-newed, came back in the fall, and then was summarily yanked right after-ward. And that *does* count as *two seasons*, nitpickers. Regardless, I was well aware that none of these shows had been a success.

In the industry, I was starting to be thought of as a guy who'd had his shot in both movies and television, failed, and was now on a trajectory downward.

Newsweek magazine was also cognizant of this aspect of my résumé, to the extent that they ran an item in a snarkily opinionated entertainment column called "Critical Moments" dated May 29, 2000, that essen-tially labeled me a show killer. Blessed with two—not one, two—sassy headlines—"TV's Not-So-New Lineup" and "If at First You Don't Suc-ceed, a Network Will Hire You"—the piece read thus: "Ever wonder why TV is so bad? Maybe because the networks keep hiring the same failure-prone actors. Some of the recycled stars returning to television next season . . ." after which its nasty little chart named me, Lauren Graham (three failed shows), Mike O'Malley (two failed shows), and Jon Tenney (four failed shows).

Once again, that's Lauren Graham, who *later that year* started a seven-season run on the beloved, acclaimed *Gilmore Girls*.

That's Mike O'Malley, who *later that year* began a choice stint on the six-season hit *Yes, Dear*.

That's Jon Tenney, who would go on to a seven-year run on *The Closer*.

Now remember, this was before the Internet had decimated the American newsweekly, so *Newsweek* and *Time* magazine were still the biggest of the four-hundred-pound gorillas in the world of news. It was pretty head-knocking to see a major publication tag you as certain death to a television series. This was a narrative, though. But no more. I felt that this insertion of me into the larger story about the state of network enter-tainment needed a measured response.

Letters Editor
Newsweek
251 West 57th Street
New York, NY 10019-1894

Dear Sir or Madam:

I, too, had been wondering why American television is so bad. So imagine my chagrin when I read your "Critical Moments" section this week and discovered that the reason American television is so bad is the fact that I'm on it.

Well, all I can say is: "Thank God!"

Thank God the crack "Critical Moments" research team has managed to isolate the cause. Now finally something can be done about it. So as soon as my "failure-prone" talents are released from my current ABC contract I shall unselfishly endeavor to inflict them on the television-watching public of some foreign power. Preferably one without the military capability to retaliate meaningfully. Right now, I'm leaning toward Finland. They are a preternaturally glum people and I hear they liked *Pretty in Pink*.

You should also be aware that since your article appeared I've been approached by several clandestine branches of our own government to be used as a TTQDD. That's Tactical Television Quality Degradation Device, to those unfamiliar with cutting-edge military parlance. The idea is that I'd be inserted in hostile territory by ultralight paraglider. Once safely in country, I would then infiltrate my host's situation comedy industry and bring it to its knees with my eminently resistible off-kilter grin, my only-semi-witty one-liners, and my not-quite-as-good-as-that-Chandler-guy prowess with physical humor.

While leaving my mother country would be devastating for me emotionally, I will do it gladly if it means that there would be hope for American television. For one cannot possibly avoid the observation that, paradoxically, while American television has descended into a foul, smelly, glutinous murk of utter trash, American television *criticism* is entering its golden age, enlightening billions both spiritually and philosophically, entertaining and educating, moving nations to action, creating entirely new paradigms of thought and revolutionizing civilization as we know it.

We who labor in the shadow of giants salute you.

Wish me luck!

Sincerely,
Jon Cryer

Chapter 25
Episodes of *Two and a Half Men*

In the year 2000, I was financially secure, got married, had a son, and bought a beautiful house.

By the year 2003, my finances were in ruins, my marriage was in the toilet, and I was three months away from having to sell my beautiful house.

Thank goodness my son was still *awesome*.

The "show-killer" tag had done some real damage. In a business where a producer needs every bit of good fortune he or she can get, hiring Bad Luck Schleprock is simply not prudent.

I'd had three whole weeks of work in three whole years.

Something needed to happen in 2003.

So I came up with a plan.

I know, I already said making plans is foolish in this business, but at this point I'd been a working actor for twenty years, and I figured that there had to be a way to leverage what I knew, what I was good at, and what I knew I was good at into a successful gig. Or at least improve my chances. First of all, I'd become adept at auditioning because of my indie-film audition experience, so I had that. I'd also learned from my Belushi pilot about how excited everyone gets when you say no. So I decided to combine the two. I was going to audition for every possible part I was even in the ballpark of being right for—big parts, small parts, good shows, lousy ones, cop shows, doctor shows, family dramas, office comedies, game shows, whatever, all of it. My hope was that at some point I'd start getting offers, and when that happened, the second part of my plan would kick in: I was going to turn them down.

Why would I do that, you ask, if I needed a job so badly? Because just getting a pilot gig wouldn't really help. Most pilots are one episode and out, because they don't get picked up by a network and turned into a series. I needed to get a show with real promise, one of the big fish, but those projects are few and far between and everybody wants them. The idea was that my rejections would put chum in the water for the sharks in the business to get excited about while I was waiting for the opportunity of a great show to come along.

And to my enormous surprise, the plan started working almost immediately. I started getting offers for shows that I really didn't think I was right for: the fiery medical examiner, the personal-injury lawyer, the stern-but-lovable dad. It just snowballed.

By the time pilot season was drawing to a close I had turned down an unprecedented nine offers. My agents were nervous, but I'd zeroed in on two big fish.

One was the new *Battlestar Galactica* for the Sci-Fi Channel, which really appealed to me because I loved the original seventies series with Lorne Greene and Dirk Benedict. I auditioned for the role of a brilliant scientist named Gaius Baltar, and the show's creator, Ronald Moore—the mastermind behind the reviving of the *Star Trek* franchise in the 1980s—was really high on casting me.

The other prospect was to play Charlie Sheen's put-upon brother, Alan, in a sitcom for writer/producer Chuck Lorre, who'd wanted me for the Belushi pilot all those years ago. Only problem was, the network (CBS) was adamant that they *didn't* want me. My agent had been told as much and had subsequently not even bothered to send me the script. An actor friend of mine, Cathy Burns, called me and said that she'd just auditioned for a part in a pilot that had a character that just "was" me and that I had to mention it to my agent. My agent made a call and was rebuffed. But pilot season was ending and casting directors were getting desperate. My agent called again, this time talking to Chuck directly, and he was willing to give me a shot.

Chuck had no memory of my doing that Belushi pilot years ago. And he *wrote* the damn thing. "I was pretty loaded then," he later sheepishly admitted.

He was also not that optimistic about my chances this time around, because, as he told me, "I've never seen somebody change Les Moonves's mind."

What I heard was that to CBS president Les Moonves, I was walking-and-talking eighties-movie-star baggage. Mind you, Sheen had that baggage, too, but two holdovers from that decade was apparently too much.

At that first audition, though, I received one more inauspicious sign: Chuck Lorre is the most notoriously generous laugher in the business at auditions, and when I read Alan Harper for him the first time, he didn't make a peep.

I had been sitting outside the audition room, and I could hear other actors taking a swing at the character of Alan and not even remotely connecting with the material. The scene that all us prospective Alans auditioned with as we read opposite a casting agent reciting Charlie's lines was the one in which Charlie has been on a bender, and Alan is informing him that his wife is divorcing him, and he needs to stay at Charlie's a few days. What I heard from the other auditioners, though, was an Alan frantic, as if he'd already begun losing his mind.

To me, Alan struck me as tightly wound, someone who pushes down feelings. It takes a lot to get him to the eruptive stage. He's like popcorn—he's got to sit in hot oil awhile before he explodes, so if he was immediately frantic, that felt wrong. Besides, Alan retains a certain judgmental air toward his lothario brother, Charlie, so he's not going to let on right away the shame he feels about his marriage being on the skids. In Alan's mind, Charlie's the fuckup, not him. Every frenzied line reading I heard through that door felt superficial and wrong, so as I walked into that room—"Hey, good to see ya, Chuck! Jim Burrows, man, how are ya?" (It was great to see Jim again; that he was directing this was a good omen)—I was pretty confident that I knew how to hit that comedy the way it needed to be hit.

But I got nothing from Chuck.

When something's dying, actors have a choice: Lie back a little and hope for the best, go big and amp up the energy, or try to connect in some other way. But as the silence from Chuck's direction began to feel louder—believe me, that description makes sense when you're a performer—I opted to stick to my guns. I told myself, *Trust your interpretation of this.* So I switched off the targeting computer, aimed for the thermal exhaust port, and let my proton torpedoes fly.

I walked away feeling slightly disconcerted, but heard back immediately from my agent.

"They want you to read with Charlie Sheen."

It was good seeing Charlie again. The last time we'd run into each other was at the ABC presentation for advertisers—called "up-fronts"—a few years prior. At that time Charlie was stepping into *Spin City* and I was hyping *The Trouble with Normal.* He had thanked me for standing up for him in the press when some were critical of the idea of his taking over for Michael J. Fox. And that day, there in Chuck's office, he was in good spirits again. I read with him, and this time Chuck Lorre let the big laughs fly.

Whew. Later on, Chuck explained his silence at that first audition. They'd been looking for Alan for weeks, he told me, and when I read, he was struck silent by the fact that someone had finally done it right.

I was getting closer on both shows. As in, all the way to reading for network heads.

At some point I'd be forced to choose.

Battlestar Galactica was incontestably going to be a cool show. My first meeting with creator Ronald Moore, of *Star Trek: The Next Generation* fame, was exciting, because it sounded like his reimagining of *Battlestar* would make it timely, political, character-driven, *and* mind-blowing.

And yet it was going to shoot in Vancouver. While it's a beautiful city—home to many television productions—it's far away for a dad with marriage troubles and a three-year-old son.

Chuck Lorre's show, called *Two and a Half Men*, sounded completely in my wheelhouse: a neurosis-based comedy that I'd get to perform in front of a live audience. I already had rapport with Charlie Sheen from doing *Hot Shots!* Plus, Chuck liked me.

And yet Les Moonves, head of the most powerful broadcast network, wasn't too keen on me. I was the show killer, remember?

I liked both options, but when each show offered test deals, I thought, *Shit, what do I do?*

Wait. You mean you don't know what "test deals" are? Let me explain this singularly unconstitutional business practice.

In a normal world, where competition between hiring entities dictates the amount of money a desired talent gets offered, I would have gone through the audition process for both shows, and if both series wanted to cast me, they'd each have to duke it out monetarily for my services. The winner? Me!

But American television operates wholly differently, like a secret cartel, with the object being to fuck over actors for money in a way that prevents them from understanding whether they're in demand or not. The networks' prime weapon, developed in the wake of soaring production costs and flagging revenues, became the "test deal": a contract one must sign just to audition at the next level. You're negotiating before you even get the part, and getting the part, of course, is not guaranteed.

It's a situation that strips an actor of any leverage. But more disturbingly, it prevents the studios from ever having to bargain against one another. An actor isn't going to tell a show, "I want more money," before he or she even auditions. The actor just wants the part. But with actors often auditioning for several shows at once, a test deal might be exclusive so that he or she can't audition for other series. Actors confronted with test deals are essentially making a decision about their future with no knowledge. A show could hamstring someone to their audition process, with the chance to say, "Bye, we don't want you!" without suffering any repercussions. It's the dirty little secret to the way networks and studios operate, and it's so shrewd in its open collusion that one imagines it being invented by an executive in a cavernous office sporting a monocle, stroking a white cat on his lap, and cackling.

I had to pick between *Battlestar Galactica* and the sitcom. Not doing the shows. Just *to get the privilege of continuing to audition* for them.

Everybody told me to pick the sitcom.

I picked the sitcom. But I suppose you already knew that.

One more to go.

It's a series of flaming hoops.

Up until you audition for the network brass, everyone hopes you're great: the creator who invented the characters as well as the studio that's always trying to get projects going. The network folks, however, sit with their arms folded wearing a "go ahead; make me laugh" expression. They're the ones you really have to win over, because the network is the buyer, not the maker. It's much more in their interest to be disinterested, because everyone's vying for the few slots in the broadcast schedule. Only the network knows what it wants, and there's always another show around the corner to try out.

Charlie Sheen and I were now in the belly of the beast: CBS Television City on Fairfax in Hollywood. The actual geographic place my ten-year-old self dreamed about! The warmth of the room when we auditioned for Warner Bros.—Peter Roth adding his ebullient laughter to Chuck's—was now replaced by a cold, upholstered, sound-deadened screening room acoustically constructed to amplify recorded sound from a TV show or movie, not normal human voices. It was like performing in the corner of a library.

Even the room didn't want to like me.

But not today. I did my thing, Sheen was on point and doing great stuff, and the CBS executives started perking up and laughing.

I walked out and saw other actors waiting to go in. It's disconcerting to be in the holding pen and see a competitor exit a door, trailed by the excited chatter of people who have just finished laughing uproariously. I always hated that asshole coming out the door. This time, I was that asshole.

The other ugly thing about test deals? Some of those actors there, who'd surely signed test deals themselves, might have been strategically signed to make a targeted actor look especially good to the network. It goes like this: When a producer wants someone in particular, but is worried that the network will make a bonehead choice if presented with even competent options, he or she might stack the deck with actors who are spectacularly wrong for the role, in the hope that the network will choose the actor the producer wanted to begin with. Sort of an antiringer. How do ya like them test deals now?

I've probably been that antiringer before as well. I wasn't that day. They booked me that afternoon.

Later, Chuck told me that Les turned around to him after I auditioned and said, "Okay, you win this one."

We had our cast for the pilot: Charlie Sheen as Charlie Harper, Jon Cryer as Alan Harper, nine-year-old Angus T. Jones as Alan's son, Jake, and as Charlie and Alan's mother . . . Blythe Danner.

At the pilot table read, Blythe was so great as conceited and blisteringly unmaternal Evelyn Harper that afterward I called my friend Jeff Greenstein, who'd been a producer on *Will & Grace*, where Blythe had guest-starred occasionally, and said, "Blythe nailed the read-through so completely she has her next three Emmys lined up."

Then rehearsals kicked off, and Blythe began trying to humanize this woman. Evelyn is casually cruel and awful, which Blythe had no problem delivering at the table read. But getting the character up on her feet, Blythe couldn't help but imbue her with spirit and warmth and humanity, and that proved to be disastrous. Evelyn was written to be blissfully, obliviously narcissistic, but the second you believe the character is capable of being better, it stops being funny.

We shot the pilot, and because she's Blythe Danner she was wonderful, and she got some big laughs. But it didn't work, and Chuck fired Blythe.

After she was let go, I was heartsick about it, and I called her that night hoping to be her Austin Pendleton. You remember the way Austin was to me when *Brighton Beach Memoirs* let me go? I was going to console this great actress over the blow of getting axed.

Blythe could not have been more unfazed. She's been in the business a long time, and seen it all. "It's a kind gesture that you called, Jon," she said, "but I'm going out to dinner." I realized how silly my call must have seemed to her, but she was nothing but gracious and touched that I would be worried she'd take it hard. It was all very "oh, you sweet, naive little man."

Two years later she won an Emmy for *Huff*. A year after that, she won another one.

Because she's Blythe Fucking Danner, people.

Holland Fucking Taylor became our new mom, and that was exciting. Years prior she and I had filmed a terrible NBC pilot about a hospital, and I've always been a fan of her work. We reshot the Evelyn scenes, and she fit right in like a comfortable pair of shoes.

Wait. I don't want to compare Holland to shoes. How about a fine mink coat?

We were talking on the set one day when she said, "Ugh, I don't know about you, but my trailer is a shithole."

"I'm so sorry about that," I said. "I'm happy with mine." At the time, I was in one half of what's known as a double-banger, a trailer split into two agreeably spacious private quarters, and a far cry from the cramped-ness of a honey wagon, which is a trailer split into sometimes as many as eight tiny hovels.

"Well, of course you like yours. I'm sure yours is great. You're the star of the show," she said. "It's frustrating for me, because I have no place to do my yoga." Holland had more free time than Charlie or I did, since she wasn't in nearly every scene. "I wish I could go someplace, instead of sitting around in my shithole."

She seemed really irritated about it, so I offered her my trailer as an option for any and all yoga needs. She could contort her body to her heart's content.

I took her outside and around the corner to my trailer. She peered in expectantly and froze.

"Oh," she said as her face fell, "this is the same as mine."

I knew CBS would pick us up for the fall season. The vibe as we filmed the pilot was very self-assured. Things clicked. Charlie and I were a solid team, and just as I'd remembered from *Hot Shots!* he was a natural at this stuff: timing a joke, selling a joke, seasoning it with just enough bad-boy charm.

On the last day of shooting the pilot in April, it was my birthday, so they brought out a cake. Very sweet gesture. I said, "My birthday wish is that all of us are still here ten years from today." Everyone laughed and applauded in that knowing way that said, "Poor kid, he doesn't know anything about show business."

Hey, I was mostly right.

I'd been in four sitcoms that made it to air but had ended ignominiously. Call it delusional ignorance, but when CBS said we'd be on the fall schedule, I was proud of my optimism. Maybe it's hereditary. I remember my broke single mom's attempts at family vacations, and how we could be lost in a snowstorm in upstate New York and she'd turn to my sister and me with that big, squinty, beautiful smile and even bigger spirit and say, "Well, this is an adventure!"

The second episode we ever shot, titled "Big Flappy Bastards," was all the proof we needed that we'd coalesced into a smooth, creative sitcom-making team. The writers crafted a really funny episode, and Chuck Lorre ran a tight ship. He was, in what now appears to be a traditional trait in the folks who've had a great influence on my life, a stern taskmaster, no doubt, and he had high expectations, but there wasn't a lot of rewriting to the tune of page-one rewrites every day, as I'd experienced on other sitcoms. On *Two and a Half Men*, writers were out by five p.m. instead of going home at two a.m. And what they were coming up with was old-school, slyly filthy, and fantastic.

The cast, meanwhile, was quickly coming together, too. When the show brought on Conchata Ferrell as Berta the housekeeper, it was immediately obvious this was a great addition. When I met Conchata, I geeked out because I'd loved her in the movie *Network*, and even the short-lived seventies sitcom *Hot L Baltimore*. As she listened to me rattle off her IMDb page to her, she laughed it off as if it were impossible for her to believe I was actually a huge fan.

I was. Am. Always will be.

———

The ratings out of the gate were great, pulling in nearly the same numbers as our esteemed, beloved, award-winning lead-in, *Everybody Loves Raymond*. The second week's numbers barely dropped. We were an instant hit, and this was something I had never experienced.

There was some guilt involved, because my wife moved out two months into that first season, so while I was feeling horrible about what my young son was having to go through at home, my professional life was going to be a source of comfort, creativity, and happiness. Knowing the show wasn't going anywhere for at least a little while was a balm, believe me.

I made a joke to someone that it took only the best sitcom producer currently working in television, the best writers, the best cast, and the best crew to finally create a show that even I couldn't kill.

———

I looked at Charlie and Denise Richards that first season, married a year, a kid on the way, and assumed they were still in postwedding euphoria. Denise did an early episode of the show, and she and Charlie were on the cover of *TV Guide*. The story inside: all about the playboy who'd finally settled down.

One day during that first season, I got a knock on my trailer door. It was Charlie. Our trailers are next to each other, right outside the Warner Bros. soundstage where we shoot.

He seemed panicked. "Dude! Dude! I need your help."

"Sure thing," I said, and ended the cell phone call I was on. "What's going on?"

He handed me a heavy shopping bag. "Denise is coming over," he said, "and I need you to hide something for me."

Oh, boy, I thought. *If this is drug paraphernalia . . .* "Is it legal?" I asked.

"What? Yeah, oh, yeah. It's legal. Hey, thanks."

He left, and I had to look. By legal, he meant barely legal. It was a bag filled to the brim with porn. Curiosity getting the best of me, I had to find out what kind of porn captivates Charlie Sheen, what decadence frightens him into having me squirrel it away for him. Grannies and trannies? Clowns? Golden-shower pictorials? German scat porn starring Federal Reserve chairman Ben Bernanke? I was prepared for the weirdest, but it really was all pretty tame, some of it just topless mags.

Really, if this was the worst I'd have to deal with regarding Charlie's vices, bring on the bags of porn for me to hide. Even when I secretly hoped for a sighting of Sheen decadence, as when we traveled to Las Vegas to promote the first season by hobnobbing with CBS affiliates from around the country, I was confronted by a pretty grounded, sober married guy. We landed in Vegas, and I was ready to get the Sin City tour from my costar. Instead, he went to his room and took a nap.

We showed up at the party for the syndicated stations, and then Charlie went back to his room to sleep. I watched our director, Jim Burrows, play blackjack. What happened in Vegas didn't have to stay in Vegas, because it was boring as shit.

As our first season of *Two and a Half Men* hit its stride, it was becoming clear to me that work was going to be my refuge. I was trudging through a divorce at the same time my character was going through one as well.

Quite a few people openly asked me if this was "fun," because I got to bring all that stuff to the show.

Uh, *no*. Not fun at all. This was not, "Yay, I get to have turmoil in my life *and* play it at work!" Of course, it brought added depth to scenes Alan had with Jake, but it's not as if I was thinking, *Thank God, the pain is so readily available!*

When Charlie heard about what I was going through at home, he very sweetly took me aside one day and said, "Hey, man, I know things are really tough for you, so if you need a place to stay, you can crash at my house."

I looked at him quizzically and said, "Thanks, Charlie, but . . . how much like the show do you want your life to be?"

"Oh, yeah," he said, smiling ruefully. "Bad idea."

———

Charlie was in his element acting in a sitcom. His comic timing was impressive. I asked him if he'd done theater. He said he hadn't. Of course, he'd done *Spin City* for two years after Michael J. Fox left, but that's never a guarantee somebody's comfortable with that format.

"I've just watched a lot of sitcoms," he told me. "I used to love 'em as a kid."

That was a real bonding moment for us. I pictured these two little boys with performing parents on separate coasts glued to fourteen-inch Magnavoxes watching Tootie get her heart broken on *The Facts of Life*. (Again, you know you watched it.) He and I laughed a lot that day about the shows we used to watch, and how ironic it was that we ended up making one together.

The first year of *Two and a Half Men* I learned something interesting, though. Where Charlie was most nervous was during the table read. Mondays we sit around a table and read the script out loud for the writers and producers. Tuesdays and Wednesdays are rehearsal. Thursday we shoot scenes in advance—whether outdoor scenes, or shots that point toward the "wall" that would be where the audience is—and Friday is when we film in front of the audience. Performance night Charlie was great, no more nervous than any of us. But what he hated was the table read.

That's because Charlie used to have a mild stutter as a kid. He's worked hard to overcome it, but he was always self-conscious about it. And since the table read is really a cold performance of a new script with no physical acting, it's like a radio play—all you have to do is say it right—and therefore more daunting to Charlie.

He doesn't like public speaking. He has anxiety about being in crowds. He didn't like attending parties. He likes "partying," but not *going* to parties. It was an interesting window into what made him tick, what might have spurred his self-medicating in darker times.

But he was sober Charlie those first few years, as far as we all knew, and he was a great, friendly, witty colleague.

As it was becoming clear that the show was turning into a breakout hit, CBS sent Charlie and me to the Television Critics Association convention to schmooze with the people who'd be passing judgment on us for the next few years. Television critics are a fiercely quirky bunch, but it was nice to see that generally the reception for the show was very positive. As I sidled up to the bar, I met a tall man with a profound widow's peak.

He shook my hand and uttered three bone-chilling words: "I'm Marc Peyser." Who the hell on God's green Earth is Marc Peyser? you ask. Well, he was none other than the television editor of (ominous chord) *Newsweek* magazine, the same publication who so casually dismissed my entire career and earned a sharply worded letter from me in response.

I tried to give him my best "Hello, *Newman*" reading as I replied, "Hello, *Marc*."

He smiled warmly and said, "I just wanted to tell you that that we all loved your letter; it got passed around the office quite a bit."

I softened. "Really?"

"Yes, we're thinking about writing a follow-up to the first article about how we got it wrong."

I softened more. "Really?"

"Yeah, we were considering putting your letter in it, and maybe even the one your dad wrote."

I blanched. "Really?"

"Oh, yeah," he replied. "His was just scathing. Looks like your dad's totally got your back."

I suppressed the lump in my throat from my father's sweetly protective gesture of parental support, assured Marc that it'd be fine if they wanted to print my missive, and marveled at how fast fortunes can change.

In the first week of November, *Newsweek* ran "The Curse of the Show Killers," a terrific piece about many of the journeyman actors who'd been unfairly tagged with the stigma. They even mentioned my dad's letter, but they didn't print it, or mine for that matter.

While work was fulfilling my days, most nights I was still coming home to an empty house. The cascade of emotions surrounding my divorce would send me into an energetic funk—a mixture of frustration, anger, and sadness that I called "full-tilt mope." I went all hermit, ordering in, surfing the Web, and watching late-night TV. One particular night I chanced upon Fuse—a channel that showed nothing but music videos. *Hey, remember when MTV showed music videos?* I mused to myself as I watched a Nine Inch Nails clip.

The next one was a song I'd never heard before. It started with a stadium-style backbeat, then a scruffy but irresistible guitar lick. The video itself was clever too, with some visual puns that instantly brought a smile to my face. Then came the chorus, a repeated admonishment to "get over it!" This was turning out to be a great song. The exact song I needed to hear at this moment. As the video ended it hit me: *Damn it, they're right! I really should just fucking get over it.* I checked the name of the band. This was the first single from a new band out of Chicago called OK Go.

I got their CD the next day and the whole thing was terrific—propulsive, playful, and hilarious. I bought ten more CDs and started handing them out to my friends at my weekly pickup Ultimate Frisbee game. (Yes, I still played Ultimate Frisbee. Again, thank you, nerd school.)

I gave one to Richard Schenkman and he became an instant fan as well, and informed me that they'd be playing one of their first LA shows at the Troubadour on April 16.

April 16?! I thought. *That's my fucking birthday!* It would be my first since the separation. As a birthday gift he bought me two tickets and instructed me to "take someone cute."

The week of my birthday we were shooting an episode that introduced the character of my ex-wife's sister, played by Teri Hatcher, who was squeezing in one last gig before filming the pilot of a show called *Desperate Housewives.* She was killing it on our show, with her warm but sardonic sense of humor, and she was beyond "cute." So I asked her to the concert. She, too, was going through a divorce at the time, so she politely declined, citing unnamed "plans," but I suspected that she wisely felt that a date for two people going through that shit concurrently was a lousy idea. I then asked a woman I played Ultimate with, who never replied to my e-mail. Another actress I invited actually laughed in my face. It was a good-natured laugh, though, a "that was a wonderful joke you made" laugh. This was not helping my spirits at all. In the end, I did go with someone "cute," and his name was Richard Schenkman.

It's nearly impossible to be despondent at an OK Go concert. They are generally pretty ecstatic experiences. But I was managing it. As they finished their song "What to Do" to deafening applause, they immediately leaped into another one, a tune I didn't recognize at first.

Their lead singer, Damian Kulash, came to the mic during its opening chords and said, "Hey, everybody, there's someone in the audience tonight who's a big fan of the band, and frankly, we're big fans of his."

Now those opening chords were ringing a bell.

As he started singing, "Caroline laughs and it's raining all day; she loves to be one of the girls . . ." my mouth dropped open. I looked at Richard, who had a sheepish grin on his face.

"Did you do this?" I yelled.

"Yeah," answered Richard. "I e-mailed Damian. These guys are so cool!"

As Damian wailed, "Isn't sheee pretty in pink? Isn't sheee?" then shouted, "Happy Birthday, Jon!" I realized that it wasn't nearly impossible to be despondent at an OK Go concert. It was actually impossible.

———

Working on a sitcom isn't just the holy grail for actors; its steady and often enjoyable employment is also the goal for all of the artists and tradesmen who compose the crew as well. And when you have the luxury of a show that is known to be a hit, you end up with a group of fellow employees who are pretty much the cream of the crop at their respective trades. So much so that you begin to take their expertise for granted. For example, you could throw a ridiculous last-minute request at our prop mistress, Lee Lee Baird, such as, "For this scene, I'm gonna need a twelve-foot cheesecake with the words 'Happy Bar Mitzvah, Ramon Garcia' on it," and without batting an eye, she'd stonily reply: "We got one on the truck."

And this was typical of pretty much everyone on the show. Even our warm-up guy, Mark Sweet, operated at a level that boggled the mind. A warm-up performer's job is to keep the audience entertained and engaged while the crew is preparing to shoot the scenes. There is a fair amount of downtime, and it's quite easy for the audience to get bored. However, Mark's capable of amping up a room of prisoners awaiting a firing squad. One Friday night there was a breakdown in the camera's "tap," the part that transmits what's being filmed straight to the monitors, so the audience can watch a rough edit live. (Sometimes the sight lines aren't great for the audience, so they need the monitors.) If that system doesn't work, there's no point in having an audience. There was much frantic hair pulling and effort to fix it, and we were down for two straight hours, which meant Mark had to keep that crowd energetic with jokes, then interaction, more jokes, maybe some magic tricks, and then even more interaction, for *two whole hours.* No comedian alive has that much material prepared and ready to go on a moment's notice.

He not only vamped like a pro the entire time, but in one respect, the audience was so raucous that by the end of it, I thought that actually resuming the show would be something of a letdown. The rest of the crew has never been asked to step up in quite that fashion, but I'm confident that these guys would have what it takes to perform extraordinarily.

———

Fridays were great at *Two and a Half Men,* because the actors usually had a couple-hour break in between rehearsals and the live taping. And that meant one thing: laser tag.

Angus T. Jones was a rare creature; even though he had an incredible facility for remembering lines, taking performance notes, and delivering punch lines, he also remained a normal kid in show business. So when I noticed the laser-tag set that I bought for my son was going unused, Angus jumped at the chance to battle me in the environs of Stage 26. The two of us had the run of the place, and as long as we didn't break anything no one seemed to mind. Some days I'd climb up into the light rigging to get a sniper-style bead on him; others it was strictly run and gun. Either way it was exhausting, and a great way to blow off steam before the show.

One night at the end of the game Angus handed over his laser rifle and said, "Will you tell your son thank you? Y'know, for letting us use his stuff?"

I said, "Sure."

Angus was that kind of kid, deeply goodhearted. The next time I picked up my son I was about to pass on young Angus's gratitude when I paused, and realized that I didn't want to tell him. That it might actually hurt him to know that the dad whom he now saw only a few days a week was playing with a pretend son at work. And even using his own toys to do it. I suddenly felt ashamed.

That night after I put him to bed, I cried that divorced-dad cry. The one where you despair that the inexorable course of your life has caused your child pain.

———

When Charlie's marriage to Denise ended during the second season—which I was truly saddened by, for obvious reasons—both Charlie and I became single at the same time. Which was . . . interesting.

Our parking spaces were right next to each other, and they were in front of the soundstage alleyway that housed our side-by-side trailers, so in the morning I'd often see him sitting outside his trailer smoking as I walked toward mine. During this time we'd have a conversation, and he'd mention that things had been going well for him romantically. "Romantically" is my choice of words, not his.

Then, as if to prove this, he'd show me a picture he'd taken of somebody's vagina. It was always a perfectly nice-looking vagina, but I would invariably think, *Why just this, and not the rest of the person?*

And what do you say in that moment? "Thank you for that vagina picture"? "How long have you been seeing . . . it"? "Please tell me she was awake"?

———

We talked about prostitutes. He'd said publicly that you don't pay prostitutes to come to your house; you pay them to leave. He'd thought this through, obviously.

I was in a bad state right after my divorce, and I certainly didn't feel dateable. I was an emotional basket case. What good was I to any woman I might have an interest in? I decided I might as well pay someone for company and certain intimate pleasures so that I could at least get my equilibrium back with the opposite sex. Charlie suggested a few online purveyors he occasionally used, as this was when prostitution was gaining a foothold on the Internet. He and I had different tastes, so I didn't go with his exact recommendations, but my forays into prostitution were about as awkward as you might imagine.

I went with an out-call for my first try, which means they come over to your house, and as I waited for her that evening, I couldn't help but think of my hooker-loving Upper West Side neighbor, Mr. Green, and his violent encounter with a tagalong boyfriend. My chosen vendor was alone, though, and she drove a white BMW to boot (nice!), plus sported a sexy Finnish accent. It was really a very friendly experience, maybe because the act of having sex is quite the conversational icebreaker. Afterward I inquired about seeing her again.

The next time I went to her place, which probably wasn't really her place, but there you go. It was pretty depressing, but that didn't matter, because we sat down, tried to make small talk, and awkwardly stumbled into a conversation about recent fluctuations in the stock market. Somehow I ended up spending twenty-five minutes of my hour helping her with financial planning. That was fine, really. I learned that the sex part of these transactions is fairly perfunctory, and that you may have a perfectly nice time chatting, but you always feel weird afterward, because you've spent all this money for the part that never lasts as long as you want it to. What I really needed to do was gear myself up to date like a normal person.

"You have to understand," she told me at one point, "I end up doing a lot more talking. A lot. That seems to be what a lot of guys want, almost as much as the other stuff."

I was also apparently one of the very few nonmarried customers she'd had. Yikes.

I suppose if Charlie's example of his evening's entertainment was best exemplified by a snapshot of lady parts, mine would be a picture of me hunched over a table of papers and telling a hot chick, "The real estate boom is building up, so I'm sounding a note of caution. You might want to diversify."

———

My first opportunity to dip my toe into the nonprofessional pool of available women came soon afterward. Rich, my trainer, one of the sweetest, goofiest guys to ever stretch your groin for a living, threw a party one night, where I met an engaging, beautiful woman—an aspiring actress and comedian—and we hit it off. I was with my son, and she got along with him, too, which was also wildly attractive to me. I asked her out, and before long we were dating regularly. It felt great. I was finding my sea legs again as a social human being, and I couldn't have been more at peace about it.

I even took the risk of bringing her to the set. I say "risk" because for most aspiring comedians, getting face time with anyone working on a sitcom is a sought-after networking opportunity. I was initially worried that she'd try to pitch the writers and make them uncomfortable, but I let that go, and when she actually met them all, she was charming and funny and they all laughed at her jokes. I thought, *Nothing to worry about here.*

I introduced her around, and we ran into Charlie, who looked at her blankly.

"We've actually met before," she said. "I was a waitress at La Moustache?"

"Right, right," he said. "Hello. Nice to see you again."

As we walked off, I thought, *Good! That was handled well.*

A few weeks later, I was sitting around on the set with a shit-eating grin on my face, and a sense that my life was coming back to an even keel, when Charlie strolled over.

"What's going on? What's with the smile?"

"Things are going good with Stephanie," I said.

"Hey, listen, we gotta talk."

He took me outside, pulled me to a place with some privacy, and said, "I've been talking to my therapist, because I don't know if I should say anything. I've been agonizing about this, dude, really. I . . . I don't know how to say this, but . . . Stephanie and I used to date."

"Oh?" I said, my grin suddenly replaced by something pursed and worried.

"I'm sorry," he said. "I guess she hasn't told you that we did."

"Well, how long did you date?"

"A month, maybe a month and a half."

"So it wasn't a single date, or even two or three. It was . . ."

"Yeah, yeah, yeah."

"Well, was it serious, Charlie?"

"No, no, not really." I could tell he was trying to play this down for my benefit.

"Okay, but was she really into, you know, drugs and stuff?"

"No, not really. I mean . . . if I had some, she would, you know? But she really wasn't into it."

I tried to gather my train of thought with this new information. "Well, I'm annoyed that she didn't tell me this. But if I may ask, how did you two break up?"

Charlie said, "Well, I wanted to bring another girl into bed with us, and she was not happy about that." And then he looked me straight in the eye, and with no trace of irony, said, "So heads up on that."

"Thanks, Charlie. I'll keep that in mind."

I went home that night and broke up with Stephanie. She tried to explain that this aspect of her past was something she didn't want to freak me out about, and that as the weeks went on she realized it was going to be a bigger and bigger deal, and that she and Charlie were never serious, and it wasn't something to get upset about, yadda, yadda, yadda. But it was something she should have said right away when we met. I couldn't go forward after that. I tried to wrap my head around the fact that I was living some romantic-comedy version of a deception, one that in the movie might end with somebody saying, "Forgive her! She obviously loves you!"

Not this time.

What's a harmless lack of initial honesty? I once dated a striking English singer who sheepishly admitted a few dates into our courtship that she was, in fact, a baroness. She said it the way you might murmur worriedly, "I used to be a Shriner." Now, that's endearing.

"I used to bang your costar"—that's up-front information, ladies.

A few seasons in, Charlie started to bellyache to me occasionally about the rewrites, and executive producer Lee Aronsohn's nitpicky notes, which admittedly can get highly specific when it comes to line readings. One time Charlie decided an actress playing opposite him wasn't attractive enough. Other times he'd call a gag he didn't like a "clam." That was his derogatory term for an unfunny joke. It was pretty small potatoes complaining, mostly to me.

Baseball terminology made its way into his comments, too. He'd call something "bush," which I assumed meant good, because of his love of vaginas. But then I realized it was short for "bush league," which meant "unprofessional" or "amateurish."

During the divorce I moved into a rented house seven minutes from work, and one day I could swear I caught a glimpse of entertainment reporter Lisa Joyner coming out of a house nearby.

Interesting.

Back in the early nineties she had interviewed me at a television press tour event, and we had an incredibly funny, breezy, and enjoyable conversation. She was a FOX reporter and I thought she was fantastic. But when she came to my place of employment a few years later when I was on *Getting Personal*, and I noticed her smoking outside the studio before her scheduled interviews with me and the cast, I was suddenly a nervous wreck with a schoolboy crush. (Again, smoking is insanely attractive to me. Just ask the Holy Name girls from my youth who puffed away in their Catholic-school uniforms as I walked by—puberty hit me badly right at that moment.) No longer blithely charming like in our first chat, I gave her a terrible interview, and it didn't even make it into the piece.

Then, a few months after that, my *Getting Personal* costar Duane Martin and I went on *Good Day LA* when Lisa guest-hosted. Duane and I had just heard that our show was canceled, yet couldn't tell anybody because the official announcement hadn't been made. We had followed through on doing the publicity out of obligation. Since we were devoid of any real purpose on the show and filled with screw-'em giddiness, we acted like total buffoons. The cameramen didn't know what we were doing, and I saw Lisa look around with a "what the fuck do I do now?" expression as we began making up songs, doing lame impressions, pantomiming illegal sex acts, whatever. . . .

Now, seven years later, she's a neighbor! I think.

And I'm single!

The KCAL van in front the next day confirmed it. I left her a note, apologizing for making a mockery of *Good Day LA* lo those many years ago, hoping she was well, and informing her that I was her new neighbor. There was also a, "Hey, if you need to reach me"—*why? Oh, just write it*—followed by every known way to contact me short of emergency numbers for relatives and a schedule of my daily routine.

Fingers were crossed.

The first actors to get Emmy nominations from the show were Holland Taylor and Conchata Farrell. It happened in our second year, and it gave us all the sense that the ball was starting to get rolling with recognition for the show. It was clear from the beginning that the A story each week—in sitcoms, that's the primary conflict of the episode—was Charlie's, whereas I got the B story, typically a purely comedic subplot. Even though this was already the clear pattern, Charlie and I had inexplicably both been submitted as lead actors for the show up to this point. So starting in the third season, I decided to submit myself as a supporting actor, because he was carrying the main story every week, and I was not in every scene, as he was. When the Emmy nominations came in that next year, we were both nominated.

I was okay with not winning, but Charlie took award recognition personally. I told him, "Look, some years voters watch the shows. Other years they don't. The Emmy voters are just like you and me. They can't see it all. They're into some things, not into others. Some years it all comes together and you're the guy they pick. Other years they don't."

"You don't understand," Charlie said. "It's all about *exclusion*, and *inclusion*."

He wanted in to what he perceived as the cool club. It surprised me that you could be a massive worldwide star like Charlie and still worry about eating lunch with the cool kids.

I didn't care about whether I had the A story or the B story each week. I've had both over the years. The quality of what I was doing was always paramount. Besides, having the A story each week is exhausting, because you're in practically every scene. If I have a well-written secondary story line that gives me something really funny to play, I'm happy. The best material comes out of an organic process, and if you encumber writers with demands like, "Give me that character's funny lines!" or, "Why don't I have more to do?" then they're writing from a place of hampered creativity and pressure. I want the writers to go where the funniest stories are, period.

I always think of Beatrice Straight as William Holden's wife in *Network*. She was on-screen less than six minutes total, and won the Academy Award. The most airtime is not the key.

———

My mobile rang, and I just saw LISA JOY on my phone display: *It's her!*

Lisa Joyner, that is. The display cut off the "NER."

She'd been in Puerto Rico filming segments for a charity fund-raising video, which was why she hadn't responded to the I'm-your-new-neighbor note I left her over a week ago.

"Hey, let me take you out to lunch!" she said.

At that first lunch, reminded of her gorgeousosity, I was so terrified that I refused to look at her, directing everything I said to the sushi chef, who must have thought I was nuts. She'd even brought me a new-neighbor package of her neighborhood favorites, like car-wash gift certificates, a café coupon, etc. It was so adorable and nice. And yet I shook her hand afterward like we'd made a deal on a new car.

But I got up the nerve to ask her on a date-date, and she said yes.

———

As the episodes of *Two and a Half Men* were piling up, I'd had cause to reexamine my character and come to the conclusion that Alan is mostly me, with brushstrokes provided by some of my friends. His cheapness comes from one pal I won't name, but he knows who he is.

Again, though, he's mostly me. Alan is so thwarted in so many aspects of his life that had I been thwarted in similarly, and not been possessed of my special self-delusional sense of destiny, I would probably have become an Alan-like mixture of uptight, judgmental, anxious, and flawed. In a way, Alan reminds me of how things could have gone.

And the writers even worked in how I sit! The mixed signals my body sends out have clearly inspired Alan's, shall we say, elastic sexuality. His odd mélange of desperate hetero and undeniably effeminate behavior has supplied the show's creators with vast comedic opportunities.

As the years would go on, they would end up throwing some heavy stuff my way for Alan as well: nervous breakdown, sexual identity, a second marriage, split personality, a heart attack. It would be pretty ballsy material to find humor in, but I loved the challenge of it, especially since our prime directive was simply to make people laugh. Chuck Lorre and the writers would keep raising the bar of how ridiculous Alan could be, and keep hoping I could jump over it. Our characters deepened in ways you wouldn't have expected from what is unapologetically an old-school sex comedy. As an actor, it's a privilege to get a role like that, one that expands with the years, rather than stagnates.

My buddy Paget Brewster had opening-night tickets to the Los Angeles premiere of Doug Wright's play *I Am My Own Wife*, starring Jefferson Mays in his Tony Award–winning role as a gay transvestite who lived through both Nazi Germany and Communism.

Now, that's first-date material.

I'm serious. It was a great play, with a great performance, and I snapped up Paget's tickets and took Lisa. There was one problem, though: For all the ways Jefferson was amazing in the role—and it was a brilliant tour de force—he was, to put it bluntly, a spitter. And our tickets were in the front row.

It may as well have been a Gallagher show for all the liquid raining down on us. Much of the play is in German, too, which is a prime linguistic enabler for excessive-saliva cases.

Seriously, whenever he'd turn and face stage right to speak, that side of the row would flinch. When he walked across, the rest of the patrons would squirm in preparation for the monsoon.

I was, to put it mildly, worried about what Lisa would think. I kept glancing at her periodically to check whether she'd become too disgusted to stay. At one point, Jefferson approached the lip of the stage shouting emphatically right in front of us. I winced as I saw my date directly in the line of fire. He got closer . . . closer. . . Yep, he got her.

"Aww, man," she said with a scowl, but as she wiped her face I heard one of the most beautiful belly laughs I'd ever experienced. She thought it was hilarious and remained a good sport about it throughout the rest of the performance.

That's when I realized that on such a moistened base, a foundation for falling in love could be laid down.

The week that seventy-nine-year-old Cloris Leachman guested on the show, I had the honor of discovering one of my comic inspirations was not only brilliant, but a little nuts. All through rehearsals, she wouldn't say lines as written, and always seemed a bit lost. She'd make jokes about not knowing what the scene's comic rhythm was, and run-throughs never seemed to nail down anything. She was funny—don't get me wrong—but we all approached performance night on Friday with a vague sense of worry. Then, when showtime arrived and the cameras were on and the audience was primed, she knocked it out of the park. If she came up with something weird, it was also wonderful—something you hadn't seen before but within the parameters of what was needed. It was amazing to watch.

Over the years the show would eventually have an extraordinary variety of guest stars: Stacy Keach, Marion Ross, Mike Connors (Mannix!), Michael Clarke Duncan, John Amos, Morgan Fairchild, Gary Busey, Martin Mull, Jeri Ryan, Judd Nelson (still strange), Jenny McCarthy, countless others. Countless! I geeked out over a lot of them. The insanely charismatic and amiable Robert Wagner told me to call him "RJ," which remains a life highlight. (I walked around for weeks repeating in my head, *Oh, my God, I'm Robert Wagner's friend!*) Carl Reiner discovered that he's got at least one fan (me) who considers his direction of *The Jerk*—an expert balance between the absurd and the deadpan—as worthy a career pinnacle as *The Dick Van Dyke Show*. He laughed at that, to which I said, "No, I mean it!" and he laughed even harder. On the show that week, my character had a bit where he had to sing an incredibly cheesy version of "Jingle Bell Rock," and this also sent Carl into paroxysms of laughter. I'm telling you, it's an indescribable feeling to crack that guy up. He'd made me giggle so often with his work, it was like returning a favor someone didn't even know that they had done for you. Virtually every time we've seen each other after we shot that episode he insists that I perform the song for him again. And I am only too happy to oblige.

"Hi, foxy!"

The words were innocent enough. But they sent an electric jolt through my body. I'd called Lisa to ask her out to a movie. When she picked up the phone and realized it was me, that was her greeting. Her salutation was significant for two reasons: 1) She was still happy to hear from me even though our first date involved getting spit on by a guy playing a German transvestite, and 2) she called me "foxy!" This was a big fucking deal. I'd long given up on ever being called that, not only because the term hadn't been popular for twenty years, but also due to the fact that

I was still pretty goofy-looking. Hearing it, I immediately regressed to my teenage years and felt all my angst from that time spontaneously heal and resolve into a warm, glowing sensation. Could it be that she actually found me attractive?

Still emotionally off balance, I struggled to invite her to the movie after that. But I needn't have worried, because she cheerily invited me over for dinner at her house instead. Her house! You know what *that* means. If things go really well . . . (porn music).

That night I discovered that Lisa was also a tremendous chef. When she asked me to help in the preparations, I jumped at the chance. All she needed me to do was roast some pine nuts.

I was secretly thrilled that it involved something so easy, as I was woefully inept in the kitchen. Just how woefully inept was about to become clear. As I sprinkled the pine nuts onto some aluminum foil and put them in the broiler, I made a few attempts at small talk. Then I leaned on her stove in a debonair fashion to emphasize my guy-helping-out-with-the-meal charm. In a flash, her eyes widened with alarm. I turned around to see flames shooting out of a vent in the top of the stove! Huge, superflamy flames! Like, set-the-ceiling-on-fire flames!

I reacted predictably: *"Ohmygodohmygodohmygod! Fire! Fire!"* I screamed, octaves above what most eight-year-old girls are capable of. And ironically, exactly as those writers on *Getting Personal* had predicted. I pulled open the broiler, only to realize that it was actually a really dumb idea to pull open the broiler, because I was just giving the already robust fire more oxygen. *Whooosh!* More flames! I became a whirlwind of panic; I was accustomed to setting *myself* on fire, not major appliances! Smoke billowed. Smoke alarms squealed. Lisa's dogs ran for the backyard. I threw open her kitchen cabinets looking for an extinguisher.

When suddenly, with the silent deftness of a ninja, Lisa grabbed a nearby box of baking soda, adroitly emptied its contents on the broiler, and smothered the inferno. We stared in slack-jawed quietude at the smoldering pile of powdered nuts on blackened foil. It seemed my fire had met its match. And maybe the king of fire gags had found a queen. (Okay, that was cheesy, but I really couldn't help it; she was very impressive.)

We'd been going on dates for a couple of weeks and I'd yet to make a move. But accidentally setting her stove on fire is not a confidence builder that often leads to nights of passion. So, once again, after a delicious dinner during which she never betrayed even the slightest irritation that I'd almost burned her house down, I excused myself with a hug.

That week, Steven Tyler, lead singer of Aerosmith, was scheduled to be on. Robin and her friend Shelly (whom we now affectionately refer to as our sister from those years living with us) were naturally excited, considering their schoolgirl Aerosmith-worship society. They got his picture and autograph.

The rest of us at the show were surprised, on the other hand, that this legendary performer couldn't get his only line right.

The setup was that Tyler moves in next door to the Harper boys in Malibu, and the front man's famous scat vocalizing—all those high-pitched *scoot-di-biddly-at-bap-baps*—is driving Charlie nuts. Finally, at the end of the episode, he makes his appearance, and Tyler has to deliver one line: "There's a lot of the seventies I don't remember."

Well, there was a lot about that one line Tyler couldn't remember. Every time the camera fell on him, he'd find some new combination of those words. "The seventies . . . don't remember them." "You know what . . . I don't remember the seventies." "Wish I could remember the seventies." Believe it or not, writers spend a lot of time crafting a line for maximum laugh potential. It was such a strange rut—thank God we were preshooting his scene on Thursday, away from an audience—that when it was all over, the cue card with his line was nailed to the wall as a memento. It's funny when someone who's such a natural performer comes completely out of his element when you give him a scripted line.

I gripped the steering wheel and stared straight ahead. We rode on silently. I'd just dropped the bomb:

"Lisa . . ." I'd said, "I have an enormous crush on you."

Now she too was staring straight ahead. She ventured cautiously: "At first I wasn't sure if you were gay or not. . . ." She looked down, then continued. "Y'know, because we've been going on dates for six weeks, and you've never even kissed me good night."

"Sorry," I said. "Just nervous."

We'd been to Casa Vega for a late lunch and were now driving into Hollywood to pick up my son from a birthday party. This was to be the first time she would meet him.

"So . . . why don't you kiss me now?" she asked matter-of-factly.

"Well . . . because I'm driving."

But now it was weird. I'd let her know that I wanted to kiss her, but simply hadn't yet. And currently I was driving and couldn't. Plus, it'd be strange for her to take the initiative at this moment and kiss me, because, again, I was operating a motor vehicle. So we spent the rest of the journey discussing how I'd pretty much dropped the ball every time I'd had a chance to make out with her. I was apologetic and tried to explain that due to my extensive history of romantic bungling, I was unlikely to handle this any better.

Finally we arrived at the party and stepped out of the car. I opened her door, and as she stepped out I went to kiss her, and even though she was clearly a little startled, she let me.

When I pulled back from the kiss I noticed an odd look on her face. Sort of a furrowed-brow mix of surprise, concern, a hint of betrayal, more than a little confusion, and finally, admiration. "Wait a minute," she said as she grabbed my shirt purposefully. "Do that again." We kissed again. I pulled back, and there was that same look. Like someone might look if they'd just found out their roly-poly accountant spouse was actually a deep-cover agent working for the CIA.

"You're *really* good at that," she said. And to this day she swears that that was the moment she knew.

———

There was a wonderfully odd moment with Janeane Garofalo when she guest-starred as a woman who hates herself after sleeping with Alan.

We had a joke where she confessed to taking her dog's sleeping pills, and Alan sympathizes because it's cheaper. It was an admittedly very sitcom joke, but a funny one. Janeane, however, who comes from a form of counterculture comedy that's about subverting the traditional tropes of humor, and finding laughs in real stories instead of one-liners, bristled at delivering it.

"I don't want to say this," she said.

"What do you mean?" I said.

"It's such a . . . jokey joke."

"Well, is it something about the line? I think it's kind of funny that the character takes her own dog's tranquilizers."

"I don't know," she said. "Who would buy that?"

Okay, I thought. *She's looking for motivation. I get it.* I said, "So you don't understand why somebody would do that?"

"No," she said. "I understand. They're expensive. I mean, I take my dog's antidepressants."

———

New Year's Eve, 2006.

Also Lisa's birthday.

The night I popped the question.

It's a packed bar at the beautiful Martini House in Napa Valley, filled with friends and loved ones staring at the ground and moving furniture.

Let me explain.

It was my sister Robin's idea to propose that night. Earlier in the year, Lisa had done a piece on a Russian psychic. At the end she asked her, "Hey, I'm in a relationship; what do you see in the cards?" The psychic said, "Now things are not so good, but next year they'll be great." Lisa said, "Did you hear the part when I said I'm *in* a relationship?"

We laughed about it, but Sis pointed out how New Year's Eve is technically the beginning of "next year," which would make asking Lisa to marry me the "great" prediction come true. Terrific idea, I thought. We got a bunch of friends to go up to Napa with us to celebrate New Year's and Lisa's birthday—the ruse!—and when the magic night arrived, I had my moment planned. I'd hidden the engagement ring, and now the box was in my pocket being nervously massaged by my fingers. When the countdown started, I'd wait for the "Three! Two! One!" and unleash the, "Remember how that Russian psychic told you that this year was lousy but next year was going to be great? Well . . . will you marry me?"

We had a pretty joyous group with us at the Martini House that night and the evening was going smashingly.

Suddenly the countdown started. "Ten! Nine! Eight!"

I nervously gripped the ring box in my pocket.

"Seven! Six! Five!"

About to open the box, I said, "Remember how that Russian psychic told you that this year was lousy but next year was going to be great? Well . . ."

"Four! Three! Two!"

"Will you marry . . ."

I opened the box, and the ring was not there. Gone. How? I'd had it when we got there!

Lisa looked at me. "Wait a minute. Is this . . . a joke?"

"One! Happy New Year!" everyone in the bar screamed at the top of their lungs.

At this moment, my sisters saw me with the open ring box, and also proceeded to scream at the top of their lungs.

It took me a second to unfreeze my face, though, and respond to Lisa.

"No! No! It's not a joke! I mean it; will you marry me?" *Where is that freaking ring?*

"Well, uh . . ."

"I don't know where the ring is!" I said, scanning the floor around me, which was unhelpfully covered in confetti and shiny decorative strips. *Why?* Oh, right, it was New Year's.

I opted for full disclosure. I announced to the crowd, "Hey, everyone! I think I've lost a diamond ring somewhere on the floor; could everyone take a look—"

This prompted havoc, since we're talking about a roomful of drunk people, all of whom began a quest for this precious piece of jewelry. Everybody in the Martini House bar was now looking for it, shoving chairs and tables aside, crawling all over one another, and getting on all fours.

I turned to Lisa and said, "Would you marry me without the ring?"

"Yes," she said unequivocally, wiping away tears, then added with a frisson of laser-focused seriousness, "But I want to see it."

Visual confirmation occurred only minutes later, when our friend Suzanne Rico located the ring amid some glittering debris below the bar, holding it up and triumphantly shouting, "What does the person who finds it get?!"

"My undying gratitude!" I yelled out, relieved.

We were married six months later in June. I was now wedded to the most wonderful woman, and starring in a hit TV show that I looked forward to working on every day.

When Charlie told me in 2008 that he had asked his girlfriend, Brooke Mueller, an attractive blond socialite turned Realtor, to marry him, I expressed joy at the news. I had bounced back from divorce myself by falling in love with the exquisite, kind, talented, and intelligent Lisa Joyner. Let's make this bliss spreadable!

"That's great, Charlie!" I said.

"Yeah, well, she made a hell of an effort," he said. "She earned it."

Earned it? That didn't sound . . . positive. In any case, I couldn't make the wedding because I was shooting a movie in Austin with Robert Rodriguez, so Lisa went in my stead. When it came time for Charlie's dad to toast the newlyweds, the esteemed Martin Sheen stood up and the crowd went silent, anticipating the matrimonial eloquence that the guy who played President Bartlet those many years on *The West Wing* was about to lay down. He took a moment, eyed the crowd, then mumbled, "Hope you kids know what you're doing," and sat back down.

More prophetic words . . . yadda yadda yadda . . .

In August, as my daughter, Daisy, was being born, she stretched her tiny gore-covered arm skyward and let out a wail. A beautiful being was emerging into my plane of existence, soon to fill my life with joy and purpose, but God help me, I'm such a sci-fi movie geek that all I could think of was how much it reminded me of Charlton Heston stretching his gore-covered arm skyward and wailing, "Soylent Green is *people!*"

I shook that off, cut the umbilical cord, appropriately beamed as she was swaddled for the first time, and gingerly held her to my chest. As I cradled her in my arms I got my first real look at my daughter's face. Of course she was sublime, a face I was already falling in love with. But the trip through the birth canal had done an outstanding job of giving her visage a noticeably compressed squishiness, and again, God help me, all

I could think of was how much she reminded me of Bert Lahr's Cowardly Lion from *The Wizard of Oz.*

Clearly I've got a problem.

It's a beautiful problem to have, though.

———

In the fall of 2009 I was driving into work one day when I heard two KROQ deejays discussing an interview Charlie had given to notorious conspiracy theorist Alex Jones, spouting crazy talk about how the U.S. government, like some really evil David Copperfield, orchestrated 9/11, destroyed the Twin Towers in a controlled demolition, slammed the Pentagon with a cruise missile, faked a plane crash in Shanksville, Pennsylvania, and made us look the other way toward Islamic fundamentalists. They played excerpts from the interview, and I thought, *What the fuck?*

When I saw Charlie at work that day, I pulled him aside. "Dude, what are you doing?" I said. "I don't really understand how you could feel this way, but even if you do, you certainly don't have to discuss it on the radio."

"Jon," he said, "there's so much going on that we don't know about."

"You mean about how the United States government, an institution that can barely deliver our mail, was somehow able to wire two of the biggest modern office buildings on planet Earth with thousands of pounds of high explosives and hundreds of thousands of feet of trigger wire, and not have any of the approximately forty thousand employees notice? Then coordinate *two* hijacked jetliners flown by amateur pilots to crash into said building *exactly* where they happen to have planted the explosives so that half an hour later they can detonate the charges and complete their evil plan?" I replied.

We continued our conversation in the makeup room that day, although arguing logic and reason against such a harebrained idea isn't

exactly like shooting fish in a barrel, because before you even start shooting you just want to stare at such poorly designed fish and say, "Really?"
Nevertheless, I aimed to ridicule my colleague, even though talking politics at work is touchy, because people care, and hierarchy colors the taking
of sides. I was surprised, in fact, that Charlie's views earned quite a bit of
support in the makeup room that day, but then, should I have been? Is
the person applying blush really going to say to the star of TV's biggest
comedy, "You know, you're actually disappearing up your own paranoid
asshole at this moment? And could you tilt your head a little to the left?"

At one point, I said, "Okay, so why destroy the towers?"

Charlie said, "Well, they wanted to destroy the documents that
revealed the plan."

"Did you see pictures of downtown Manhattan afterward?!" I said.
"It was littered with documents! Pretty dumb way to keep your documents secret—by spreading them all over the lower third of one of the
world's most populous cities! What happened to just going to Office Depot and getting a shredder for thirty-nine dollars?! It's only thirty-four
dollars if they used their Office Depot Rewards card!"

This went on for a while, but then I backed off. That Charlie stood by
this was hard to fathom, unless . . . unless *they'd gotten to him.*

Actually, I teased him about it whenever I could after that—someone
remarking that the craft service table was out of something might incur
a snotty, "Damn you, neo-cons!" from me. But it did really seem as if
something wasn't right.

———

On Emmy night in September 2009—my fourth year in a row as a nominee for supporting actor in a comedy—I was seated off to the side of the
Nokia Theatre, and frankly, I understood why. That's where the peren-
nial losers go. *That's fine*, I thought. *It cosmically fits Alan's persona to be*

in the loser role. Lisa and I sat next to female supporting actor nominee Kristen Chenoweth. Ah, I figured, they don't expect her to win either.

Then she won. Were we in the lucky section?

Then I won. We were!

Years before, the year of my first Emmy nomination for playing Alan, I'd come up with what I thought was a funny acceptance line, but as I kept losing I filed it away in the back of my memory. Now, in the flush of a win I didn't expect, I was walking slowly to the podium because I wanted *desperately* to remember that line. *Then again,* I remembered, *there's nothing more embarrassing than outlasting your applause. Better hurry to that stage!* Fortunately it came back to me, a joke about how I'd never thought of awards as much. Until right then, of course.

It was an exhilarating night. To be recognized by your peers is a truly wonderful feeling, and the fact that we were entering our seventh season of *Two and a Half Men*—and logging our first Emmy win for acting— seemed to bode well for the continued health of the show. On top of that, the addition of Daisy to our family was already exponentially increasing the joy at home.

This was a good time to be me.

Jon Cryer, winner at the Emmys, winner at life. I could settle in for a continued existence of absolute normalcy and nothing weird ever happening at all.

Chapter 26
The Tsunami Is More Important

I had been enjoying Christmas Day of 2009 so much with my family around me that I somehow managed to stay away from all Internet-connected devices for much of it. It's the holiday present that doesn't announce itself, really. You just wake up from concentrated yuletide merriment at some point and realize, *Hey, I haven't been online at all today. Sweet!*

Then, of course, you give in, check a news site, and read that your costar "Carlos Irwin Estévez" has been arrested in Aspen, Colorado, for spousal battery.

Alarmed and freaked-out, I texted him: *Dude, my thoughts are with you. If you need to talk, give a call; if you've got bigger problems, call me when you get back.*

A few minutes later, Charlie texted back: *Thanks bro. Yikes—fukk me, wut a bad day. . . . I'm flying home tonite. I'll try to call over the weekend. Shower rape was bad but the food was okay. Hair and makeup for mug shot got there too late. . . .*

He followed that with: *And I had same bail bondsman as Kobe.* . . . *No joke* . . . *:)*

I took the sense of humor about shower rape and sharing Kobe Bryant's bail bondsman as a good sign, although it seemed pretty clear my friend and colleague wasn't sober anymore. We exchanged "Merry Xmas" texts, although mine had a question mark, to which Charlie texted back, *I'll take it!*

I knew the media would want a quote from me, and Charlie's manager, Mark Burg, called me to say that any statement of support I could offer up would be great. I told him I would be happy to, but that it sounded like Charlie wasn't sober anymore, and I hoped he'd get on track again. Situations like this are rough on your sense of friendship and loyalty, because the allegations are serious, yet you know Charlie and Brooke are a drug-troubled pair, and Charlie's your longtime friend who was proud of his sobriety, but that doesn't mean he didn't do something to her, and you should give a woman the benefit of the doubt when she's been abused, and oh, boy . . .

This would put everybody at the show in a weird position, I realized.

In January, at the first read-through of the script after his arrest, Charlie made the Kobe joke again, everybody laughed, and it was as though the whole incident was forgotten. Things seemed almost normal, with a low-level fog of denial settling in, although I could sense a slow-boil fury in Charlie. He felt persecuted. In February I got a knock on my trailer door one day, and it was Chuck Lorre. I invited him in, and he said, "Jon, can you talk to Charlie? I hear he's going off the rails."

Chuck himself is a recovering alcoholic, and open and honest about it. This was such a sincere plea that I knew I had to consider it. "I can try," I told him.

The next day, though, Charlie went into rehab, so we never got to

have that conversation. Charlie did, however, have a different kind of pro-
ductive conversation—with Warner Bros. business affairs. Despite falling
off the wagon, a rocky marriage, looming felony charges, and possible
time behind bars, he managed to secure a massive raise, fully three times
what I was being paid.

I immediately began contemplating a series of well-publicized
drunken brawls in retirement homes, or possibly leading cops on a de-
structive car chase along Santa Monica beach, just prior to my next contract negotiation.

When Charlie's punishment came down that fall regarding Aspen, it
felt like a slap on the wrist: thirty days in rehab, thirty days of probation,
and thirty-six hours of anger management—the therapy, not *Anger
Management* the TV series, which didn't exist yet, but would eventually
because of upheavals such as this.

There was a brief time when it was thought Charlie's sentencing
would involve his serving time at a community theater in Aspen, the news
of which led me to think, *Wow, they managed to find the only thing that
sounds worse than jail.*

———

Person or persons unknown have pushed Charlie's expensive German
sedan off a cliff.

"Damn you, Bush!" I wanted to say to him, but didn't.

I'll admit, this incident sounded fishy. How could someone break into
Charlie's gated, security camera–festooned Mulholland compound and
make off with a Mercedes-Benz, the steering of which they don't seem to
know how to operate?

I thought, *If he comes in to work with scratches, I'll know he was actually driving the car, and that he went off a ravine in a drugged-out stupor.*
Charlie arrived a little late, but looked the same, and when I said hi to
him he must have thought I was trying to guess his weight, the way I was

eyeing him up and down. Then I blurted, "Hey, shake!" and extended a hand, only so I could grasp his and turn it over, looking for cuts or bruises. None that I could see.

When he talked about the incident, I asked if there was anything of value in the car for someone to steal. He said, "Well, I'm pissed because all my VHS copies of *Spin City* were in the trunk."

"Well, there you go," I said. "Cops should be able to canvass the last VCR owners in the city, no problem."

We laughed about it and chalked it up to freakishly creative young vandals saddled with outdated video recorders.

Then it happened again.

Charlie didn't look so good as we started our eighth season in the fall of 2010—gaunt, pale, sallow, even sweaty occasionally. He started talking to himself. But most of all he just looked thinner, in a not-good way. Watching the new episodes at home, Lisa could tell how terrible he looked, and said as much.

Even his teeth looked bad. They looked like they were going to fall out of his mouth.

His timing started to go off, too. The pauses were now a little too short. He was rushing lines. He was still remembering them, at least, but there was now an incrementally more manic energy that threw his rhythm off by microseconds. These might not have been perceptible differences to the vast majority of viewers, but to me they felt substantial. Charlie just wasn't hitting the jokes the way he used to. It was as if his psyche had been sped up.

One time during rehearsals to choreograph the movement for a scene, he asked, "Can I just stand next to this couch?" He wanted to hold on to it for the duration of the scene.

so *that* happened

During a week off in October 2010, I was in New York for a birthday party for my mother, and Charlie was there as well, taking time to see Denise and the kids. He invited me to go see the Broadway production of *Mary Poppins* with them, but I told him I couldn't. Charlie texted me the next day that the kids had to wake him up forty-eight minutes into the show, and that they were "ready to bolt."

I'm not saying *Mary Poppins* always has a calming, cheerful influence on everybody, but it appeared Charlie had his own interpretation of the kind of spoonful of sugar that helps the medicine go down, as I learned the following day when I read about Charlie's Plaza Hotel "booze-and-blow binge"—so described by the *New York Daily News*—and the "semi-pro" escort found naked and locked in the closet of his trashed hotel room.

I texted him asking if he wanted to talk, and he texted back, *Thanks, bro. . . . Shoulda stayed for the whole Poppins show. . . . Oops . . . :)*

I began to imagine scenarios in which I enthusiastically agree to go to *Mary Poppins* with him. Then afterward, when he says, "Thought I'd head back to the room with a prostitute, get really fucking high, decimate the place, then toss her in the closet," I say, "No, I don't think you should do that." Then he says, "You're right. Let's get ice cream." Then everything is better.

Back in January, after the Colorado arrest, Charlie had been legitimately worried about how the audience would receive him. And yet they roared their approval on Friday night at the taping. The applause had been thunderous, as if, forced to make a choice between the polite clapping of reserved judgment and "we support you" raucousness, they openly took his side. And Charlie had been nervous. Yet there appeared to be no moral consequence. They wanted their Charlie Sheen.

Then, after the Plaza insanity later that year, and the obvious conclusion that he was openly partying again, all of us at the show assumed his tabloid notoriety was going to result in a ratings drop. I even told Chuck, "Look, I don't know when this stops being funny for people. We keep making jokes about the fact that the Charlie character's an alcoholic on the show, and yet the real Charlie's actually got an addiction problem. When does it stop being funny?"

Then the ratings went up, and Charlie said, "Yeah, look at that! Look at that! How's that, motherfucker?!" He was rejoicing in the fact that his off-camera exploits were in no way hurting the show's appeal.

This only added to the surrealism, to say the least.

Chuck Lorre came to me again about having a talk with Charlie. But this time it was clear that Chuck was desperate. His eyes were rimmed with tears. I told him I would.

As Charlie and I arrived on the set the next morning, I pulled Charlie aside and said, "Hey, man, do you have some time later to talk?"

"Yeah, yeah," he said. "We can talk now, right?"

"No, I really want to talk to you privately."

"Can't we talk now?" *He's onto me,* I thought. He wanted us to have this "talk" in front of everybody. Since he probably knew what it was about, he figured I wouldn't actually say anything negative with crew people around. And it would be short.

"No, it's a private thing," I said.

When our first five-minute break came that day—with Charlie around these were common, since he'd want a smoke, which meant going outside—he said, "Hey, can we talk now . . . ?"

He was like a child sensing that a parent was mad at him, concerned about the seriousness of the topic, but eager to reduce the circumstances that could make it an uncomfortable powwow. I said no, but later, during another five-minute break, I acquiesced and followed him outside for his smoke.

"Here's the thing, dude," I said. "It used to be that you could party all night and show up here and still hit it out of the park. Those days are gone. People can tell now."

"Really?" Charlie took it in, nodded, puffed, then said, "Okay, okay. I guess I gotta change things." It sounded sincere, as if he'd listened.

"Good," I said. "We're all rooting for you to fix it. Everyone's here to help."

That was in December of 2010.

———

When your star can't make it to rehearsals, your production doesn't just stop. As Charlie's appearances for table reads and rehearsals became more and more erratic, the producers resorted to rehearsing the scenes with Charlie's stand-in, Jim Marshall.

For me, performing with Jim turned out to be an unexpected treat. His impossibly droll delivery of Charlie Harper's lines proved to be hilarious. Plus, rehearsals just went more quickly because Jim didn't take smoke breaks.

Often, our Sheen-less run-throughs would get more laughs than the real thing. It was a testament to the talent of the writers (and, of course, Jim) that the material still worked equally well with diametrically opposed performances. When Charlie did manage to show up at Stage 26 he was transparently making an effort to appear sober. But he was overdoing it. He'd be eagerly good-natured all the time, smiling and laughing excessively. Hugging bewildered crew members. I'd spend my time trying to decide which was more disturbing: Sheen loaded or Sheen "sober."

At this point Charlie started complaining about the show more.

But again, only to me, it seemed.

On a Tuesday, Charlie came to me, rolling his eyes about the script that week. "What the hell are we doing here?" he said. "This is just a train wreck." He was even vocal about it to our director, Jamie Widdoes.

As we went through rehearsal, Charlie was actually his usual professional self. When the writers and Chuck showed up for the run-through for them—typically the time when changes are suggested—I got nervous, looking at Charlie, then Chuck, then back at Charlie, wondering when the blowup was going to happen, when he'd let everyone know about the "train wreck." But instead Charlie kept quiet, and the scenes got a lot of laughs. As the writers migrated back to the writers' room, Jamie and I were there to see Charlie walk up to Chuck and say, "Hey, this stuff is great this week. Thanks."

Jamie and I looked at each other with expressions that could only be described as, *What the* fuck? What happened to the "train wreck" comment?

This further stressed to me the fact that Charlie was genuinely afraid of confrontation. But on a show like ours, when you have less than a week to get the thing up and running, letting people know your concerns isn't confrontation—it's collaboration. Over eight years, I had absolutely let it be known when a joke didn't sit right with me, or an entire act didn't work. The great thing about our writers is that when you let them know this, they do their damnedest to come up with something else. It wasn't as if you could never let them know that you didn't want to do something a certain way.

And Charlie, as the guy making the biggest of the big bucks in sitcom land, should have known that his criticisms would carry a lot of weight.

But Charlie wants people to like him. For eight years he'd been fun, charming, and smart. And nice. I guess I didn't want to think about the fact that something was bottled up inside.

As 2010 became 2011, the promise of a brand-new year ahead still barely a blink in destiny's eye, sin looked kindly upon Charlie Sheen and beckoned him to its namesake city in the Nevada desert the weekend before he was supposed to report back to work. Vodka shots, willing babes, and steep tabs awaited, and if you didn't know any better reading about his weekend bender on gossip sites, you'd think he was the star of a show called *Back in Vegas*.

I decided to passive-aggressively "live text" him throughout his debauched January weekend, interrupting what I figured were M. C. Escher–style sexual permutations to alert him that he should make some time during the weekend to see *The King's Speech*. I might have casually suggested he try not to marry anybody, either.

I joke, but I was worried. With TMZ reporting these excursions of his as they were happening, I knew that he was being watched by the media, as an adoring pet owner would hover with a camcorder over a cutesy-wootsy kitten in the hopes it'd do something oh, so cutesy-wootsy.

Then I started to get the surveillance treatment.

I was the colleague of the incident-prone, off-the-wagon star, after all, so obviously my jogging, dog-walking, and stroller rituals needed to be scrutinized. I began noticing cars driving aimlessly around my neighborhood. Then there'd be a car at the end of the street, parked perpendicularly in the middle of an intersection, with the telltale circle of a massive zoom lens poking out the side window.

Whilst I was walking my dogs, I'd invariably notice the lense right after one of my canines had dropped a steamer on the sidewalk. Then I'd be faced with the dilemma of how do I pick up this poo, knowing that whatever I do will be photographed with the highest-quality equipment available and almost instantly posted on the Internet for worldwide consumption. Do I whip out my plastic poo bag, adopt an Abercrombie & Fitch male-model pose, and try to sell this as a casually handsome, responsible dog owner deep-knee bend? Do I go for a balletic arabesque with a J. Crew expression of comely approachability? Do I curtsy?

Occasionally I'd get the "nice" paparazzo, who starts off with, "Sorry to bother you, Jon . . ." as I'm doing my daily run. And up until this point in my life, I hadn't minded the occasional walk-and-chat with a TMZ guy. Maybe that was why they were polite initially. They figured I'd talk. But then they were standing at the edge of my driveway yelling out questions when my kids were in tow, and I don't live in a gated community.

"Hey, what do you think, Jon? You think Charlie's guilty?"

"Did Charlie beat up his wife?"

"You got anything to say to Charlie?"

Meanwhile, my kids didn't know anything about Charlie Sheen and his vices. This was beyond the pale. I called the police on these lurkers once, because if there are guys sitting outside your house taking pictures of your kids, you don't know if they're paparazzi or pedophiles. (You suspect the former, but love the excuse to call the police that the latter gives you.) When the cops came and ticketed one guy for being parked partly in a red zone, I felt all warm inside.

But still, their following me on my jogs or while I was walking down the street was getting obnoxious. Then my wife, an experienced entertainment journalist, clued me in on something essential about the relationship between pestered celebrity and dogged reporter.

"If you don't speak to them, they have nothing," she said. "It's when you open your mouth, even to say, 'No comment,' that gives them a clip." And she's right! If I just run by, or walk by, or whatever, wherever, all they have is a shot of me being ambulatory—not so sexy! The video guys really don't like that. Now I just pretend it's a long tracking shot in a movie, and I'm the actor pretending the camera isn't there as I make my way through the airport, or down the sidewalk, or along the ledge of a building when I'm deep into my parkour training. (That last one is a joke, people.)

I went to the drugstore one day with a very particular shopping list, and as I was putting my items on the counter, I heard the *click, click, click* that can mean only photographic attention. *Oh, shit,* I thought. Then I looked up and was relieved to discover that it wasn't me they were after; it was Britney Spears, who had entered the very same CVS. Whew. I looked back down at my purchases: a Duraflame log, a jar of mayonnaise, and an enema kit. What tabloid headline had I just narrowly escaped?

It was starting to get to me. Having my life intruded upon set me on edge in a way I'd never experienced. And it was all the more galling that it wasn't even anything I'd done that warranted this crap. Around this time *Theater Geek,* the book about Stagedoor Manor, had come out, and to take my mind off the intrigue, I picked up a copy. Its portrayal of my youthful stomping grounds was spot-on, and provided some much-needed levity. I could even laugh off the egregious historical inaccuracy that attributed my subway improv to one Robert Downey Jr.

But I also read something that genuinely shocked me: that our beloved artistic director, Dr. Jack Romano, the man who'd changed my life with his craft, passion, enthusiasm, and respect for acting, was not only never a graduate of the Royal Academy of Dramatic Art, but he wasn't even a doctor. It had all been a lie. I guess he'd gotten the job based on a résumé that was, to say the least, padded.

I was already awash in an ocean of bullshit and now this. At first I felt betrayed, of course, but it occurred to me that his particular brand of bullshit was used to inspire children and give them the skills to pursue their dreams, not tear people down and hurt them. And it also occurred to me that the letter to the Royal Academy that he wrote for me must have really been something, 'cause it fucking worked. Learning this about Jack, who had died in 1993, taught me about the duality of bullshit: It always stinks, but sometimes something great grows from it.

———

As it was increasingly apparent that my famous workmate was taking a turn for the worse, I was facing the fact that things weren't going so well for my childhood friends, either.

For a while David Dennis had really seemed to be doing well. He'd been running the Plaza Hotel's Oyster Bar, and had turned it around from a money loser into a hot spot where the Yankees gathered after they won the World Series. He'd gotten married and adopted a daughter. But then he began abusing prescription drugs—"Hey, at least I'm not drinking," he'd throw out as a qualifier—and his addictions took their toll, to the extent that his visits to California invariably involved all manner of strange behavior. He stopped making sense when he talked. He'd rent a car and get into an accident, then walk away from it. He'd come to the set, then fall asleep in my trailer. He also kept trying to get close to Charlie, under the impression that the two could bond over sobriety issues, but Charlie thought he was mentally ill and kept referring to him as "Prozac Dave." I love my friend, but it was getting harder and harder to have him around the way I used to.

Then Artie, who I'd always assumed was a highly functioning alcoholic, called me in the middle of the Charlie craziness with a tale of woe. I hadn't really kept up with Artie. I would typically find out about him through David. But then out of the blue Artie phoned me saying his marriage was falling apart, and that a storage facility was selling off his stuff because of a billing screwup. He needed a thousand dollars to keep his possessions from being sold.

That was a no-brainer. If he needed a thousand dollars, I could give him a thousand dollars.

The blue Nissan Versa stayed behind us the whole way.

It was there when Lisa, the kids, and I pulled out of our driveway, and it was still there on the freeway as we headed north toward Santa Clarita.

My son was trying his best to enjoy this spy-movie moment with some very persistent paparazzi, but Lisa and I could tell that underneath, he was actually scared. Another freeway and one exit later, there was no way to look at our tail as fun in any way. I was beginning to get pretty riled. When would this shit end?

I pulled into my sister Robin's driveway, got out, and looked back at the Versa, after which it peeled away and down the street. Thank God. The kids ran inside, and Robin's husband, Phil (remember the PA who got screwed out of his driver's license? Well, he ended up marrying my sister), asked me to help bring some firewood inside from the trunk of his car.

Screeeech, click, click, click, vroooommm.

With all the urgency of a drive-by shooting, they pulled up, rattled off a fusillade of photos, and tore off as if I were about to give chase. They'd come all this way for what had to be the most incredibly lame photo exclusive of all time. Unless they were from *Firewood Monthly*. I never found out. I guessed there'd be no escaping a headline this time: "Cryer Sports Wood with Male Companion!"

There's a long history in Hollywood of performers with addiction issues being enabled and even abetted by the studios they work for. But on *Two and a Half Men*, the time had come for Warner Bros. honchos Bruce Rosenblum and Peter Roth to get involved. A couple weeks into January, Chuck Lorre informed Charlie that at the end of that week's show taping on Friday, Bruce and Peter were going to have a meeting with him. If Charlie was only nervously apprehensive about me wanting a word with him last month, this kind of official-meeting shit would drive him up a wall.

Backstage, he was talking to himself, and getting madder and madder. Gabe and Janice, his respective makeup and hair people, were trying to do their jobs while he fidgeted and smoked. He started to get manic as he psyched himself for what he assumed was a meeting of incredible importance. It was so tension-filled backstage, I thought he was going to come to blows with someone.

I walked up to him and said, "What are you worried about?"

"All these assholes are gonna come, they'll spend two hours giving me shit, and I'm just gonna have to nod and say yes. I'm tired of all the bullshit!"

"Okay," I said. "Then do you want to give them a reason right now to give you even more shit, or do you want to buckle down and do the show?"

He looked me in the eye and said, "Yeah, you're right. You're right."

Things didn't start smoothly once the show began. We did a scene with the two of us sitting on a couch, and Charlie screwed up every line. He could not remember anything he was supposed to say. It was hard to comprehend what I was seeing, because Charlie had always prided himself on getting it done on show night. It was like watching HAL go haywire in *2001: A Space Odyssey*. Mark Samuels, our assistant director, who is the soul of diplomacy and quiet competence, said to Charlie, "Do you need a minute?" (Over the years, Mark had acquired a courteous way of answering a frustrated director's "Where's Charlie?" query. He'd say, "He's been invited.")

Charlie paused, then said, "Wait a minute; just give me a second."

Somebody handed him the pages, and as he went over them, the rest of us were extraordinarily uncomfortable. The audience was here, after all. And then a rather astonishing thing happened. On take two, Charlie completely nailed it. Every beat. Every line. When he absolutely had to focus, he did. It was a strange and impressive thing to behold.

Instead of sticking around for the meeting with Bruce and Peter, however, Charlie chose to walk out, still in full makeup, get in his car, and have his driver take him home. He left Bruce Rosenblum and Peter Roth just standing by his trailer. And with that, we all accepted that something was truly broken here, that Charlie couldn't be counted on to even go through the motions anymore.

That was also the last episode of *Two and a Half Men* Charlie would ever shoot.

I, meanwhile, stayed late to film a scene in which I was dressed as a woman, and, I would like to add, got quite a few compliments on how good I looked in return. Just sayin'.

"Artie's dead."

"What?"

"He died yesterday. We've been trying to get in touch with you."

I had gotten several voice mails from David, but long before, I'd come to the realization that his behavior had become so erratic that I had to stop listening to them. This call was actually from his brother Eric, who was undoubtedly overwhelmed.

Only a month before, Artie and I had had our conversation about the storage locker. Apparently he had had a seizure, then gone into a coma; then a lung infection ran rampant through his body. It was very shocking. Although Artie was prone to mystery ailments, he had lived the last five years with a neurological disorder that would paralyze his leg occasionally, then go away, but leave him in debilitating pain. He was also drinking enormous amounts of alcohol. Even David, who spent lots of time with Artie, couldn't tell when Artie was drinking or how much.

The funeral for Artie was a sad, odd affair. Artie's friends did their best to emphasize the joyful parts of his life, because Artie was such a funny guy. But it was a disconnect emotionally for me: seeing all these people from my childhood, which on one level was comforting, but tied to the fact that we were all there for a terribly tragic reason. It made me feel dazed. When David showed up—we all heard the *thump, sssshh, thump, sssssh* of his caned walk before we saw him—he wore dark glasses, and looked pale and wan, in a way almost the picture of a grieving widow. Artie's death was a loss for me, but for David it devastated him to his core. He clearly wasn't going to be channeling his usual enthusiasm toward a light, celebratory story about his dear departed friend.

To this day, the mention of Artie triggers a flood of tears in David.

———

During an off week for the show, Charlie was hospitalized with abdominal pains. We were now at the stage when Chuck and I and others at the show were all pretty sure this was the overdose we'd been expecting. Charlie wasn't answering my texts.

What followed, as I understood it later, was that after Charlie was released, he got a visit at his home from Bruce Rosenblum and Les Moonves, who told him they'd have a private jet ready to take him to a rehab facility out of state so he could get help and have some privacy. This wasn't a suggestion. It was either this or the show would be stopped for the season. We'd filmed sixteen episodes already out of a twenty-two-episode season.

Charlie agreed, then the next day changed his mind and said he'd complete a rehab program at home with a highly regarded sober coach, and a sober companion. But Chuck Lorre, who'd been keeping close tabs on everything, talked with the coach, and when he learned Charlie was going to do it all at home, he came to the conclusion that it wouldn't work. Chuck's view was that Charlie needed to be taken out of his comfort zone to effectively deal with his problems. This, naturally, pissed Charlie off.

All of this I learned later. What I knew at the time was that we were shutting down production for a few weeks—the second time in two years—in the hopes that Charlie could get better and we could complete four more episodes instead of six. I was hopeful, and made plans to visit Charlie at his Mulholland house on the first weekend in February. I had to see how all this was going down.

He greeted me at the door with, "Welcome to Sober Valley Lodge." He hugged me, then said, "I gotta go pee in a cup." I watched him walk off with a doctor.

Denise was there, as was one of the "goddesses," the label he'd given his nubile Vegas companions. The one there that day was Natalie, the bikini model for *High Times* magazine who looked like a fourteen-year-old, not Bree, the porn star who looked like a fourteen-year-old. The sober companion was there, too, as well as the sober coach, who didn't look like a fourteen-year-old, and answered my query as to what I could do to help with, "Just coming to visit is great. Keeping him involved in the world that worked for him sober would be great."

Charlie seemed in good spirits that day—more coherent and clear-eyed than he'd been in a while—although his voice was completely shot for some reason. He was happy to have company, but I couldn't help feeling that this was still an existence in which everything he wanted (save drugs and alcohol) was around him, his needs were being catered to, and issues weren't being addressed. I worried that whatever this arrangement was at Charlie's house, it wouldn't truly be effective. But hey, with addiction, most of the time none of it works. Maybe trying anything different is better than nothing.

And yet, I asked Charlie as I was leaving, "What is it you ultimately want?"

"I don't want Chuck on the show anymore," he said. "I'm tired of his shit."

"Really?" I said. "I'm sorry that your relationship with Chuck has deteriorated like this. I didn't know your problems ran that deep." The whole time I was thinking, *When was this head-butting between Chuck and Charlie happening?*

Charlie said, "I want Don Reo to take over the show." Don, a sitcom veteran who'd created *Blossom*, had been on *Two and a Half Men* only a short while, and while I liked Don, I knew that *Two and a Half Men* without Chuck Lorre would suffer. I said as much, and Charlie added, "Oh, well, Chuck can still run the writers' room. I just don't want to deal with him ever on the set."

This was something of a shock to me, because I simply did not have that kind of relationship with Chuck. I worked well with him. I told Charlie I couldn't stop him from airing his grievances about Chuck to the network, but that if he was looking for us to band together on this campaign, it wasn't going to happen.

"Okay, okay," he said. "But I want you to know I'm going to pay you for these two shows we're not doing."

"Thanks, Charlie, but that's a lot of money."

"I'm gonna pay you, we're gonna come back, and I'm gonna get everybody paid. Either I'll pay you, or I'll get Warner Bros. to make sure you get paid." He seemed genuinely intent on this point, especially his concern that the crew was losing two weeks of pay. "Anyway, we're coming back. Next week! I'm feeling great. I'm back next week."

———

The theory going around at the time was that Charlie was desperate to get back to work because he needed the money. Yes, yes, I know: How does someone who makes that kind of dough suddenly "need" money? Well, as the speculation went, all the high living had taken its toll. If you've reached the point where paycheck-to-paycheck living isn't a matter of hundreds of dollars, but millions, you might just go off the deep end about missing out on that weekly scratch.

Then the rants started. On February 14, he went on Dan Patrick's radio show and offered up the image of a ready-to-work, one hundred percent clean-and-sober Charlie Sheen blithely showing up to the studio lot to earn his keep, only to find an empty workplace, like a ghost town right out of an old Western. He's banging on the stage door, a lone figure of responsibility and promptness howling to an uncaring, soulless corporate entity, "Where is everybody?"

That was actually kind of funny. Completely untrue, but funny.

The reality, as I later learned, was that Chuck Lorre knew a week and a half of home rehab wasn't enough, and wouldn't sign off on cranking up production again that quickly. It angered Charlie so much that he felt all he could do was take his fight to the airwaves, calling out the show executives as the ones not ready. "Bewildered" doesn't begin to describe my feeling at listening to this interview.

I would like to clarify something, however, that was misinterpreted by the by-now steady drumbeat of coverage on Charlie's antics and the show's turmoil. The night of that Dan Patrick interview, the season's last (although we didn't know it yet) episode aired, and in Chuck Lorre's vanity card at the end of the show, he listed a litany of his own examples of healthy living—exercise, good food, doctor visits, no drink or drugs or smoking—and ended with a joke that read, "If Charlie Sheen outlives me, I'm gonna be really pissed."

To almost everybody, this came off as a barbed retort, a deliberately antagonistic response to Charlie's accusations. But in actuality, that vanity card had been written weeks before, and we'd all laughed about it on the set. Even Charlie.

The paps were now showing up when I dropped my son off at the school bus and when I took him out for a frozen yogurt. They were tailing my car whenever I drove to Disney to do voice work, and chasing my wife and me in and out of local stores. They'd even started to follow my assistant, Sarah. Two guys trailed her to her apartment complex, parked out front, and just waited. After several hours they finally took a break to get some food. My keen-eyed assistant picked up her cell and dialed. Turned out they'd parked with eight whole inches of their car blocking the apartment complex driveway. They returned, hoagies in hand, to see a tow truck pulling away with their piece-of-shit Prius dangling off the back. And my assistant laughing her ass off.

———

The insane rumors were flying fast and furious: that Charlie was spiraling, that he was being extorted by an underage girl who had video, that he sent former New York Met Lenny Dykstra (soon to be indicted for fraud) over to Warner Bros. Studios with a list of demands including Chuck Lorre's dismissal, yet another pay raise, and that Bruce Rosenblum, only the head of Warner Bros. Television, be barred from the lot.

It occurred to me at that time that Lenny Dykstra would actually make a fantastic process server. Who wouldn't open the door for a three-time all-star?

———

A-a-a-a-and we're back to Alex Jones.

Because when you have truly berserk shit to say, where else do you go?

Charlie returned to Alex Jones's radio show, and this time unloaded on Chuck. Labeled him a "charlatan," claimed he'd turned Chuck's "tin can" of a show into "pure gold," and called him "Chaim Levine," which while technically Chuck Lorre's actual Hebrew name, to the ears of an audience not out of its mind might as well have been "Jewy Jewerson."

What the fuck was going on with Charlie? Was this an attempt to embarrass Chuck, or coerce him into leaving the show of his own volition? The gambit seemed ill-advised. As I mentioned earlier, regular protocol in the TV world—and this has happened a lot—dictates that an unhappy star simply go to the network brass and say, "Hey, I can't work with this person any longer. Can you make a change?" The producer then steps aside, still retaining his or her massive paycheck, and goes to Fiji.

But Charlie hated confrontation. Loved doing plenty of drugs, stewing about shit, and having a meltdown on the radio. But not strolling over to an office and asking someone to take care of a little problem. Charlie Sheen would not have made a good Mafia don.

I learned a lot from Charlie out of that Alex Jones interview. Charlie's a Vatican assassin. He's addicted to winning. He's our new sheriff. He's got poetry in his fingertips. Alcoholism is a false construct. And Thomas Jefferson was a pussy.

I couldn't let that last one stand. I texted him that day, *If u say ANY-THING about Ben Franklin, I am gonna lose my shit!!*

He texted back, *four eyed wig thief.*

I tried to ascertain what exactly Charlie was after. I sent him back a text asking what his plan was, what was behind this "PR stuff," as I gingerly called it. He responded with a long text screed about Chuck, calling him a "cancer that needs to be punished" and ending with a twisted kind of life lesson:

> *hatred is fuel.*
> *fuel is god. . . . .*
> *or is it; dog. . . . . ?*
> *hmmmm. . . .*

Last, I tried to let him know that he was letting anger consume him, that he would lose all his power if he did that. Then he sent a cryptic response:

> *oh but dear man,*
> *most of it is all an act,*
> *I have a much bigger plan*

that will benefit us all . . .
trust me.

It was our last text exchange. CBS announced that day that they were halting production on the show for the rest of the season, and shortly after that, on March 7, Charlie was fired.

Once again I was living my particular actor's nightmare: Something had happened that had absolutely, irretrievably stopped the whole fucking show.

At home, where I had mostly spent my time awaiting all news via text, alert, e-mail, phone call, and news flash, my iPhone had become a terrifying object. What was once a sparkling portal to a whole new world of communication and information was now some dark conduit of notification hell. And I really hoped it wouldn't be the delivery system for the worst possible news of all regarding Charlie, because even though it appeared I had just lost my job, that this incredible run of eight seasons was over, what was on everybody's mind was our colleague's potential imminent death. How had this friend who seemed so proud of his sobriety gone completely off the rails?

The day after Charlie was fired, my publicist, Karen, called me to ask if I wanted to put out a statement. "You don't have to say anything," she said, "but if you want to, now's the time."

I thought about it, and decided I wanted people to know how much I was going to miss working with Charlie, that I wanted him to get better, that he and Brooke deserved peace. We began crafting a statement: "It's my hope that Charlie can find a way to focus on his sobriety again. Working with him was a pleasure, indeed an honor . . ." and as I'm literally hashing out this statement with Karen, my fingers on the keyboard, she stops me.

"Wait. Here comes something," she said, reading an alert on her computer. "Okay. Get ready. 'Charlie Sheen lets loose on Cryer, calling him a troll.'"

"Maybe we should put a pin in the statement of support," I said.

———

I mentioned earlier that you have to be careful about narratives created about you, or that you fashion for yourself. I've always been just an actor. I never had a public narrative, and I certainly didn't want to create one by being on, say, a reality show. Nobody cared about me personally anyway, and that's how I like it, says the guy writing a memoir.

But with Charlie's "troll" crack—he also added the alliterative sobriquets *turncoat* and *traitor*—I saw an opportunity to address the situation in a way that gave me control of the narrative. On the one hand, Charlie was a man suffering from an addiction that seemed to be getting worse, yet on the other, he was being patently ridiculous and needed to be ridiculed. I had to come out and say, "You know what? You got me, Charlie. I'm a troll." Maybe then he'd realize how far gone he was.

My publicist, Karen, got in touch with Conan O'Brien's people and asked if they'd be interested in me coming on and doing a humorous response on his show. They were willing, so between their writers and me we came up with a bit in which I'd walk out from behind the curtain— surprising the audience—and confess to being a troll. The spiel being, my parents didn't know. I'd spent all kinds of money on electrolysis, reconstructive surgery, and hair dye to hide it. We don't drink the morning dew from buttercups . . . all really funny stuff. One of the writers came up with a fantastic ending, a tweak on the "It Gets Better" public-service messages that were geared toward the LGBT community.

When I made my entrance on *Conan*, I got the same thunderous applause Charlie got after his return from ignominious arrest. It was that same feeling. The audience was in on a story. They realized they were in the room with the guy from the headlines that day, and could now voice their support for this new narrative: the good soldier who stood by the friend as he fell apart, and who was taking the craziness in stride with humor, and maybe showing said friend that he was acting like a jackass.

———

And then choosing to be part of the narrative revealed its own unique side effects.

The day after my *Conan* appearance, everyone around the world learned about the horrific devastation that had taken place in Japan, when an earthquake unleashed tsunami waves that killed thousands. I was at my computer in the morning reading up on the latest when my son came in and asked me about what had happened. I told him that a terrible tragedy had occurred, and brought him closer to the screen so he could read about it.

He looked a little closer at the CNN.com page, and noticed that under the headline "Tsunami Hits Japan, Thousands Dead" was a second headline: "Jon Cryer: 'I Am a Troll.'"

Yep.

Very few moments in life present themselves as instantly teachable, so I gathered myself for this golden opportunity, turned to my oldest, and said, "Son, there's the Internet for you. Information of actual substance and magnitude shares space, almost equally, with incredible triviality. As you go through life, you'll have to use your judgment to figure out what's more important. But here's a good foundation for that judgment: In this case, the tsunami is more important."

———

Charlie's $100 million lawsuit against Chuck and Warner Bros. was another instance in which you just wanted to shake him and say, "Get help! Not lawyers!" Suddenly crew members were being approached and offered astronomical sums in order to cull horror stories about Chuck, and I started reeling at the prospect that I would be called to testify.

I knew that my testimony would not help Charlie, but I was also pretty sure that he wouldn't be dumb enough to subpoena me.

As the bad press about Charlie's behavior and firing continued to flow, Chuck called me. "They're going to ask you about what I had to do with this, and I hope you'll let them know how hard I tried to get him to get help," he said.

"I know, Chuck," I said. "Of course I will."

But the media didn't want to hear that there was no feud between Chuck and Charlie. A feud needs two sides. If the McCoys are just firing away at the Hatfields, and the Hatfields are standing around saying, "Huh?" it's not really a feud. I have told many people this over and over. Shouted it from the rooftops. It was one guy simmering in his own anger for years before it exploded. His complaining once that an actress isn't pretty enough doesn't constitute long-standing hostilities.

———

America's—indeed the world's—reaction to the meltdown was cacophonous and unsettling. Opinions ranged from righteous indignation to purple-faced outrage. The bellicose underbelly of the Internet was unleashed. After Charlie gave Chuck's phone number to a radio host during an interview, Chuck received so many death threats that he had to hire personal security.

The Web was boiling with anger about Charlie's dismissal. Predictably, there were those who were angry because they felt it had been way too late, that his alleged crimes demanded this action long ago, but surprisingly there were also those who felt it was unjustified. An astounding number of people stood up for Charlie, as though people should be able to show up to work rarely, if at all, verbally abuse their coworkers publically with anti-Semitic slurs, get arrested on a regular basis, as well as abuse drugs to the point where they can barely function, and not have their incredibly high-paying jobs threatened. They directed their fury at Chuck, but also at me, with hundreds of comments about how I'd betrayed Charlie, that I was a "homely fag," and that they'd never watch a show with me as the lead. As ridiculous and horrifying as those sentiments were, it was impossible for me not to feel their effect. And even if I could dismiss their specific comments, I was filled with sadness that there actually appeared to be thousands of people who felt this way.

The most disgusting group of folks were the rubberneckers who were just enjoying watching Charlie's drug-fueled self-immolation for the entertainment value. And goading him further with "go, O.J., go!"–style cheer-leading.

America's faceless corporations didn't acquit themselves particularly well either. They began clamoring to capitalize on the marketing opportunity that Charlie's epic flameout was presenting. A company called Ustream gave him a webcast platform to continue his rants in a monetized worldwide fashion. LiveNation immediately offered him millions to go on a stage tour across the U.S., which he christened his "Violent Torpedo of Truth."

I knew that Charlie, while being a gifted actor and a remarkably smart man, didn't have the slightest fucking idea how to put on a live stage show, even when he wasn't loaded, but I figured he must have at least one person in his retinue of managers and hangers-on who knew what they were doing in that respect. Turns out, I was wrong. His first few dates were spectacularly incompetent. They resembled exactly what happens when a bunch of assholes throw money at a drug addict to make him dance like a monkey.

A curious phenomenon was bubbling up in the media as well. Entertainment culture had become so stultifyingly repetitive, mechanical and predictable that Charlie's antics felt like a breath of fresh air. To some authors, commentators, and bloggers, seemingly intelligent people, he was a rebel, a truth teller willing to poke his masters in the eye. They defended his baleful screeds. (I'm looking at you, Bret Easton Ellis.) Of course, Charlie wasn't those things. He was simply lashing out at the people who told him the party was over. That he was actually just a human being with a monumental drug dependency mattered less to the pundits than his value as something to write about to alleviate their collective boredom. The fact that he could very well be dead soon was not their concern. In fact, it'd just give them more to write about.

Charlie was never an insurrectionary guerrilla fighting the established order. He was a guy who got everything he had ever wanted from it. He even texted somebody at the show once, "I think they gave the wrong guy too much money." That shows even he had the occasional flicker of self-awareness.

And hey, Bret Easton Ellis, don't be a dick.

—

My agent, Sarah Clossey, was on the line.

"I just got an offer for you, but before I tell you about it, I want you to know that you're doing it."

I stammered, "Um . . . okay."

About three weeks before, I'd become the most famously unemployed actor in America, and my agents were now urgently trying to rectify that situation.

Sarah continued. "They're doing *Company* at Lincoln Center with the New York Philharmonic. The cast is insane, and they want you too!" My mind raced. I loved the show. *Company* was one of Stephen Sondheim's most sophisticated and beloved works of musical theater. But I hadn't done live musical theater since Stagedoor Manor. And this was the New York fucking Philharmonic!

I queried, "Who else is in it?"

"Well," she continued, "there's Neil Patrick Harris, Patti LuPone, Stephen Colbert, Martha Plimpton—"

"Jesus," I interjected.

"I'm not done. Christina Hendricks, Anika Noni Rose, Craig Bierko—" She rattled off a list that was a veritable murderers' row of Broadway heavy hitters. Then she went on. "It's going to be a benefit for the Philharmonic. They're doing it under an Encores contract. You need to do this!" Encores referred to a style of production where actors perform the show in front of the orchestra with the script in hand. Many Encores revivals of popular musicals had turned out to be very successful, boasting Tony-winning best musical *Chicago* as one of their premier efforts. The advantage to that kind of production is that the shows can be thrown together with very little rehearsal. And since the actors are required to be on script with minimal staging, they end up having a very loose, fun flavor to them.

"But the last time I sang live was at summer camp. I can't perform with—"

"You're doing it!" she insisted. Sarah was a member of an elite minority in Los Angeles: agents who are also trained opera singers. I'm pretty sure it's a minority of one, actually. She was show folk, and she would allow no disagreement from me. This was an opportunity I needed to seize. In times of crisis, when the world is in chaos and all seems lost, only one thing can save us: musical theater!

I agreed and hung up with great trepidation. I was still reeling from my show's demise and the maelstrom that was the Sheen meltdown. But I consoled myself with the idea that at least this was going to be a relaxed, just-for-fun one-off that would benefit the New York Philharmonic. It'd give me an excuse to visit my mom, reconnect with my roots, and maybe get my head out of the madness.

My first inkling of trouble was a call I got from the show's director, Lonny Price.

"Your first choreography rehearsal will be tomorr—"

"My what?" I interrupted.

"Your choreography rehearsal. You've got a few numbers—"

"Wait. There's choreography?!"

Lonny carefully explained to me that this show was NOT going to be a loose, fun one-off with the actors bumping into one another with scripts in hand. It was going to be a fully staged production, without scripts, that would be performed four times in Avery Fisher Hall and then filmed for release in movie theaters! I had misunderstood. It was going to be done under the Encores contract, but not in the Encores style. I had cavalierly committed to appearing in the equivalent of a Broadway show.

"Holy shit! Are you kidding me?"

He wasn't kidding me. And he had a nice capper. "Stephen is coming to see it." And he didn't mean Colbert. I slid into fretful apoplexia. Stephen Sondheim, one of the most admired writers in the American musical canon, was coming to see the first time I'd ever sing professionally. With the New York fucking Philharmonic.

And speaking of the other Stephen, Colbert, I was nervous enough simply to meet him, much less perform with him. He, Jim Walton of *Merrily We Roll Along*, and I were going to sing "Sorry/Grateful" together. As far as I was concerned, Stephen Colbert was a comedic genius. Jesus, I was in over my head.

I flew into JFK with wife, Lisa, and my one-and-a-half-year-old daughter, Daisy, in tow. Paparazzi pelted us with questions as we got to baggage claim and sprinted after us as we headed to our town car. We decamped to my mother's apartment and unpacked our suitcases in my childhood bedroom.

My second night in New York, I ran into Colbert at Comedy Central's Comedy Awards and got up the nerve to ask him, "Did you know this was going to be a fully staged production?"

He let out an aghast, "No! I thought we were going to have scripts! I only found out when they told me I had to go to fucking karate practice!"

His character and Martha Plimpton's have an elaborate karate battle in one of the opening scenes of the show. I felt better knowing I wasn't the only one out of the loop. And at least I didn't have to learn karate.

The cast would have only two weeks to rehearse for this show. Two weeks! No one puts up a Broadway musical in two weeks. Compounding that was the fact that everyone in the cast was so busy (Neil was still shooting *How I Met Your Mother*, Christina, *Mad Men,* and Stephen Colbert was taping his *Report* daily) that the cast could never be in the same room at the same time. I was the only one with enough free time to be at all of the sessions. Lonny got around this by bringing in a bunch of musical theater majors from Pace University and having them learn the entire show and then stand in for whoever was missing that particular day. Their enthusiasm was inspiring, but it would never quite feel like the real thing.

We worked out of Pearl Studios on Eighth Avenue, where the hallways were packed with performers either working on shows in other rooms, generally kibbitzing or waiting nervously to audition for other productions. It was instant total immersion in the New York theater community, and it was great to be back.

Patti LuPone remembered me from my days backstage at *Evita* with my dad, and she was warm and welcoming. And also a bit of a drill sergeant. I discovered while working with her exactly why she's so good at what she does, because she sweats the small stuff and doesn't stop working until it's perfect. That's why she hired a piano-playing premed student to spend months working with her on the songs before we even started.

The music of *Company* is very difficult to learn. When it was written, it was considered bizarre and avant-garde. Many of the rehearsals were spent exploring the vexing minutiae of it. That it all comes together into one of Sondheim's most crowd-pleasing scores is part of its singular appeal.

Martha Plimpton sang the shit out of it. Which was only surprising because I didn't know she could sing at all. Colbert and I shared a certain dismay about our own vocal abilities. We were in the midst of the most formidable voices on Broadway, and we were concerned we'd stick out like atonal sore thumbs.

Midway through the first singing rehearsal with conductor Paul Gemigniani, we had a break, and Patti casually stood up and announced, "I'm getting something to eat in the other room. Anybody need anything?"

"I'll take some water," Colbert offered.

She nodded and was headed out when I piped up helpfully, "Actually, Stephen, there's a whole box of bottled water right over there in the corner."

Patti registered that and continued on her way.

Colbert whirled on me with an exasperated whisper, "What are you doing?!"

I lamely began, "I was just—"

"I almost got Patti LuPone to get *me* water!'"

As I looked at him mystified, he explained, "Don't you get it? Broadway is like prison. Your first day in, you gotta jack the biggest guy in the room!"

That night I shared a cab with Martha back up to our respective digs on the Upper West Side and asked her whether she had been aware this was going to be a fully staged production. She blurted, "No! I only found out when they told me I had to go to goddamn karate class!" It appeared that particular miscommunication was not uncommon.

We spent the first week practicing the show without our lead. Neil Patrick Harris was playing Bobby but was still in Los Angeles working on his TV show. I couldn't imagine how he was going to play such a large role with perhaps the least amount of rehearsal of all of us.

We'd all received MP3s of our vocal tracks as well as ones with just our tracks removed so that we could practice either way. We'd also been sent video of our dance moves performed by choreographer Josh Rhodes. So all you had to do was plug in your headphones and your iPhone would become your virtual rehearsal partner.

When Neil showed up he leaped right in, already up to speed on the music and most of the staging already. Somehow, while shooting *How I Met Your Mother*, he managed to prepare meticulously. He and I had never worked together before, but he was just as I imagined: effortlessly charming and dedicated. He made it all look maddeningly easy.

Every now and then I'd look at Martha and Stephen and notice that the three of us all had a similar deer-in-the-headlights expression as we struggled to adjust to the idea that we were doing this show for real. In those kinds of situations sometimes a performer will half-ass it, sort of signal to everyone that this is not what they signed on for, that this wasn't going to be them at their best. But not this bunch. Even though several other cast members were in the same boat as we were in terms of their expectations, every single one of us was committed. We were going to put on a show! If a bunch of eleven-year-old Jewish kids from Long Island could put on *Jesus Christ Superstar!* in two weeks at Stagedoor Manor, then dammit, we could put on *Company*.

The show had become a hot ticket; all four performances sold out near instantaneously. I was informed that there was another hot ticket in town, Charlie's "Violent Torpedo" live show was to play Radio City Music Hall on the same night that we had our second performance.

Now whenever the paps saw me, they'd ask: "You gonna see Charlie's show?" and "Is he gonna see yours?" Which struck me as kind of a funny idea as I don't think he's much of a Sondheim guy.

At my mom's place, my daughter, Daisy, had come down with a stubborn lung infection. And even though she loved spending time with her grandma, it was becoming clear that she and my wife would have to head back to LA. My workdays had been grueling, and I was having a hard time assimilating my dialogue, so I was not as attentive to our sick daughter as

I should have been. Now it would just be my mom and I, like it was when I made my Broadway debut some twenty-seven years before.

As the night of our first performance arrived, we got our dressing room assignments at Avery Fisher. I found out I'd be roomies with Stephen Colbert. And to answer the question on everybody's mind: boxers.

Our first and only dress rehearsal was distinctive for another reason. It would mark the first time the whole cast was in the same room at the same time. It was bumpy as hell. This was not one of those everything-just-came-together moments; the fact that we'd never performed as an ensemble was very apparent. Afterward Lonny introduced Stephen Sondheim to the cast. Turns out, he'd been watching the dress rehearsal but hadn't wanted to be a distraction. He was vaguely complimentary, stressed the need for lyrical crispness, and then was gone as mysteriously as he'd arrived. I spent that evening doing lip exercises. I intended to be lyrically extra crispy.

Our first performance was marked by the occasional jarring imperfection. But we got through it. My "Sorry/Grateful" was shaky, but I enunciated it within an inch of its life.

After the show Elaine Stritch, who had originated the role of Joanne, now played by Patti LuPone, came backstage and hugged me like we were old friends. She asked if I was okay, then gravely intoned, "If you see Charlie, tell him I'm worried about him."

"I will," I promised.

As I exited the stage door at Avery Fisher, there were the cameras.

"Have you seen Charlie?! Are you going to Radio City?!"

"Are you still a troll?!"

"If you saw Charlie, what would you say?!"

Elaine Stritch is worried about you almost came out of my mouth. But in a gesture I was becoming adept at, I walked past without comment.

On Friday night, as we arrived at the theater a half hour before showtime for our second performance, New York media was abuzz with Charlie Sheen anticipation. Word was that he'd gotten his act together out of town. That he'd worked on his show and that this one at Radio City was going to be the turning point of his tour.

Company began with its opening number, fittingly titled "Company," at eight p.m. sharp; meanwhile ticket holders at Radio City were still milling about in the lobby buying T-shirts emblazoned with Sheen catch-phrases such as "I'm Not Bipolar" and "#Winning!" As I managed to nail my part in "Sorry/Grateful" with unusual confidence, downtown Charlie took the stage about a half hour late.

He opened with a joke about being back in New York: "Surprise! I'm not staying at the fucking Plaza Hotel!" and got a big laugh. But a mere five minutes later, as Christina Hendricks, Chryssie Whitehead, and Anika Noni Rose were singing "You Could Drive a Person Crazy" at Avery Fisher to enraptured applause, the crowd at Radio City began turning on Charlie. He'd started by telling his side of the story about the prostitute who had accused him of assault at the Plaza, but was now meandering conversationally.

The heckling and catcalls commenced at low volume but only in-creased as it became clear that Charlie had no show. He was just rambling on the audience's dime. And even worse, he no longer seemed like the fuck-'em-all provocateur he'd been hyped as. By the time Neil was bring-ing down the house with "Marry Me a Little" on Sixty-sixth Street, hoots of "BOR-ing" could be heard on Fifty-first.

As we were starting the second act with a show-stopping "Side by Side by Side," over at Radio City, Charlie's act was not yet over, but patrons were streaming up the aisles toward the exits anyway.

A heckler howled one last zinger before hitting the lobby: "This is the worst thing I've seen, ever!" and added only somewhat hyperbolically, "This is worse than Chernobyl!"

That second night of *Company*, we had our everything-just-came-together moment at exactly the right time. The response was euphoric. If I thought the applause at *Conan* was something, this was another beast entirely. When you throw twenty-seven hundred New Yorkers Neil Patrick

Harris, Patti LuPone, and Stephen Colbert singing Sondheim with the New York Philharmonic, you get an ovation that registers on the Richter scale for a ten-block radius. Backstage after the show, Stephen Sondheim appeared to be beaming. I have to imagine that it's wonderful to hear that particular reaction to a musical you wrote more than forty years ago. I was glad that this was the performance he'd come to see.

I was on a high. As I made my way out the stage door and headed to Broadway to hail a cab back to my mother's apartment, a group of five guys spotted me.

"That's Alan Harper! That's that guy! Hey, *Two and a Half Men!*" one of them shouted while urgently pointing.

They approached and surrounded me. I murmured polite hellos. I noticed two of them had "Violent Torpedo" tour T-shirts.

"You gonna party with Charlie tonight?!" one of them barked at me.

The other yelled, "We just saw Charlie! You're gonna party with him, right?"

Without waiting for an answer, he demanded, "Here, give me a picture!" He wrapped his arm around my neck and brought up a smartphone to take a selfie. As he posed I could smell something sweet and powerfully alcoholic on his breath; he was missing a couple teeth up front as well.

He got off a photo, then released me to show the picture to his friends "I got him! I fuckin' got him!"

I turned to keep walking uptown and heard him shout after me: "Fuck you, *Two and a Half Men!* Fuck you! You fuckin' homo!"

And then let out a banshee wail of "WINNING!!!"

Chapter 27
React to the Good Part

The text from Chuck Lorre read, *Lee and I have gotten together, and we may not be done yet.* That's Lee Aronsohn, who cocreated and co-ran *Two and a Half Men* with Chuck.

I wrote back, *Well, I hope Charlie's okay.*

Chuck's reply: *But I said we may not be done yet. React to the good part!*

Yes, it was great to hear that the guys who'd invented this wonderful role for me were angling to continue giving the character things to say and do, but I was unsure. Since they were being cryptic, I didn't know if that meant Charlie was coming back, or there'd be a spinoff with Alan, or what. Alan Harper's a genuinely funny character, but I'm not sure I'd want to watch a show centered completely on that guy. Taking another flawed, hapless sitcom icon as an example, would you tune in to a series focused solely on George Costanza?

When I got back from New York, I had to call Chuck and pick his brain on this. "Where do you think we can go?" I said.

"Well," he said, "we thought, we've got to find somebody with that same Teflon charm, whom people love no matter what. Lee and I talked back and forth, back and forth. 'Who could possibly do this?' Then we thought of Hugh Grant."

I burst out laughing. "Well, of course *Hugh Grant*! But come on, Chuck, you're not going to get Hugh Grant!"

"He's flying in next week," Chuck said. "Would you want to meet with him?"

———

Ballsy choice, I thought.

Hugh's an international star, blessed with great comic timing, and, like somebody we all knew, could win back hearts, minds, and box office after consorting with a prostitute. As I drove up to Peter Roth's house for the meeting with Hugh, Chuck, Lee, and *Two and a Half Men* producers Eddie Gorodetsky and Jim Patterson, I also thought about the live-theater aspect of filming—was Hugh much of a theater guy? Then again, his payday would be incredible, surely. Landing Hugh Grant would be a serious coup.

I had learned that the character for Hugh would be an incredibly charming Brit who tells Alan he works for the British consulate and is looking for a place to stay so he can be near his daughter at USC. Alan, needing a renter or he'll have to sell the Malibu house in the wake of his brother's death, quickly says, "Welcome, roomie!" only to discover that the man's a fraud, but a damned charismatic one. He can pay his rent, though, so Alan's stuck with him, and eventually the two grow to like each other.

I suggested making Hugh's character an eccentric, like that British boyfriend of my mom's who used to walk around the house naked. Chuck seemed to take a liking to the idea.

As I parked, I texted Chuck and suggested that if Hugh agreed to do the show, Chuck should let me know by texting *some cool code phrase like 'The* Eagle *has landed' or something.*

I like it, he sent back.

Walking into Peter's house, I still wasn't convinced Hugh would even be there, but he was. Chuck had prepared two scenes for Hugh and me to read, but I could tell Hugh had questions about the character he was going to play. Chuck, meanwhile, looked to me to sell him on what doing a show like this entails.

"First of all, Hugh," I said, as we sat ourselves down at Peter's dining table, "it's the best job for an actor in show business, because you get to build a character over many episodes. You get real interaction with the writers, and you have input as things constantly change. As a way of life it's great, because the hours work for someone with a family."

But as I said all this, I could tell Hugh was hesitant about the open-endedness of the character—of the whole process in fact, that it *wasn't* strictly defined yet. Here was a movie actor used to getting a screenplay with everything he'd need for the character in it. Even British television shows—usually only six episodes to a season—are typically written all in advance, and by one person. As we threw our ideas to him, including the naked gag, he'd respond well, but then settle back into a reserve I took to be apprehension. He also admitted openly to anxiety issues about performing, which, as you now know, I had too. I offered him tips, and he was incredibly gracious.

Overall, Hugh was in good humor, friendly and appreciative of everyone's interest, but after he left and Chuck asked me what I thought, I told him, "I'm not sure he's going to say yes, but who knows? Maybe it's a deal he wants to make."

"Well, we have a plan B," Chuck said.

"Maybe it's time to think about plan B," I said. "Who is it?"

"Les Moonves wants me to consider Ashton Kutcher."

Uneasy looks went around the table.

Chuck continued. "I don't know a lot about his work, but I know he played an idiot on *That '70s Show*. It's the only thing of his I've seen, and that character doesn't interest me."

My first reaction was concern. We'd gotten so much comedic mileage on the show from having two main characters who were both facing the dilemmas of middle age but responding in different ways, that I just didn't see what would be the new dynamic. I didn't know how our roles would relate. But the more I thought about it, the more open I got.

"People loved him on that show," I said. "He's comfortable with doing sitcoms. And he's got a sense of humor."

I informed Chuck, Lee, Jim, and Ed that Ashton had been the architect of one of the most inspired pranks I'd ever seen on television—the now legendary episode of *Punk'd* featuring Beyoncé unwittingly destroying the Christmas gifts of a gaggle of orphans. Even my meager retelling of it had them laughing.

The prospect on our minds at the moment, though, was the English movie star who'd just driven away. We had all been just a bunch of men, standing in front of a charming Brit, asking him to love us. (What, you don't like *Notting Hill*? Have a heart, people.)

—

Checking in with the rumor mill again, this time around they were saying that Charlie had been chastened by his firing, that the continuing rants were just bluster, and that his reps were desperately trying to arrange a peace summit for Charlie and Chuck. Charlie was supposedly looking to apologize, and there were many who felt that there had to be a way to get Charlie back on the show.

Meanwhile, there hadn't been a peep in the media about our British visitor. I waited on tenterhooks for his reply.

I received a single-word text from Chuck the next morning: *Yes.*

I sent back, *Really?!??*

He answered, *Really. Negotiations start now.*

What about our cool code phrase? U blew it! I whined.

I forgot. What was it?

"The Eagle has landed." Jesus.

Right, right. Sorry.

By nine a.m. the next morning, I'd gotten definitive word: The negotiations were successful; Hugh Grant and I would be the stars of *Two and a Half Men* going forward. I sat back and tried to get used to the idea.

Then, at eleven fifteen a.m., I got a call from Chuck.

"He's not doing it. The deal was done, but he changed his mind."

That was a real whiplash day.

———

The other surprising thing I found out that day was that my mom's doorman had heard about the Hugh deal falling through before I did. As it turns out, Mom's doorman often knows things before any of us do. Many a time Gretchen Cryer has strolled out of her building to be greeted by Ronnie Clemmons providing an update on my life—Sheen madness updates, renegotiation bulletins—as reported in the tabloids or the trades or on the Internet or from a band of traveling Gypsies.

Needless to say, Mom has occasionally called me after these briefings, slightly appalled that I haven't clued her in first. But what can I say? This is the age we live in. And yet, aren't you pleased to know that my mother's building, once a way station for petty criminals, is now fancy enough to have a doorman?

And that building gossip Norma Vogelstein has been reincarnated as one of them?

When word hit the media that efforts to replace Charlie were very real, he responded quickly. His public statement began: "Good Luck, Chuck, *my* fans may tune in for a minute, but at the end of the day, no one cares about your feeble show without me. Shame on you." He was aggrieved, unrepentant, furious, and near delusional. He reminded Chuck that the show that had made them both rich had been based on his "awesome life," and continued, "You sad, silly fool. A-hole pussy loser. Put on the gloves, you low-rent, nutless sociopath; I'll beat your chickenshit soul in a courtroom into a state of gratitude. A state of surrender." He finished the missive as hatefully as he began: "Wow, I'm sure your children are *so proud* of you. You can teach 'em how to be a stupid bitch. A narcissist. A coward. A loser. A spineless rat. I'm out here with my fans every night. The message is crystal clear: *No Charlie Sheen. No show.*"

So much for "chastened." It made me sick to my stomach. It was all over. There would be no turning back. According to Charlie, he'd done it all by himself. He was the only one who mattered. He'd just insulted me and everyone else who'd ever worked on our show. The same one that had given him a chance at rebirth, and had made him the highest-paid actor in television.

For a moment I thought about what this must have felt like for Chuck. He had thought for all the world that he and Charlie were friends, and that he was simply trying to help his friend find his way out of addiction.

———

Pursuing Ashton felt like the next step. Although I'd been defending him the previous day, one thing was bothering me: the age difference. How could Alan relate to this young, superhandsome guy? What would unite us?

But then Chuck watched all of Ashton's movies, and called me up with the sound of possibility in his voice. "You know what? I think he's got something that might work. I had this idea about a very damaged, emotionally handicapped guy who's a famous sitcom actor. Alan saves him from a suicide attempt, and becomes his assistant or something like that." It sounded like a) the *Teddy Z* premise all over again, but also b) maybe a slight reference to a previous cast member? "He's not going to be Charlie Sheen," said Chuck. "He's not an asshole."

Then Chuck met individually with Ashton, and called me even more energized. "I love this guy!" he said. "He's great. He's funny, supersmart, and gets it. I don't want to do the sitcom idea anymore. I want him to be an Internet billionaire."

———

After a meeting with Ashton and the writers, we converged again, this time at Chuck's house. At this time Ashton was sporting his expanding kabbalah beard, but what he also had was a wife I had dated when he was seven years old. I didn't know if he knew this, so I kept quiet and just tried to get to know him, because you can't force sparks in a creative partnership. Fortunately, Ashton is incredibly fun and personable. But, *Jesus, does he know?* was in the back of my mind.

Afterward, I walked out with him to his car and did my best at a positive-vibe sendoff: "Hey, man, this is gonna be fun! It'll be an adventure. That's for sure!"

He opened the driver's door, but stopped short of getting in. He turned and came back to me. "Oh, man, I just want to say, Demi told me you guys used to date. Totally cool. Don't feel weird about it."

"Oh, hey! Heh, heh . . . okay, great! It was really nothing!" He was in the car, driving off. "I mean, it was just a little while! We were doing a movie together! You know how it is!"

———

I had really been despairing for the nation when I heard about people buying tickets to Charlie's "Violent Torpedo of Truth" tour. That it was a mess didn't surprise me. But then the bidding war for Charlie's sitcom services had me shaking my head again. When he eventually made the deal with Lions Gate for *Anger Management*, I was pretty surprised. Here Warner Bros. made a moral, gutsy move against their own financial interest in firing Charlie, and what's the response in Hollywood? *Hey, everyone, he's available!*

———

When everybody came back to work in the summer of 2011 for a ninth season of *Two and a Half Men*, it also felt like we were shooting a pilot all over again for something new. The stakes seemed so high, and you could feel the anticipation. Would it work?

The first read-through with Ashton, however, quickly dispelled a lot of the worries. For one thing, it was a really crackerjack episode: funny, deeply impure, and in Alan's bit where he keeps spilling the deceased Charlie Harper's ashes, admirably disrespectful—in a strange kind of respectful way, mind you—toward all the craziness that had led us to this point. Plus, Ashton's natural comfort with sitcoms put everybody at ease. Charlie never liked read-throughs, and missed them occasionally—that wasn't where he shone. Ashton knew how to slam-dunk at a read-through. That felt new and exciting.

One of the hardest things to get used to was the fact that Ashton was so very punctual and dependable. As he was always at rehearsals on time, there was no need for me to work with Jim Marshall, Sheen's comically deadpan stand in. And frankly, I missed him.

The buildup to our first audience show, however, had its own pressures. We knew the coverage of our first show with Ashton would be intense. In rehearsals we worked extra hard to get every beat right. We had one nagging problem, though: My naked-Brit-walking-through-the-living-room memory had made it all the way to this incarnation with Ashton as tech billionaire Walden Schmidt. After Alan offers to dry Walden's sodden clothes, the forlorn industrialist nonchalantly drops trou and hugs Alan bare-assed. The question was, How were we going to handle having Ashton walk around nude in front of a studio audience?

It's more difficult a problem than you think when you factor in the expected laughter from a surprised audience. If we slapped tiny flesh-colored briefs on Ashton—well, ideally Ashton would do that himself—then it wouldn't come off as outrageous. And yet real nudity was out of the question.

Out of nowhere, Ashton said, "Well, I do have a huge prosthetic penis in my trailer."

We all laughed, and he said, "No, no. I do."

Apparently our new family member (heh, heh, member), in his past role as a television prankster, had had a fake man part constructed for a punking in which someone had to run around in public naked. Since public bare-assedness is actually illegal, a prosthetic was created. I won't bother to speculate why Ashton still had this, and why it was in his trailer at that very moment, but he went to retrieve it. It. Was. Huge. Ashton was willing to wear it on taping night. Warm feelings all around.

That first Friday in front of the cameras again after what had been a truly bizarre roller-coaster twelve months was really pretty special. Surrounded by friends, colleagues, and crew who had endured everything, and perhaps assumed we wouldn't return, I stepped back into Alan's shoes ready to do everything I could to give this show a new lease on life. Would people accept us again?

They did. And when Ashton unveiled his anatomically correct strap-on—that's "anatomically correct" as a general biological descriptor, mind you, not pertaining to Ashton specifically (as far as I knew)—I heard a soundstage-wide scream of shock and dirty joy from the fans that told me everything was going to be just fine.

Three years later

In June of 2014, I got a call from Charlie's ex-manager, Mark Burg. He told me Charlie had called him up and apologized for everything—Mark had been fired and rehired and fired and rehired by Charlie countless times— and that my former costar had been sober for a while and wanted to make amends to me.

Hmmmm.

The years since Charlie's departure had been kind to both me and the show that he was so certain could not survive. Ratings had remained strong. I'd been awarded another Emmy—this time as lead actor—and even Charlie Harper finally got one. That is to say, Kathy Bates won Outstanding Guest Actress playing Charlie Harper's ghost.

My actor's nightmare no longer haunted me, as both that play in London and my TV show had survived and even flourished despite their respective interruptions.

I'd also come to a place of peace. The crucible that was the Charlie Sheen shitstorm had seared away many of my petty concerns and given me some much-needed perspective.

Mark's offer seemed questionable, but I accepted it anyway, and drove up to his Tuscan-style villa in the Hollywood Hills. When I stepped inside, Charlie was already there, and I could immediately tell he looked better. He'd gained weight, for one thing—he wasn't that muscular but wraithlike being from his last season on the show.

The small talk was awkward. Mark and his dog made for helpful diversions, an uncomfortable pause settled in, and then Charlie volunteered, "Hey, man, I'm sorry about the bullshit."

"Okay, but you understand 'I'm sorry about the bullshit' doesn't exactly hint at the enormous amount of bullshit that went down."

He nodded, took that in, paused for a long while, then said, "I'm *really* sorry?"

I recounted the list of things that had pissed me off, and he responded to each one with some variation of apology: "Yeah, I'm really sorry about that." "You're right; I have no excuse for that." "Yeah, that was a bad one." "Yep, I'm so sorry; I have nothing to say to defend myself."

He'd really only torn into me that one time with the "troll" outburst, but while he apologized publicly the next day, the media weren't interested. But he never called me personally to atone, to say he didn't mean it. I was still bugged that he'd endangered my job and the jobs of others, irritated at the way he'd treated my friends and spoken ill of Chuck and Ashton. These were the issues I brought up, and I tried to get some explanation from him. "Why now?" I said. "What's changed for you?"

"Just some things in my personal life that made me realize I had to change. I stopped drinking alcohol."

"Fine, but what was the source of the anger?"

"Well," he said, "I was using testosterone. I was using the cream. Three times a day you rub the cream on your thighs, and it's deceptive, because you feel the same, but suddenly you're flying into a rage."

(So the ad would go, "Side effects of testosterone cream may include: losing your multimillion-dollar sitcom starring role.")

I confessed to him that I'd never been more shocked than the day Warner Bros. fired him. Charlie admitted a great deal of surprise as well. Mark piped in: "You probably shouldn't have sent Lenny Dykstra over there with a list of demands." Charlie grimaced.

"Why did you get so angry at Chuck?" I asked.

"I just felt like the show was going so well, and every Monday we'd hit it out of the park ratings-wise, and then we'd come in on Tuesday and I'd see all these dour faces on the writers, worried about how the show was going to be this week."

Now he seemed to be reaching. No one's going to say Chuck isn't occasionally a hard-ass about making the show as great as it can be, but it invariably has led to better scripts. Coming into *Two and a Half Men*, I'd worked on a number of shows where dud weeks were common. I don't recall a single dud week on *Two and a Half Men*. Besides, the vast majority of the twelve years I worked on the show were fun, and for the first eight of those years, working alongside the guy in front of me that day was a great part of why it was fun. Chuck simply didn't deserve that vicious unloading. I was convinced there was something Charlie wasn't saying. But he seemed genuinely contrite, and eventually the real reason behind the meeting became clear: He wanted to revive his relationship with *Two and a Half Men* and give some closure to the fans.

That amount of bridge repairing, I thought, would require a congressional appropriation and the Army Corps of Engineers. My sentimental, "give a guy a chance" attitude liked the idea of Charlie returning, but my practical side knew it was close to an impossibility.

But there was supreme irony in Charlie's wistfulness that day, in the sense that he knew he'd lost something. That's because the demands he was making in the last days—Chuck off the show, Bruce Rosenblum off the lot, Don Reo taking over as showrunner—all eventually happened of their own accord. Chuck stopped being the day-to-day maestro, falling back into a plot-approval position while he tended to his burgeoning sitcom empire (*The Big Bang Theory*, *Mike and Molly*, *Mom*). Bruce left to run another company. And Charlie's buddy Don Reo stepped in to oversee *Two and a Half Men*.

If Charlie had just kept his fucking mouth shut, he'd have gotten everything he wanted.

As for whether Charlie's last wish about the show came true—returning to it in any capacity—publishing schedules prevent me from seeing into the future at this writing to be able to acknowledge whether that happened or not.

But if Charlie Sheen didn't come back, are you sad?

And if he did, was it everything you wanted?

And if he relapsed, huffed a bunch of glue, hijacked a stretch limo, freed a bunch of zoo animals, and led them with a caravan of prostitutes to Vegas, is it on video?

Coda

As I said, narratives are tricky. Especially since they're mostly in our heads. We weave our lives' events into a story because it allows our brains to grasp them, infuse them with meaning, and then gives us a tale that we can relate to others. Like a celebrity memoir. But let's face it: It often seems to me that the reality is that we simply keep on living and a lot of crazy shit just happens all at once. That would explain a fair amount of what's in this book. Certainly the Carol Channing incident.

And if the act of gathering all this stuff together and presenting it to you has given you some insight into life, love, comedy, entertainment in general, sex, Puerto Rican girls, contract law, Courteney Cox, children's multivitamins, male prostitutes, *Mary Poppins*, and fake bird shit, well, then God bless you. It all seems kind of random to me.

But if the idea that life must have a narrative is something you simply can't enjoy this book without, there is hope. In 2003 a British philosopher from Oxford University named Nick Bostrom (yes, they still pay people to be philosophers in England) published a paper that made a shockingly plausible case that the universe we live in is, more likely than not, a numerical computer simulation created by an ultra-advanced "posthuman" civilization. I know, if it's true, these "ultra-advanced" folks totally stole it from *The Matrix*. But bear with me, people; I swear there is a reason I'm telling you this.

I won't bore you with the details, but in a nutshell, he bases this on some not-at-all-crazy assumptions, a few convincing calculations of probability, and one somewhat iffy postulate.

The assumptions are: 1) that computer technology is advancing at such a pace that it is inevitable that at some point our descendants will have the computing power to simulate an entire universe, at least as it is perceived by a single consciousness (okay, I buy that); 2) that beings with that power will almost definitely use it (*shyeah*, wouldn't you? I'd also build an orgasmatron); 3) that the most popular simulations we humans of today run are "ancestor" simulations, or replications of life in our distant past (hello, Assassin's Creed); 4) that the number of simulated universes will vastly outnumber the total of unsimulated ones (that being one, the real one, not the one we think we are in) and—oh shit, I'm boring you with the details; well, just let me finish; I'll be done in a sec—and here's the iffy part: that in order for all this to work, consciousness needs to be "substrate independent," or able to exist based either on biological structures (like our brains) or some other— Oh, fuck, I'm already confused, and I went to nerd school.

The freakiest thing about this idea is that it is being taken seriously by physicists and mathematicians, not just because they are probably geeks and it sounds gnarly, but because it would actually explain the many aspects of our known universe that currently remain inexplicable! Namely, the fact that mathematics appears to be the irreducible language of the universe and, of course, the Fermi paradox, which asks— Oops, damn you, nerd school, damn you! Sorry.

Bottom line: This whole thing, my whole life, this whole universe,

Los Angeles, my dogs, Justine Bateman, everything, may very well be a huge, very intense, very realistic video game. Which would sort of make sense to me. I figure I spent my youth wanting so badly to be a part of the movies and TV I loved that I ended up living a game where I got to experience all of it—this despite the fact that I was such a dork to begin with. And, like any self-respecting dork with a video game, I guess I, well, won it.

On September 27, 2011, that kid who stood on the walk of fame wondering when Mary Tyler Moore would show up to clean her star got one of his own. He was inducted by none other than one of his boyhood comedic heroes, Carl Reiner. And yes, he made me sing "Jingle Bell Rock" again.

My mother, father, and stepmother were in attendance, as were Ashton and my remaining castmates, my friends, my agents, my managers, my lawyer, Richard Schenkman, Chuck Lorre, the writers of *Two and a Half Men*, several hundred tourists, and a bunch of waitresses from Hooters (I had scored a primo location for my star, mere feet from the beloved buffalo wingery).

I went home to a boisterous party at my house in a part of Los Angeles where I love to live, full of the amazing friends I've acquired in thirty years of performing. We talked about a million things, some of which I've just told you, and reflected on how even the very worst of a life spent in movies and TV is still pretty great. We watched the relaunch of *Two and a Half Men* as it played to the largest audience it had ever garnered, and I was embraced by my wonderful sisters, my beautiful, hilarious children, not to mention my wife, who fills my soul with love and trust, just happens to be the most stunning woman I've ever laid eyes on, and is also a maniac in the sack.

See, it all seems a little far-fetched.

Like if it was in a book, you might not believe it.

Appendix

Robert Altman's Famous Mock Bird Shit Recipe

INGREDIENTS

2 quarts sour cream
1 large mixing bowl
4 tbsp. ground black pepper
2 oz. black rubber bands

Add sour cream to mixing bowl.
Mix in ground black pepper.
Finely mince black rubber bands until pieces are roughly ⅛ inch long.
Add rubber bands to mix.
Stir vigorously.

Take palette knife, scoop up generous dollops and drizzle eager young actors with Mock Bird Shit. They will be grateful. Trust me.

Acknowledgments

The word "collaborator" acquired a negative connotation during World War II, when it signified allegiance with the Nazi-led Vichy government in occupied France. "Collaborators" earned the hatred of millions of Frenchmen as they worked with the Nazis to facilitate crushing the French Resistance, enforcing draconian Nazi edicts, as well as exposing Jews and turning them in to local authorities.

Well, Robert Abele was such a wonderful collaborator during the writing of this book, that he almost completely rehabilitated the term. I say "almost" due to his bizarre penchant for turning in Jews to bewildered clerks at the West Hollywood Department of Motor Vehicles.

That quirk aside, his masterful writing, artful editing of my work, extensive interviewing, tireless transcription, copious research, and generally fantastic attitude made him absolutely indispensable in the writing of this tome. To say that I couldn't have done it without him would be like George Steinbrenner saying he couldn't have won the World Series without the Yankees. Technically true, but just saying it would make me a gigantic asshole. Robert also maintained a nearly inexhaustible supply of Fresca at his workplace, which spurred my creativity to such an extent that it might as well have been grapefruit-flavored peyote.

So, many thanks to Robert and his lovely wife, Margy, who we were both trying to impress throughout this process. Also much gratitude to Jennifer Schuster, my editor at Penguin, who was a deep well of valuable guidance.

Max Searle and Matt Ross are two writers from *Two and a Half Men* who contributed some very funny ideas and Jeff Greenstein provided immensely helpful feedback. Richard Schenkman also reminded me of some important tidbits that made their way into this memoir and David Quinn was my source for all facts Stagedoorian. David Quinn also insisted that I mention that he ended up being one of the founders of Allrecipes.com and is now wealthy beyond his wildest dreams. There, I said it.

Some folks have asked me why I don't talk about my children more in this book. Since many in the media have decided that my children no longer have a right to privacy simply because I appear on a television show, I'm trying to preserve what little of it they have left. But rest assured, they are genuinely mind-boggling and beautiful, and I love them very much.

I want to thank my mom for, well, everything but also for her exceptional recall. And Howie Deutch for his insight on one of my formative filmmaking experiences.

I'd like to thank Charlie Sheen for seven great years, and one pretty lousy one. I'd also like to thank Ashton Kutcher for both teaching me how to be fearless and for saving my job as well as those of a lot of my favorite people.

I want to thank every writer who ever worked on *Two and a Half Men*, and every member of the crew and, of course, Chuck Lorre And Lee Aronsohn for creating Alan Harper, a guy I grew to love dearly.

My managers, Connie Tavel and Vera Mihailovich, as well as my agent, Sarah Clossey, were instrumental in convincing me to write this book, and I hope their faith in me has been vindicated. I didn't think I could do it. Or that anybody'd want me to. But I guess I was wrong. Thanks, ladies!

Lastly, I want to thank my wife, Lisa, for facilitating the enormous amount of time that I needed to work on this. Thanks, honey. I'll try to return the favor when you write your book.

Wait. . . . Okay, I was mistaken, one more: I'd like to thank you, the reader, and express my hope that you've ended this experience feeling that your book-purchasing dollars were not misspent, and if you come away with anything at all from this volume, let it be this:

The subway improv was mine!